Miracles
AND Pilgrims

Miracles AND Pilgrims

POPULAR BELIEFS IN MEDIEVAL ENGLAND

RONALD C. FINUCANE

ST. MARTIN'S PRESS
NEW YORK

First published in Great Britain by J.M. Dent & Sons Ltd.
and in the United States of America by Rowman & Littlefield, 1977.

First paperback edition, with a new introduction, published
in the United States of America by St. Martin's Press, 1995.

Library of Congress Cataloging-in-Publication Data

Finucane, Ronald C.
  Miracles and pilgrims : popular beliefs in medieval England /
Ronald C. Finucane.
      p. cm.
  Originally published: Totowa, N.J. : Rowman and Littlefield, 1977.
  Includes bibliographical references and index.
  ISBN 0-312-12528-3
  1. England—Church history—1066-1485. 2. Miracles. 3. Christian
pilgrims and pilgrimages—England. 4. Christian saints—Cult-
-England. 5. Christian shrines—England. 6. Popular culture-
-England—Religious aspects—Christianity. I. Title.
BR747.F56 1995
274.2—dc20   94-41007
                                                        CIP

First St. Martin's Paperback Edition: May, 1995
10 9 8 7 6 5 4 3 2 1

Contents

Acknowledgments

Most of the research which went into this study was carried out during my tenure of a research fellowship in the Graduate Centre for Medieval Studies at Reading University, and I wish to thank the Resarch Board of the University for their support. Two of my colleagues at Reading, Ralph Houlbrooke and David Farmer, read and commented on particular chapters. I owe thanks, too, to William Urry of Oxford University for suggestions about the cult of Thomas Becket, which has provided us with with a congenial topic of discussion for several years. Finally, Ivan Roots of Exeter University has my gratitude and my sympathy, for he took on the onerous task of reading through the entire manuscript and offering very helpful comments and suggestions.

RCF

Maps

Introduction to the Paperback Edition

It is gratifying to discover that one's work has been of some assistance to fellow scholars, and to learn that the approach adopted, and the questions asked of the data, have been useful to historians working in other regions. There is, for example, the interesting study by Pierre-André Sigal, *L'Homme et le Miracle dans la France médiévale* (Paris, 1985), in which several explicit comparisons are made between my analyses of English cults and Sigal's examination of the cults of medieval France. The approach taken in *Miracles and Pilgrims* has also found echoes in recent research by Christian Krötzl, who draws upon Scandinavian hagiographical materials in his *Pilger, Mirakel und Alltag: Formen des Verhaltens im skandinavischen Mittelalter* (Helsinki, 1994), a superb survey of cults from the twelfth to the fifteenth centuries that invites comparison between the northern and the better-known western European cults and pilgrims and miracles. A succinct analysis of four south German/western Austrian cults was presented by Barbara Schuh in *'Jenseitigkeit in diesseitigen Formen': social- und mentalitätsgeschichtliche Aspekte, spätmittelalterlicher Mirakelberichte* (Graz, 1989). Other examples of the dramatically heightened and maturing interest in medieval saints, their cults and 'popular' religion, are Peter Dinzelbacher and Dieter R. Bauer's (eds.) *Heiligenverehrung in Geschichte und Gegenwart* (Ostfildern, 1990) and Thomas J. Heffernan's *Sacred Biography: Saints and their Biographers in the Middle Ages* (Oxford, 1988), which takes a look at theoretical matters associated with the composition of saints' lives. Other recent works are *Les fonctions des saints dans le monde occidental (IIIe-XIIIe siècle)*, [Actes du Colloque, 27-29 October 1988], Collection de l'école française de Rome, 149 (Rome, 1991); *Santità e agiografia* [Atti dell'VIII Congresso di Terni a cura di Gian Domenico Gordini], Ricerche Studi e Strumenti, 24 (Genoa, 1991); Paolo Golinelli, *Città e culto dei santi nel medioevo Italiano*, Biblioteca di storia urbana medievale, 4 (Bologna, 1991); and an extremely helpful guide by the late Dom Jacques Dubois and Jean-Loup Lemaitre, *Sources & Méthodes de l'Hagiographie Médiévale* (Paris, 1993). A handbook by Réginald Grégoire, *Manuale di Agiologia: Introduzione alla letterature agiografica* (Fabriano, 1987), is particularly good on basic hagiographical concepts and the development of the genre in the early Christian centuries.

As for changes that I would make to *Miracles and Pilgrims*, chapter 2 would undoubtedly have benefited from the work of Patrick J. Geary, *Furta Sacra: Thefts of Relics in the Central Middle Ages* (Princeton, 1978, rev. 1990), though his study does not emphasize English saints and their relics. If rewriting chapter 2 now, I would eschew the use of anthropological terms (even though in using them I acknowledged that they were outmoded) such as 'mana' and 'tabu' to characterize the atmosphere round shrines. A different tack would probably have been taken after reading Peter Brown's short but elegant work *The Cult of the Saints: Its Rise and Function in Latin Christianity* (Chicago, 1981).

Much has appeared since 1977 on the subject of the third chapter, pilgrimage. Many of these studies turn to non-European regions, where pilgrimage is still very much a part of life. Exemplary works in this genre are those of Christian W. Troll's (ed.), *Muslim Shrines in India* (Oxford, 1989) and Ann Grodzins Gold's *Fruitful Journeys: The Ways of Rajasthani Pilgrims* (Berkeley, 1989). Other representative studies of non-western pilgrimage are provided by Susan Naquin and Chün-Fang Yü (eds), *Pilgrims and Sacred Sites in China* (Berkeley, 1992), and P. M. Currie, *The Shrine and Cult of Mu'in al-din Chishti of Ajmer* (Oxford, 1989). In addition to insights that can be gained by these examinations of non-European regions, the anthropological overview provided by Victor and Edith Turner, *Image and Pilgrimage in Christian Culture* (Oxford, 1978), would have been a beneficial vade mecum in constructing my analyses of medieval pilgrimage at English cult-centers. More recent works include Alan Morinis's (ed.) *Sacred Journeys: The Anthropology of Pilgrimage* (Westport, 1992) and Linda Davidson and Maryjane Dunn-Wood's *Pilgrimage in the Middle Ages: A Research Guide* (New York, 1993). A thorough examination of some modern European shrines that tends to confirm—for me at any rate—the element of continuity in the cultural history of western Europe is Mary Lee Nolan and Sidney Nolan's *Christian Pilgrimage in Modern Western Europe* (Chapel Hill, NC 1989).

Pilgrims usually purchased some sort of badge or token at shrine-centers, as described in chapter 3. Readers who would wish to follow up this subject are now referred to Brian Spencer's *Pilgrim Souvenirs & Secular Badges: Salisbury & South Wiltshire Museum Medieval Catalogue*, Part 2 (Salisbury, 1990). This finely produced catalog is much more than a descriptive summary of some 325 items; it also provides a historical background to the various types of metal pilgrim badges, ampullae, livery badges, pendants, love tokens and noise-makers (such as bells, whistles and rattles) used on festive occasions and even pilgrimages. It also includes a bibliography of approximately 170 entries. Pilgrim badges and medals from medieval times to the nineteenth century are discussed and illustrated by Heidelinde

Dimt in 'Heiligenverehrung auf Münzen und Medaillen' in Dinzelbacher and Bauer, *Heiligenverehrung*.

Chapter 3 also deals with the process of canonization, which began
its development into procedural maturity in the thirteenth century.
Here I must recommend a short but enlightening essay by an
acquaintance from my Oxford days, Patrick Daly (who, after obtain-
ing his doctorate, went off to the priesthood and a job in Rome examining the dossiers of prospective saints), 'The Process of canonization
in the thirteenth and early fourteenth centuries', *St. Thomas Cantilupe:
Essays in his Honour*, ed. Meryl Jancey (Hereford, 1982), pp. 125-35.
Sections of chapter 4 should be read in conjunction with Nancy G.
Siraisi's admirable work, *Medieval & Early Renaissance Medicine: An
Introduction to Knowledge and Practice* (Chicago, 1990). As for the distinctions between sacred and secular curative techniques mentioned
here, and for additional food for thought concerning the relationship
between Christian and non-Christian cultures in early medieval
Europe, see Valerie I. J. Flint's *The Rise of Magic in Early Medieval
Europe* (Princeton, 1991).

If rewriting chapter 5, 'Saintly Therapy in Action: Shrine-cures and
Home cures', I would probably stress even more the distinctions
between the two types of cures in its title. This is a difference of
substantial importance and should be recognized as such. Indeed,
this distinction was made in one of the most important books to have
appeared in this field since 1977, by André Vauchez, *La sainteté en
occident aux derniers siècles du moyen âge d'après les procès de canonisation
et les documents hagiographiques* (Rome, 1981). For Vauchez, the shift
away from shrines, and away from material relics, in the working of
miracles in the later middle ages, represents an important psychological shift in attitudes toward sanctity itself. Chapter 5 also considers
dreams and visions as they relate to saints, pilgrimages and miracles.
Dreams as stimuli to pilgrimage, or as occasions of visitations by
saints sometimes followed by cures, are discussed by Maria Elisabeth
Wittmer-Butsch in *Zur Bedeutung von Schlaf und Traum im Mittelalter*
(Krems, 1990).

In some reviews of *Miracles and Pilgrims* I was taken to task for,
among other things, attempting in chapter 6 to identify too specifically the ailments and disabilities that were reported by the pilgrims
or, to express it more accurately, recorded by the registrars who main-
tained lists of miracles at the shrines, or elicited from sworn witnesses
giving testimony at papal canonization inquiries. Other reviewers
faulted me for not being more specific and mathematically detailed
concerning the accidents, ailments and other hazards reported by pilgrims. These conflicting opinions lead me to conclude that perhaps
my approach was adequate after all: rather than trying to determine

what was 'really' wrong with the medieval suppliants, I continue to believe that the most appropriate methodology is the one I set out on p. 103: 'We will follow the clues given by the registrars and pilgrims and classify ailments not by what we think they 'really' were, but according to the symptoms and signs as given in the miracle collections even if this only conveys a vague idea of the events going on at the shrine.'

In approaching the problem of types of events associated with particular individuals and groups of pilgrims, discussed in the eighth chapter, I would now perhaps be more tentative about assigning suppliants to particular 'classes' within medieval society. In addition, it would be interesting to see how the figures derived from these English cults would compare with those from, say, Italian cults. Secondly, in recasting chapter 8 I would probably pay more attention to the question of expectations: how did preconceptions of 'miracles' carried around in the heads of the 'unsophisticated' majority of pilgrims differ from those entertained by educated, privileged or clerical pilgrims, or between men and women; and to what extent did these assumptions about what 'miracles' were *supposed* to be, amongst various pilgrim types, predetermine the context and character of their 'miracles'? Though I stated that medieval pilgrims worked their own miracles, it would be interesting to explore further the implications of this apparently unremarkable conclusion. Finally, now that I have had the opportunity to examine continental and particularly Italian cults, I find that the concept of 'shame' is one worth additional investigation. On pp. 149-50 I indicated that some pilgrims at English shrines were embarrassed about their infirmities, and that these tended to be the wealthier, privileged, even noble pilgrims. Subsequently, I have found in such collections as the one edited by Nicola Occhioni, *Il Processo per la Canonizzazione di S. Nicola da Tolentino* (Rome, 1984), that this tendency to be ashamed of certain illnesses, debilities or even accidental deaths was also present among the townsfolk of central Italy, and not necessarily the richest or most honored townsfolk. Variant cultural expectations about 'shameful' situations in England, and in Italy, would repay further examination.

The communication of ideas about 'new' saints is the subject of chapter 9. As to particulars in this chapter, it should be stressed that one of the virtues of the many Becket miracles is the fact that they were recorded over a relatively short period of time; consequently I would now give even more weight to the geo-temporal patterns elicited from the overlapping lists created by Benedict of Peterborough and William of Canterbury, in spite of the problems of their composition.

The pursuit of the cult of Thomas Cantilupe, Bishop of Hereford (d. 1282), featured in chapter 10, has taken me deep into the Herefordshire countryside in search of deserted villages, ruined chapels and nearly vanished fishponds in an effort to reconstruct the medieval ambiance of several of his best-documented miracles. I must acknowledge the encouragement provided by my companion on many of these rambles through the English countryside, my wife, Lynette Folken. This process of examining the locations mentioned (in meticulous detail) in the sworn statements recorded by papal commissioners in 1307 has helped me to make more sense of the testimony about several of the 'miracles.' I presented some of the fruits of this field-walking at an international roundtable in Krems, Austria, published a few years later as 'Pilgrimage in Daily Life: Aspects of medieval communication reflected in the newly established cult of Thomas Cantilupe (d. 1282), its dissemination and effects upon outlying Herefordshire villagers', in *Wallfahrt und Alltag in mittelalter und früher Neuzeit* (Wien, 1992), pp. 165-217. Some details requiring emendation in my chapter on Cantilupe are found on p. 174. There I state that the bishop's body was interred in 1282, but I now recognize that this occurred in 1283; in 1285 six, not three as stated, bishops provided indulgences for prayers for his soul, and in 1286 not one more, but five more, bishops offered further indulgences. These details arose from perusal of a Vatican manuscript *(Vat. Lat. 4016)* that deals not with Cantilupe's canonization, but with his purported excommunication by archbishop Pecham. Perhaps this is the appropriate place to suggest that since the longest extant papal process of canonization for any English saint is contained in the companion manuscript *(Vat. Lat. 4015)*, and that none of 4016, and only sections of 4015 have been published (with many errors, in *Acta Sanctorum*), it would seem that both of these manuscripts are worthy of transcription and publication in toto.

In dealing with late-medieval shifts in sensitivity toward holy places and figures (in chapter 11), Vauchez's *La sainteté* is particularly perceptive. A rather different aspect of the problem is considered by Richard Kieckhefer in *Unquiet Souls: Fourteenth-Century Saints and Their Religious Milieu* (Chicago, 1984), in which the author is less concerned with cults than with the individuals who become sanctified. Along these lines, another relatively recent work on the late medieval period is Aviad M. Kleinberg's *Prophets in their Own Country: Living Saints And the Making of Sainthood in the Later Middle Ages* (Chicago, 1992). Michael Goodich has just completed a study of the inter-relationships between fourteenth-century miracles and saints' cults and the violence and anxieties of that age. This work, to be published shortly, will no doubt helpfully augment our understanding of yet other ways in which the natural and supernatural worlds intermingled in the Middle Ages. In rewriting this chapter I would now, when touching on the subject of Mariolatry and the Virgin's cult in general, be able to draw upon the prolific harvest of recent studies on medieval women, one of the many areas of scholarly research that has been enriched by feminist history.

This book's final chapter, on the English Reformation and fate of the saints' cults and shrines, should now be read in conjunction with Eamon Duffy's *The Stripping of the Altars: Traditional Religion in England 1400-1580* (New Haven, CT, 1992). Though the title leads one to expect that the book is a study of English iconoclasm, it is this and much more; in fact nearly two-thirds of its pages are dedicated to an examination of late-medieval belief and ritual (and therefore appropriate to the eleventh chapter of *Miracles and Pilgrims*), while the last third or so takes up the history from 1530 (thus useful for chapter 12). Margaret Aston's *England's Iconoclasts* (Oxford, 1988) is a thoroughly researched, excellent study.

In addition to comments I make in the final chapter about the treatment of the holy dead in Henry's reformation of the Church (and the more harsh treatment accorded statues and images), I would now take an even closer look at correlations between the decline and destruction of English shrines and greater popular recourse to curative alternatives such as springs and baths, and the 'cunning' men and women found in so many villages, as well as their less fortunate manifestations, witches, whose pursuit and condemnation was a marked characteristic of post-Henrician England.

* * *

Although in 1977 I recognized some of the people who had assisted in the preparation of this book, I take this opportunity to augment that list of acknowledgments, which should begin with Professor Emeritus Gavin Langmuir of Stanford University, who, by introducing me during the 1960s to the cult of 'little' William of Norwich (d. 1144), drew me into the world of posthumous cures at medieval shrines—from which, it seems, I've never escaped. His assistance, in many ways, has been invaluable. Others to whom I remain grateful are the late William Urry, my research director at Oxford whose wry humor livened up many a discussion of Becket's cult and Marlowe's escapades, and at Cambridge the late Christopher Cheney, one of the most exacting scholars, and kindest men, I have ever known, and who after the appearance of the book encouraged my exploration of procedural aspects of canonizations. Among the many scholars (some already mentioned) to whom I am indebted for publications of particular value in my research both before and after *Miracles and Pilgrims* first appeared, or for correspondence, conversations and suggestions that have been especially helpful, I must not neglect to mention Christopher Brooke, Patrick Daly, Pat Geary, Michael Goodich, Thomas Head, Christian Krötzl, Lionel Rothkrug, Barbara Schuh, André Vauchez, and Benedicta Ward. I should also mention Peter Shellard, who guided the first edition of this book into print for Dent and Sons in 1977, and who has remained a respected friend ever since. Thanks are due to the editorial staff of St. Martin's Press and to Simon Winder, Senior Editor, for agreeing to publish this reprint as a paperback, thereby bringing it within range of a larger segment of the reading public and, one hopes, of university students interested in studying these important aspects of medieval history and culture or the mechanisms of 'faith healing' in general.

R. C. Finucane
Rochester, Michigan
March, 1995

Introduction

This is a study of about 3,000 medieval people who claimed that they had experienced a 'miracle', in most cases a miracle of healing. A great many of them received their supernatural assistance after praying to Thomas Becket or going on pilgrimage to his tomb. Today, innumerable English and foreign tourists wander through the cool vastness of Canterbury cathedral, stopping for perhaps an hour on their way to London or to a summer's holiday at the seaside, pausing to gaze through the space where Becket's shrine once stood. Six centuries ago a visitor might have caught the notes of pipe and drum on the green as a worldly group of pilgrims arrived, having started out, perhaps, from an inn called Tabard in Southwark; he might have heard their raucous, holiday-maker voices as they filed in to visit Becket's monumental shrine at the apex of steps and altars, where for a few coins they could have seen the canopy of the shrine raised up to reveal gold and silver ornaments and gems and rubies that burned blood-red. After viewing the sights of city and cathedral and spending a night at an inn they would move off next morning on the homeward ride, with badges and phials of Canterbury water to prove to their neighbours that they had really seen the famous tomb. Going back to the early 1170s, however—before Becket's shrine and cult had become embellished, encrusted with 'respectability'—all was different.

A modern visitor, magically transported to the darkened crypt of this ancient church, would probably be astonished if not repelled by the sight of wretched cripples writhing on the floor at Becket's simple tomb, by the screams of fettered madmen straining at their bonds and the low moans of lepers and the blind, and by the characteristic odour of the Middle Ages, the stench of poverty and disease. The pious would pray noisily in the dancing shadows of the crypt or offer their hard-won pennies and home-made candles. An uncouth peasant gesticulates wildly as he tries to explain his miraculous cure to the monk in charge of the tomb; he knows no Latin, no French, and his English dialect is scarcely comprehensible to the guardian-monk. The recorder of the miracles, perhaps a monk named William of Canterbury, scribbles briefly on a scrap of parchment and waves away the pilgrim, who shrugs and shuffles from the crypt and goes up into the Kentish sunshine. A small deputation from Flanders arrives to describe and swear to the miraculous recovery of a child drowned but resuscitated after prayers and vows to the saint: the crowded crypt is hushed by foreign accents piping from the little girl herself who praises the great Saint Thomas Becket who had saved her life. After the rejoicing dies away a few noblemen, with a clutch of clerics, step forward to present their gemstones, their silver images, their models of human limbs and animals made of wax, their testimonial letters with pendant seals to be copied into the great book of miracles, *liber miraculorum,* placed alongside tales told by peasants who could only speak *Anglice,* in English.

The focal point of all this activity was the corpse of an archbishop murdered in his cathedral in 1170, to modern eyes a mere human skeleton, to medieval eyes one of the most famous relics of western Europe, the almost integral remains of an undisputed saint. But what was so special about a dead man's bones, not merely those of Becket, but of all the other saintly corpses revered in the Middle Ages? Why did these mouldering remains draw crowds of pilgrims; why should anyone pay for the privilege of kissing an ancient toe bone or touching the cold marble of a tomb? It is hardly satisfactory to say that these things occurred 'naturally'; there is little in the New Testament to suggest that the bones contained in reliquaries would loom so large in the popular religion of medieval Europe. Yet even today at Christian pilgrimage centres the shrivelled remains of saints are on display to crowds of eager visitors.

As we examine the historical and ideological background to beliefs about pilgrimage and saints, their relics and miracles, it will become clear that from the earliest Christian centuries there were conflicts about the extent to which these beliefs should be encouraged, even permitted. This running battle was fought not only between clergy and laity but within the Church itself. But 'the Church' is really a convenient expression almost devoid of meaning. At its extremes it embraced the Church of the Lateran in Rome and the Church as known, say, to the medieval villagers of Oxenton in rural Gloucestershire. There was not only an Italian and an English medieval Church, as a modern historian has emphasized,[1] there was a French Church and a Spanish, an Icelandic and a German, each with its own history, traditions, liturgical uses and saints. Within these Churches were hundreds of divisions subdivided again into thousands of smaller units, ending at last with a semi-literate cleric in some rude chapel in the midst of inhospitable forests or fields, surrounded by peasants who muttered charms over their ploughs and whispered magic words at crossroads. It was a very long way from pope or prelate to peasant-priest, a long way in distance, education and attitude. This is why there was contradiction, misunderstanding, fraud and credulity within 'the Church'; why popes defined and pseudo-friars defiled the concept of 'saint' or 'relic' or 'miracle'; why there were conflicts about these aspects of popular religion. We are apt to forget this diversity when discussing 'the Church', but in such a gigantic organization the wonder is that there was not more dissension in the Middle Ages. And outside this convoluted corporation the laity stood excluded, an exclusion which grew as the power of the clergy grew. As we shall see, these conflicts about popular beliefs were more or less resolved in England in the sixteenth century during the Reformation when the sources of discord were removed by sweeping away both the shrines and their thaumaturgic relics.

Faith-healing at the shrines of medieval saints[2] cannot be separated from this changing historical background, nor from the people who were actually involved. To appreciate the popular beliefs and rites which centred on curative shrines we need to know something not only about the particular saint and the origin and development of his cult,[3] but also about the pilgrims affected by his miracles, their social status and sex, where they lived, what particular 'miracle' they enjoyed. Some of the posthumous miracles provide extraordinarily intimate views of English life, detail down to the red laces of a peasant girl's new shoes.[4]

Our emphasis is upon English saints whose popular cults emerged between the Conquest of 1066 and about 1300. Although drawing upon more than 3,000 posthumous miracles—wonders attributed to saints after they had died—associated with a score of saints, both English and foreign, the main conclusions will be based on nine 'major' cults, seven English and (for comparison) two French, in which slightly more than 2,300 miracles were registered.[5] These were, in the twelfth century, the cults of William of Norwich, Thomas Becket, Godric of Finchale, and Frideswide of Oxford; in the thirteenth century, Wulfstan of Worcester, Simon de Montfort, Thomas Cantilupe of Hereford and, in France, Edmund Rich and Louis of Toulouse. Of the nine, five were officially canonized by the pope. These nine cults were chosen for three reasons. First of all, at least 100 posthumous miracles were registered in each cult. Secondly, the cults developed in the twelfth and thirteenth centuries, rather than in some legendary period for which we have very little historical evidence. These two criteria ensure that there are sufficient miracles for each cult from which to draw general conclusions, and that, excepting the cults of Wulfstan and Frideswide, the pilgrims were contemporaries of the saints to whom they attributed their miracles. The saints were 'real' people, the

1   The seven selected English cults: (1) Thomas Becket, Canterbury (2) Frideswide, Oxford (3) Thomas Cantilupe, Hereford (4) Wulfstan, Worcester (5) Simon de Montfort, Evesham (6) William, Norwich (7) Godric, Finchale

pilgrims were 'real', regardless of what may be concluded about their miracles. Thirdly, and related to the second point, is the fact that these were all 'new' cults. It is a commonplace that from a very early period the medieval universe was peopled with a multitude of saints; Britain was no exception. The Anglo-Saxon writer Aelfric boasted of the great numbers of English saints of his own day. With the Conquest England lost some of the old Anglo-Saxon saints but gained a great many from

Europe. In the twelfth and thirteenth centuries the English peasant who stood in his parish church on a Sunday would have been surrounded by the images of a score of saints to whom he might turn in his hour of need; they were part of his world, they were 'received' from earlier ages. But each of our selected saints' cults was something new to contemporaries, a fresh addition to the legions of spiritual helpers. We have chosen them because in them we can observe the impact of a novel saint upon society, as his cult takes shape. The evidence of how these 'new' saints affected the people of their regions lies in the posthumous miracles. We have chosen to examine only posthumous wonders because the miracles reputedly performed by a saint during his life tend to be far fewer in number and, as the product of a single admiring biographer, far more 'literary' and imitative than posthumous miracles. In our records, on the other hand, it is not the saint but the pilgrims themselves who work their 'miracles'.

Admittedly the pilgrims who reported these miracles represent only a fraction of all of the people who visited shrines, the registrars exerted a filtering effect upon what the pilgrims reported, and the whole concept of 'miracle' presents innumerable difficulties to many modern readers. These problems will be considered in due course. In our examination of the pilgrims and their miracles at medieval shrines we shall discover not only that there were characteristics common to all miracle-touched pilgrims, but also that the miraculous cure or other wonder reported by any given pilgrim tended to be related to the sex and social class of that pilgrim; the incidence of certain illnesses was not the same for all classes and sexes. We shall also discover that shrines might attract their own social 'types' and that the ratio of men to women varied, sometimes strikingly, from shrine to shrine. In other words, the people involved in miracles in different saints' cults were not all alike. Finally, our study will lead us to conclude that each saint's cult had its own history: at different periods a saint's shrine performed different functions in medieval society, and furthermore as those functions changed, so too did the characteristics of the pilgrims.

Perhaps the most primitive and immediate need which shrines satisfied was that of healing but, since this depended upon human enthusiasm, it was the most quickly extinguished and transient of all characteristics. Rather more long-term was the way the shrines served the needs of special-interest pilgrims who visited and attributed miracles to the entombed as honoured individuals, for example for political reasons. But as new generations replaced the old and the memory of the dead man or his cause faded, this appeal ceased too. Shrines also served medieval society as funds of spiritual comfort. Beyond the many subsidiary needs satisfied by the enshrined saints, medieval pilgrims, both the sick and the well, found relief in the assurance that they had spiritual protectors not only in earthly matters but also in that more important, everlasting world to come.

In the event this spiritual function outlasted all the others. Some saints, such as Becket, continued to the end of the Middle Ages to perform this service and attract pilgrims for that reason. This is not to say that society outgrew the need for curative shrines, which continued to appear in England up to the eve of the Reformation. But at almost any shrine the 'spiritual' vitality of the place might continue centuries after the miracles once performed there were only a memory.

The events at curative shrines are worth studying because they provide a glimpse of the behaviour of medieval people at centres of popular religion and an indication of what sorts of people were involved. They illuminate many aspects of the beliefs of the Middle Ages in a way that other historical sources—theological, liturgical, even (strictly speaking) hagiographical—cannot do. This has been recognized in recent years by a few European historians,[6] but so far there has been very little substantial work of this kind dealing with the English saints' cults, and it is hoped that the present study will stimulate further historical research into a fascinating body of documentary material. In addition, perhaps the information provided by medieval curative cults may appeal to those interested in modern 'faith-healing' and other alternative therapies in both the West and the East. Some of the findings may elucidate the behaviour of pilgrims at shrines which still play an important part in the lives of many people, as in India for example, where more than 1,800 holy places draw ever-increasing numbers of pilgrims every year. Whatever may be the other 'applications' of this study, however, the main purpose will be to find out how medieval people interacted with their spiritual heroes, the saints. We shall examine not only their beliefs, but also the actions which flowed from those beliefs. Finally, we shall look at the conditions of medieval life which reinforced this faith in wonder-working saints, and made them so important to the people who lived and died so many centuries ago.

Part One

Historical Background

Chapter 1

Dark Age Christianity: Miracles in the Missionary Epoch

As for Chlodobert, they placed him on a stretcher and carried him to the church of Saint Medard in Soissons. They set him down before the Saint's tomb and made vows for his recovery. He died in the middle of the night. . . .

Gregory of Tours (sixth century)

Christianity was born into a world already familiar with wandering healers and soothsayers; it developed in an atmosphere heavy with magic and miracle. Apollonius of Tyana, for example, a famous pagan wonder-worker of the first century A.D., was credited with miracles which included the resuscitation of the dead. There were cures at pagan shrines centuries before Christ's time, and Jews as well as pagans had a very ancient tradition of thaumaturgy or miracle-working; many wonderful deeds are chronicled in the Old Testament, like the dead brought to life by Elijah and Elisha or the cure of Naaman's leprosy. The four Evangelists reported cures wrought by Christ but, contrary to what one might expect, his miraculous powers were not fully extolled and exploited during the first three centuries A.D. since the Christian apologists knew full well that the *pagani* had a much older claim to thaumaturgic abilities. The pagans, in fact, looked upon Christ as just another itinerant magician or ordinary healer, and they were always ready to pit the wonders of Apollonius or Apuleius against those attributed to the Son of God.[1] And not only Gentile pagans, for in the New Testament certain factions of the Jews had claimed that Christ performed miracles not with the celestial assistance of Jehovah but through the infernal machinations of Beelzebub. In the mid-second century St. Justin Martyr had to combat the Jewish taunt that Christ was a mere 'magician who misled the people'.[2] Miracles, then, before the fourth century, played an ambiguous part in Christian propaganda. Yet by the early fifth century one of the most influential of all Christian writers, St. Augustine, Bishop of Hippo in north Africa, was eagerly publicizing miraculous cures wrought by the relics of the saints.

Although saints' relics were being venerated in the second century, if not earlier, the great boom in *miracles* associated with Christian relics seems to have begun during the fourth century, after Christianity was declared to be a tolerated religion by Emperor Constantine, in A.D. 313.

St. Augustine was present in 386 when the bodies of two martyrs, Protasius and Gervasius, were opportunely discovered in a basilica outside Milan by the bishop of the city, Ambrose. The holy remains were moved into Ambrose's new basilica where miracles then began to occur through the intercession of these newly-found 'saints'. Augustine, though not yet a Christian, was very impressed with all this, and in his autobiography he commented that a blind man was cured and demons cast out by the two saints. He became a Christian very soon after these events—within the year, in fact—and he never forgot them; perhaps they even had something to do with his conversion. Several years later (in 404) he wrote to a friend, Paulinus, 'Is not Africa also full of the bodies of holy martyrs? Yet *we do not know of such things* [*miracles*] *being done in any place here'* (that is, around Hippo).³ After 415, however, when the remains of St. Stephen the Protomartyr were found in the Levant and sent to north African churches, St. Augustine had ample opportunity to observe, at first hand, cures with relics of the sort which were to become so common in the Middle Ages; his is in fact among the first substantial collections of posthumous miracles in the west, sparked off by the reception of Stephen's relics. In two years he published accounts of more than seventy miracles for the Hippo area alone and he claimed that many more went unrecorded. He delighted in the details of the wonders performed by the relics, which he kept behind a protective metal grill in his basilica. Once, he was preaching to his congregation about one of these cures

> when lo! as I was proceeding, other voices are heard from the tomb of the martyr, shouting new congratulations. My audience turned round, and began to run to the tomb,

where they found that another miracle had occurred.⁴ Miraculous tokens of saintly power became common currency in fifth-century Christendom: the web had expanded, binding European cities and Constantinople in mutual veneration and exchange of miracle-working relics, encouraged by the leading clergy of the Mediterranean world. Relics—saints' bones, or objects associated with them, even bits of material which had touched their tombs—were not merely miraculous, they were fully mobile, too.

As posthumous miracles became part and parcel of popular Christianity in the fourth and early fifth centuries, appropriate rituals were established at curative shrines, and candles and incense, once prohibited by the Church as too 'pagan', now burned at saints' altars, while wax or silver offerings (often representing the anatomical parts cured) were brought by grateful pilgrims.[5] It is likely that the growth and spread of these traditions from the later fourth century was not only the result of the enthusiasm of certain prelates, but also of an increasing flow of pagans into the Church, especially after many found it prudent to observe the edicts of the Roman Emperor Theodosius— who in effect made Christianity the *only* legitimate religion of the Empire, in the late fourth century. Although pagan temples and altars were closed down, converted or destroyed, the old cures, visions and miracles of the healing god AEsculapius, or Apollonius, still occurred at Christian shrines under the patronage of a new spiritual hierarchy, the martyred saints.

Some Christian leaders reacted adversely to these trends. Even St. Augustine became more cautious in his old age, suggesting in his *Retractions* of about 427 that though miracles still happened they were not of the same order as those of Christ's time; Christians, he wrote, should not over-emphasize visible wonders and grow contemptuous through familiarity with them.[6] As the circles of Christianity widened, orthodox theological principles were qualified by less sublime inter-pretations of the hereafter and of the powers of the dead. Scattered beliefs about spirits, healing, magic and prayer, which varied according to the new convert's own region or tribe or social status or native scepticism, were re-interpreted along Christian lines. Nevertheless, it was not merely pressure 'from below' which brought miraculous relics into the Church.[7] All through the fourth century latent tensions developed as 'the Church' encouraged the principles but condemned the excesses of popular veneration of saints and their relics. The seeds of ambiguity, of paradox within the 'official' Church were already taking root, thrusting through the writings of bishops and theologians. The inherent conflicts were to re-appear in the non-Mediterranean, 'barbarian' world where faith in the power of holy bones became for many the very core of Christianity. By about A.D. 400 the first phase in the development of this side of popular religion was ending, the second about to begin.

Whether they were executed by Roman provincial officials in times of persecution or travelled the Roman roads unmolested to preach the good news in times of toleration, Christians were from the very beginning subjects of the Roman Empire. That gigantic bureaucracy, struggling for survival since about A.D. 200, finally succumbed to internal corruption and 'barbarian' hordes in the early fifth century. Alaric's Gothic rabble ravaged Italy and Rome in 410, and by 476 the line of Western emperors had come to an end. Yet something of tremendous significance remained, namely an organized network of believers—the Christian Church—which had evolved while the political machinery of the State was falling into confusion and which even imitated the imperial administration in some points. Some historians, like Gibbon (whom Boswell disliked because of his 'sneering infidelity'), have suggested that one of the causes of the fall of Rome was its adoption of Christianity. Although it has become evident since their days that the causes of the decline and fall were far more complex, this was an old idea long before the eighteenth century, with adherents as far back as the time of St. Augustine of Hippo whose own north Africa was ravaged by Vandals shortly after his death in the fifth century. He had written *City of God* to refute pagan claims that Rome fell to the barbarians because the old pantheon of Greco-Roman gods had been displaced by Christianity. It is in his meandering, voluminous work, thirteen years in the writing, that Augustine discussed the miracles which proved that God, independent of the rise or fall of mere temporal states, had not abandoned his own. Augustine could not have known that some day the barbarians, pacified and converted in their turn, would consider themselves the true Christians.

In the wake of the mass folk-movements of the fifth and sixth centuries, the migrations and wanderings of the Ostrogoths, Visigoths, Vandals and others conveniently comprehended by the term 'barbarians', the Christian missionaries who went out to convert these rude inheritors of the Roman Empire introduced them to a religion impregnated with miracles and saintly wonders. In Gibbon's caustic sentences,

> If, in the beginning of the fifth century, Tertullian, or Lactantius, had been suddenly raised from the dead, to assist at the festival of some popular saint . . . they would have gazed with astonishment and indignation on the profane spectacle which had succeeded to the pure and spiritual worship of a Christian congregation.[8]

It is likely that this worship was seldom pure or spiritual even in its earliest forms but it was this very 'spectacle', which so annoyed Gibbon, that was characteristic of the Christianity taken to the 'barbarian' tribes of Germany, Gaul and England.

Miracle was one of the most expedient of all missionary devices. In common with Elijah, who was told (after performing a miraculous cure), 'Now I know for certain that you are a man of God', many missionaries used their powers of faith-healing to prove that they had a special relationship with their Creator. For example, Germanus reputedly cured a crippled child in fifth-century Britain by running his hand over the afflicted knee, perhaps in the same manner as any modern faith-healer, at which 'the crowds were overwhelmed by the miracle *and the Catholic faith strengthened* in all of them'. The eighth-century English missionary to the Germans, Boniface, also converted many by 'sound doctrine *and miracles*'.[9] To the barbarian congregations who could barely grasp theological principles—such as they were—simpler methods of convincing them of the truth of Christianity were to perform miracles (usually of healing) or demolish their temples; the message could not then be misunderstood. Christian missionaries were labouring in this way among the *pagani* even before 410. In Gaul, for instance, St. Martin, Bishop of Tours, brought about conversions by preaching, healing and knocking down pagan shrines: the sight of burning temples convinced many barbarians that 'Martin's god should be worshipped and the idols ignored, which could neither save themselves nor anyone else'.[10] Sometimes, however, it was prudent to preserve heathen temples. In the early seventh century Anglo-Saxon idols were replaced by Christian altars and relics though many of the old familiar buildings were unmolested:

> The temples of the idols in that nation ought not to be destroyed; but let the idols that are in them be destroyed . . . For if those temples are well built, it is requisite that they be converted

so that the heathen English might more readily come in to learn about the new faith.[11] In these words Pope Gregory the Great suggested a generous compromise with traditional beliefs.

Pope Gregory (d. 604) himself 'contributed more than anyone to bridging the gap between the sophisticated past of the Roman Empire and the new barbarian society of the west'.[12] He was truly a man of his times: on the one hand a competent civil administrator in the Roman tradition, on the other a sincere believer in the miracles wrought by saints' relics. He begins his *Dialogues*, for instance, by noting the many miracles at the tomb of Fortunatus, where people were cured if they arrived 'with a lively faith'; we are drawn deeper into the miracle-world with every chapter of the *Dialogues*. Gregory wished to introduce the Christian faith to the strange men of the north whom he knew as 'Angles'. In well-known passages Bede describes how Gregory sent an Italian monk, Augustine, to the English in 597, how the missionaries, solemnly chanting and bearing a cross and a picture of Christ, met King Ethelbert of Kent on the Isle of Thanet—then actually an island—and how, some time after this meeting, the king was converted to Christianity and Augustine settled down in Canterbury as the first archbishop. Augustine's missionary-monks were admired for their exemplary way of life and 'delightful promises which, *by many miracles*, they proved to be most certain'. Unfortunately the power to perform cures seems to have gone to Augustine's head, since Pope Gregory admonished him, in 601,

> It is necessary that you . . . rejoice because the souls of the English are by outward miracles drawn to inward grace; but that you fear, lest, amidst

the wonders that are wrought, the weak mind may be puffed up in its own presumption.[13]

Though the pope acknowledged the utility of miracles in the task of converting men from the worship of Woden and Thor to that of Christ, there were other churchmen who were calling attention to the dangers of unregulated thaumaturgy. Alcuin, an English intellectual at Charlemagne's court who played a leading role in the Carolingian Renaissance, wrote that 'the ministry of preaching the Gospel is to be preferred to the working of miracles and the showing of signs', though he had to admit that country folk were usually more impressed by physical wonders than preaching.[14]

The consequences of employing miracles in the work of conversion is at once apparent: for the novice barbarian Christians, miracles and saints' relics attained a significance far beyond what the missionaries may have intended. The beliefs promoted by missionaries in the heat of conversion were often an embarrassment to later generations of churchmen in a peaceful Christianized Europe when the battle to evangelize had been won; but by then the damage had been done.

For the moment, however, relics streamed away from the shores of the Mediterranean, across the Alps and by sea, to assist missionaries in their work. Some fourth-century churches had been built over the graves of martyrs, but it was far easier to disinter the martyrs and transport their remains to a church and place them under the altars, which also allowed several individuals to be venerated in one place. This practice was called *translatio*, the translation or movement of a corpse or lesser relics from one place to another, usually more honourable, location.[15] For instance, when Constantine established a new city on the site of the old Greek town of Byzantium, martyrs' remains were sent for and by 357 Constantinople (as the place came to be called) had received the relics of SS. Andrew, Luke and Timothy. Relics were translated not only from country to country but also from one location within a church to another, commonly into a more elaborate shrine in a more prominent place. This custom of shifting relics here, there and everywhere—which gave rise to various abuses—was to be followed in England throughout the Middle Ages.

Sometimes what seem to us to be rather curious circumstances surrounded these translations. It was reported of several saints raised from their tombs in the Middle Ages that as soon as the lid was lifted from their coffins a sweet odour seemed to pervade the air, the 'odour of sanctity'. Whether these odours arose from traces of aromatics (balsam, for example) used in embalming, or from the imagination of the excited bystanders, cannot now be determined. Sometimes an even more striking discovery was made on these occasions, namely, that the corpse of the individual in question had not completely deteriorated to dust and bones. Even in France during the eighteenth-century 'Enlightenment' such discoveries aroused the same responses: when a woman's well-preserved but century-old body was dug up in a Breton church '*la nouvelle d'un miracle se répandit dans la contree*'.[16] This miraculous preservation—a mark of sanctity—could be known in the Middle Ages only by opening the coffin, and generally speaking only the coffins of presumed saints were unsealed, usually for a translation, so the occasional finding of an 'uncorrupted' corpse among purported saints was rather to be expected. Theologians fell back on biblical references to account for the uncorrupted body, but apart from their explanations it is likely that embalming, which was usually reserved for upper-class clergy and laity—crudely done though it was—may have left its mark. It is also probable that in many such cases the environment favoured the transformation in damp, hermetic conditions, of body fat into a waxy substance known as adipocere, which resists deterioration. In any case modern ideas of 'preservation', typified by the way our dead are presented as rouged dolls displayed in their best clothes in lined caskets, are very different from those of the Middle Ages. The fact of death was not so easily ignored then; people were far more accustomed to the sight of human bones and corruption than we are.[17] Even the slightest evidence of resistance to dissolution would have seemed a 'miraculous' confirmation of sanctity.

Throughout the early Middle Ages the bodies of martyrs and confessors (those who had suffered for their faith but had not actually been martyred) were unearthed and mobilized in defence and exaltation of the faith. At Rome itself the invading Ostrogoths, Greeks and Lombards destroyed many holy shrines but had thereby released even more relics from their hallowed graves. Benedict Biscop (d. 689) made six trips from Rome to England bringing books and relics for the enlightenment and comfort of his colleagues. The old Roman laws protecting the sanctity of the grave had long been—one might say—a dead letter; the traffic in relics increased in the seventh century, and in the eighth century Pope Paul I was magnanimously opening graves and giving away bones, while St. Boniface repeatedly carried relics from Italy to his German churches.

In this way, among the barbarians, the powers of holy men both living and dead took the place of abstruse doctrine and theological subtleties. 'The atmosphere of primitive Germanic Christianity could . . . only be that of belief in the miraculous, the hourly expectation of supernatural events.'[18] This situation was clearly the result of the export of the cult of saints and miracles from the world of Mediterranean Christianity to a new and robust Europe:

> It was only in this world of Christian mythology—in the cult of the saints and their relics and their miracles—that the vital transfusion of the

Christian faith and ethics with the barbarian tradition of the new peoples
of the West could be achieved.[19]

The 'vital transfusion' was well under way when in the sixth century
Gregory of Tours was collecting records of hundreds of relic-miracles,
and it was complete by the time Bede was writing in the early eighth
century. Saints' bones performed a variety of wonders like those that
thrilled St. Augustine of Hippo three centuries earlier, and which
Thomas Aquinas would discuss with scholastic detachment five
centuries later: Bede wrote, for instance, of tomb-dust mixed with
water as a healing elixir, of pregnant women safely delivered with the
aid of a miraculous belt, of demons who fled at the sight or touch of
relics, of wonderful springs of curative water which welled up where
holy men had died, and of bodies which lay for years in their coffins
without decaying and emitted a heavenly, sweet odour when disturbed.
In Bede's pages the new mythology appears as a fully-developed
system.

Such were the fruits of missionary zeal, the harvest of Christian
folklore. Missionaries won converts by reciting stronger charms,
routing braver devils, and performing greater wonders with objects
more powerful than rude idols. From Rome to Lindisfarne the powers
of holy bones were recognized by the simplest Christians, innocent of
theology, and for a thousand years these beliefs, though sometimes
challenged, would dominate much of the folk-Christianity of Europe.

Chapter 2

The Holy Dead and their Relics

The true religion of the Middle Ages, to be frank, is the
worship of relics.

A. Luchaire

An outstanding characteristic of the 'barbarian' Christianity of the
early Middle Ages was the belief in relics that worked wonders, but the
preservation and veneration of holy bones was hardly a Christian
innovation. The head of the Egyptian god Osiris was kept at Abydos,
the ancient classical world boasted several tombs of Aeneas, and in the
very first book of his great *Histories* Herodotus wrote of the quest for
the bones of Orestes. Many pagan relics were supposed to work
wonders and cure diseased suppliants, properties which were appropri-
ated by the bodies of Christian martyrs especially during the fourth
century as paganism fell to minority status and then became illegal.
Early imperial legislation prohibiting the removal, sale, or cutting up of
the dead was disregarded by those anxious to obtain even particles of
such powerful and valuable remains, and for the rest of the Middle Ages
they were bought and sold, bequeathed as heirlooms, stolen or counter-
feited, given as gifts, fought over and hoarded in secrecy. When the
corpse of William of Norwich was translated in the twelfth century, a
monk furtively removed a few loose teeth he found in the sarcophagus.
He later confessed that he committed this 'pious theft', as he called it,
so stealthily because

> I naturally feared that if it became known that I was in possession of the
> teeth . . . it might also happen that I should be deprived of them.[1]

Although it was their curative powers that were most widely
acknowledged, relics had many other uses. At one extreme, in twelfth-
century Rochester a man claimed that he had driven flames away from
a house with a Becket relic fixed to the end of a long pole,[2] at the other
relics were used in oath-taking since it was firmly believed that lying
would be taken as a personal affront by the saint, sometimes punishable
by death. Relics played a part in the trivial and the great controversies

of the age, in a minor property dispute where one of the parties came to court with holy bones instead of living witnesses, and in one of the most significant battles of the time, when King Harold lost both the realm of England and his life after breaking his oath sworn on the relics of Bayeux cathedral. It was no coincidence that William the Conqueror charged the Anglo-Saxon shield-wall near Hastings wearing those same holy objects round his neck. A twelfth-century writer claimed that the Welsh were far more cautious about oaths sworn before relics than those sworn on the Bible, an attitude no doubt shared by the English as well.[3]

Relics, especially the integral skeletons of widely-known saints, emitted a kind of holy radioactivity which bombarded everything in the area, and as early as the sixth century it was believed that objects placed next to them would absorb some of their power and grow heavier.[4] They affected oil in lamps which burned above them, cloths placed nearby, water or wine which washed them, dust which settled on them, fragments of the tomb which enclosed them, gems or rings which touched them, the entire church which surrounded them, and of course the hopeful suppliants who approached to kiss, touch, pray before and gaze upon them. In the earlier centuries they were sometimes placed in circular crypts so that pilgrims could perambulate in an orderly manner and share equally in the beneficent aura. Relics made an impact on the beliefs of medieval Christians and even altered the physical setting of their congregational rites.[5] After about A.D. 800 it often happened that holy remains were raised from under the altars, probably because the numerous relics imported by Frankish prelates excited competition between churches and so prompted the 'elevations' of their saints. Usually a shrine was placed directly upon the altar which (once reserved for the Eucharist), gradually changed from a cubical into a rectangular table, with the shrine as a kind of centrepiece or primitive reredos. As shrines became larger and more elaborate, they were placed immediately behind the altars on separate bases. Thus altars for the first time had a 'back' and a 'front'. Many churches were rebuilt or extended in the eleventh and twelfth centuries and, with the coming of larger choirs, shrines were detached from their altars and set in a more eastern or 'holier' location which at the same time allowed easier access. In the twelfth century, for example, Abbot Suger explained that he rebuilt St. Denis to provide more space for pilgrims to move around the relics.[6] In some churches this evolution was retarded until a relatively late date: cubical altars were still in use in Alsace in the thirteenth century, and it was not until 1345 that the prior of Tynemouth disconnected Oswin's shrine from the high altar 'so that pilgrims could walk all round it and more easily and more freely pay their devotions thereat'.[7] Not all relics passed through these stages, for some remained permanently under the altar, while others rose from a simple tomb to a magnificent shrine without intermediate stages.

The level at which a saint's bones were placed or the height of his monument usually provided a rough measure of his importance. In 698, eleven years after Cuthbert died, the brethren decided to place his body in a new coffin 'but above the pavement, for the honour due to him'. Another, later, example is provided by the twelfth-century monks of Norwich cathedral who split into two factions in the matter of the gravestone of William of Norwich, the quality of whose sanctity was debated: should it be allowed to project a few inches above, or should it lie flush with, the ground?[8] The bones of really famous saints were sometimes elevated almost out of reach of the pilgrims, as in Westminster cathedral where the remains of St. Edward the Confessor still repose some six feet above the pavement in a thirteenth-century shrine. Pilgrims lodged themselves in the large niches in the base of Edward's shrine in order to be as near to the corpse as possible. Originally, as in St. Osmund's 'shrine' at Salisbury and Becket's first tomb, these niches were simply holes cut in a protective stone box built over the tomb.

The removal of certain saints to nearly inaccessible, elaborate shrines not only emphasized their elevated sacral status but in a way consolidated their *mana* (supernatural power), and made them even more *tabu*, to use some old-fashioned anthropological terms. Fear, seldom absent from feelings of reverence, was especially evident in attitudes towards certain famous relics. When Gregory the Great refused to send St. Paul's head to Empress Constantina he cautioned her against disturbing such powerful saints and provided horrific examples of their destructive vengeance.[9] In contrast to the small relics which people carried about on their caps or in rings, many of the enshrined saints could only be approached after undergoing rituals that were meant to surround the suppliant in a protective shell. Ordinary pilgrims were expected to be without mortal sin when they drew near the holy dead, and when a saint was to be translated to a more honourable shrine the officials who were to take part usually prepared themselves with a three-day ritual of prayer and fasting before daring to touch the remains. Even after observing all the precautions, certain bodies were approached in fear and trembling. When in 1198 Abbot Samson of Bury St. Edmunds picked up the shrouded skull of his patron, Edmund, he prayed with many loud groans that the famous martyr would not damn him because 'I, a miserable sinner, now touch thee'. He had good reason to tremble and groan, for one of his predecessors had interfered with the same corpse to his lasting regret:

> A certain abbot . . . wished to know for himself whether the head that had been cut off at [Edmund's] martyrdom had been reunited with the

body . . . To his danger, he learned all this by sight and touch; with one
at the head and the other at his feet, he pulled to see how [Edmund] was
and determined that the body was solid. But soon after he wasted away
with a permanent palsy of both hands.[10]

This striking scene—an English abbot and a monk, tugging away at the
feet and head of a corpse—could only have happened in the medieval
world of relics and saints. But, just as saints punished anyone who
disrespectfully fingered their remains, so they favoured those who
treated them with due honour—one reason why, when the body of St.
Edmund Rich was translated to a new shrine in the thirteenth century,
a devoted cleric carefully arranged the hair on the head of the sanctified
corpse.[11]

Monasteries and cathedrals were the greatest repositories of relics. In
1116, for instance, the rich Benedictine house at Abingdon claimed to
possess, among other things, five relics of Christ, pieces of six apostles,
bits of thirty-one martyrs, assorted remains of thirty-nine confessors,
and particles of sixteen virgins.[12] Even this collection was modest when
compared with the astounding number of relics in Canterbury
cathedral at the close of the Middle Ages. The desire to enhance the
reputation of their cathedral or monastery or even village church
plunged many clerics into compulsive relic-gathering. While visiting the
French monastery of Fecamp the saintly Hugh, Bishop of Lincoln (d.
1200), thought nothing of chewing off a piece of Mary Magdalen's arm
'with his incisors and finally with his molars' while onlooking monks
hopped about in anxiety wailing *O, O prob nefas*, for shame, for shame.
Hugh replied that if he could touch the Divine Body of Christ in the
Mass, surely he should be allowed to apply his teeth to Mary's bones.
On another occasion he obtained a relic of St. Nicasius by pulling a
little bone out through the holy eye-socket.[13] With respectable prelates
indulging in these practices it is little wonder that the lesser clergy
followed suit. This attitude justifies the statement that in 1274,

> Thomas Aquinas, lying on his deathbed at Fossanova, thinking his last
> syllogism, can hardly have been unaware of eyes contemplating his
> body, minds thinking what a splendid relic he was about to become.[14]

The great scholastic philosopher did indeed provide splendid
relics—which worked miracles—after the flesh had been boiled from his
bones. This was often the fate of notable personages who had died far
from home; to facilitate transport the body was dismembered, the flesh
and viscera were removed and buried usually near the place of death,
and the skeleton was packed up and taken to the home-country for
ceremonious burial. This was so common that Bishop William Durand
the Elder (d. 1296) thought it unnecessary to reconcile (ritually
reconsecrate) a church after bloodshed—if that blood had been spilled

while a corpse was being 'dismembered in the church or embowelled, that perhaps one part may be buried in one place, and another in another'. Evidently the pope disagreed, for in 1299 Boniface VIII forbade the eviscerating, dismembering, and boiling of human bodies in churches.[15]

Yet even within a monastery or cathedral saints were sometimes dismembered in order to establish subsidiary shrines. A thirteenth-century English chronicler claimed to be horrified that monks at Pontigny (in central France) had cut an arm from the corpse of the Englishman, St. Edmund Rich, and placed this limb in its own reliquary,[16] which allowed more pilgrims to honour the saint and thereby attracted greater contributions.

Sometimes a great deal of money was at stake. Becket's golden, bejewelled memorial at Canterbury, for example, was one of the greatest concentrations of portable wealth in England. Sir Simon Burley (a tutor to Richard II) was even accused of trying to steal it. Froissart reported that for some people his downfall and execution in 1388 were not unconnected with this suspicion. In many churches there was a noticeable correlation between the acquisition (or translation) of saints' bones and new building projects financed by the pilgrims' offerings. The nave of Hereford cathedral was enlarged or strengthened thanks to the oblations at Cantilupe's shrine, the west front of St. Albans was built with offerings to the imaginary St. Amphibalus, and the body of Edward II turned out to be a 'gold mine', as Coulton called it, for the Gloucester monks.[17]

For financial as well as other reasons some famous relics caused prolonged disputes between towns or rival monasteries. Glastonbury and Canterbury contended for St. Dunstan's corpse into the sixteenth century and Dorchester and Winchester both claimed the bones of Bishop Birinus, just as in the early Middle Ages the monks of Poitiers and Tours disputed energetically about the body of St. Martin. There are diverting tales of nocturnal thefts and crafty substitutions of bodies, as well as battles over the possession of a few bones, in the chronicles of many countries. The strife was sometimes 'resolved' by the production of duplicates, which might account for at least a few of the heads of St. John the Baptist and other saints. Occasionally duplication arose quite innocently. After a relic communicated its power to other objects, over the years these secondary relics could become confused with the original, especially if placed in reliquaries which disguised their true form. For instance, a head-shaped reliquary might be called a 'saint's head' even if it contained only a sliver of skull, so that several 'heads' of the same saint might co-exist. This is not just a medieval phenomenon: until 1954 'two skulls' of Joseph Haydn were in existence, two of Emanuel Swedenborg up to 1958 and as recently as

1965 two of Friedrich von Schiller.[18] Moreover, even after the relics were translated people often continued to worship at the original burial site, thus adding to the confusion. Though Becket's bones were taken upstairs to a new shrine in 1220 pilgrims continued to go down into the crypt to venerate his empty tomb, which had itself become a relic—no doubt to the delight of the Canterbury monks.

There was ample opportunity for deception from the moment bodies were moved, and when they were cut up the possibilities became infinite. Abuses, and attempts to curtail them, increased together as the centuries went by. As early as the sixth century doubtful relics were liable to trial by fire since it was believed that the genuine article could not be destroyed by flames. The eighth century was the great era of faked relics in the Frankish realms.[19] Since missionaries had created a demand among their converts the supply of relics—real and fake—increased to meet that demand. In relatively peaceful conditions, fostered by strong Frankish rule, not only merchants and priests, but imposters and relic-mongers could more easily cross the forested lands of Francia, encouraging churches to vie for notoriety as relic-museums by displaying their treasures conspicuously upon their altars. The almost inevitable abuses grew more serious, and so did attempts to end them. In 811, to cite but one of many similar laws, Charlemagne ordered his ministers to keep an eye on anyone dealing in relics, and a few years later a Frankish Church council reiterated this. As an example of the frauds perpetrated with so-called 'relics', in the early eleventh century a certain enterprising grave-robber used to gather up a load of miscellaneous bones and then

> sell them widely as relics of holy martyrs or confessors. Eventually he fled from Gaul into the Alps where folk were not particularly bright, assumed a false name, and then as was his custom collected human bones, put them into a shrine, and claimed that an angel had revealed that they were the bones of a martyr, 'Justus'. As soon as the word spread, the simpletons began to gather.[20]

Credulous people who paid their small fees for the privilege of bowing before such objects—touted about almost like a travelling 'peep show'[21]—were never in short supply. But there were various ways to protect the simple (both among the clergy as well as the laity) besides trial by fire, such as the inspection of any writings or other tokens of authenticity which might be found with the relics when their shrines or reliquaries were unsealed. This was often left to local or visiting prelates. During one of his visits to England at the end of the eleventh century Anselm (soon to become Archbishop of Canterbury) was asked to authenticate the bones of a certain St. Neot. After opening the carrying-case or feretory, he verified the remains, removed an arm—which later ended up in Cornwall—and took away a small portion of the saint for his own use, then

> carefully closed and locked the bones in the case and took the key away
> with [him] to the church at Bec where it is diligently preserved to this
> very day.

The process of control was extended and, in the twelfth century, for
instance, the rules concerning relics became part of canon law, or at
least were included in Gratian's collection of ecclesiastical law, the
Decretum, and a church council at Westminster decreed that relics were
not to be venerated without episcopal approval.[22]

Even so, public demand for relics was far stronger than public
obedience to church regulations. After the fall of Constantinople in
1204 the churches of the East were ransacked and crate upon rattling
crate of bones was sent to the West. The subsequent relic-inflation
sometimes had bizarre results, to say the least: some Western churches
claimed to possess Christ's breath in a bottle, his tears or blood, Mary's
milk, even the tip of Lucifer's tail. The Venetians were ready to display
a molar from the capacious mouth of Goliath.[23] Europe went through
its last great age of relic forgery as unscrupulous laymen and clerics
took advantage of the confused situation. The Church tried to rise to
the challenge, and in 1215 Pope Innocent III ordered that no one
should 'presume to announce newly-found relics unless they shall have
first been approved by authority of the Roman pontiff', a regulation
already implicit in some earlier papal decrees. The English prelates
followed Innocent's lead, repeating his mandate at a number of
thirteenth-century councils. But the laity and lower clergy were too
strongly addicted to relic-collecting for these efforts to be effective,
and even well-educated, responsible ecclesiastics sometimes accepted
objects as undoubted relics, without proof. Obviously, authentication
of the remnants of primitive saints who had died centuries earlier,
perhaps a thousand miles away, would have been very difficult to
obtain, and even if they knew they were fakes, medieval collectors may
have looked upon them as they looked upon forged documents, which
were nearly as good as the real article and served a useful, even godly,
purpose. Now and then this pragmatic attitude was openly acknowledged.

Just as prelates and even emperors found it necessary to approve
relics, control their acquisition and regulate their use, the rites of
saint-veneration became increasingly subject to the pastoral and
administrative offices of the Church. This regulative function had
appeared in the very earliest stages of saint worship. Even the pious
mother of St. Augustine of Hippo was turned away from a Milanese
basilica in the fourth century:

> When my mother had once, as she used to do in Africa, brought to the

churches built in memory of the Saints cakes, and bread and wine, she was forbidden by the door-keeper . . . lest an occasion of excess might be given to the drunken; and because these anniversary funeral solemnities resembled the superstition of the Gentiles.[24]

There were, then, two objections: such rites were too much like 'pagan' ceremonies, and in themselves they were inappropriate to the solemnity of the occasion since they might lead to drunken behaviour (which St. Augustine proscribed elsewhere). If regulated, however, offerings of food might be acceptable to the saints, or so Pope Gregory the Great thought in 601 when he allowed Anglo-Saxon converts to slaughter cattle for religious feasts provided the meat was offered not to devils but to God. Not everyone was ready to permit such rites; two centuries after Gregory, Charlemagne prohibited 'animal sacrifices which foolish men perform according to pagan rites near churches in the name of the holy martyrs'.[25] This was the sort of behaviour the early medieval Church wished to control. Rustic tendencies to overdo saint-worshipping grew more irksome and embarrassing as the hierarchy settled into sedate and self-conscious respectability in the post-missionary era. Ailred of Rievaulx possessed a sensitive and refined clerical intellect; we can only wonder what he was thinking that day in 1164 as he watched the enthusiastic denizens of Kirkcudbright trying—unsuccessfully—'to make a burnt offering of a bull to St. Cuthbert'.[26] Here, in the inhospitable Scottish environs of the Solway Firth, the two extremes of medieval Christianity—in effect, the two religions—faced each other. It was not the first time that reason and theology confronted popular belief and rite, nor would it be the last.

Bishops, called upon to determine whether relics were genuine or false, in the course of time had to distinguish between true and spurious saints as well. Though this would not have been much of a problem while Christians were being persecuted and martyred, after 313 A.D., the date usually taken to mark the official toleration of the Christian religion, genuine martyrs and unimpeachable confessors would gradually become something of a rarity. It was still true that if someone died violently as a result of his Christian beliefs (such as Boniface, martyred in Germany about 755) the Church almost automatically accepted him as a saint, but by the central Middle Ages, generally speaking, the primary route to sanctity no longer lay through self-sacrifice and death. The 'measurement' of holiness itself had become conjectural. It was often a matter of popular opinion whether a particular individual was, or was not, a saint, but the Church itself naturally claimed the right to make the decision. The working of posthumous miracles at a shrine or tomb usually convinced the uncritical that 'their' man was a saint; and occasionally popular canonizations were also suggested, and some official saints were confirmed, by the discovery of an 'uncorrupted body'.

The problem of official versus popular saints seems to have been especially serious among the English, who persisted in honouring their heroes regardless of ecclesiastical cautions. In the eleventh century Archbishop Lanfranc purged the post-Conquest English Church of several Anglo-Saxon saints such as Maerwynne, Mellitus, Aldhelm, even Dunstan, Aidan and Theodore (some were later reinstated). Lanfranc also wanted to dispense with Archbishop Alphege, killed in 1012 by raiding Vikings who used him as a target for the refuse of their banquet table, but Anselm dissuaded him. When he himself succeeded as archbishop, however, Anselm also intervened in popular saint-veneration when he ordered the Romsey nuns to stop honouring the remains of the Anglo-Saxon Earl Waltheof.[27]

Waltheof, executed as a traitor by William the Conqueror, represents the species of unofficial saint who created problems for kings and prelates alike, the 'rebel' leader cut down in battle or executed by royal command. Simon de Montfort was the best-known English political saint, killed in battle in 1265 while fighting against the king's army; another was Thomas of Lancaster, 'martyred'—actually executed under Edward II—in 1322. In both cases public veneration of their remains (around which miracles were said to have occurred) was prohibited by civil as well as ecclesiastical authority. The political function of these 'saints' comes out clearly in an incident in fourteenth-century Bristol. After the execution of some rebels certain men,

> wishing to alienate the affection of the people from the king [Edward II] . . . pretending that miracles had been performed at Bristol at the places where the bodies hung, have made and published idolatrous tales there.

Their methods were quite uncomplicated: they stood around the gibbet loudly discussing 'miracles' wrought by the remains and one of them paid a local child two shillings to say that he had been cured of blindness. A more famous case involved Archbishop Scrope of York, executed as a rebel in 1405. Henry IV prohibited veneration at his tomb, where miracles were reported, and sent four men-at-arms there to keep the people away.[28]

So far we have examined beliefs about saints' relics and the 'official' attitudes toward those objects and toward the saints themselves. Perhaps the dreams and visions of medieval folk will enable us to discover some of the common, *unofficial* assumptions about the saints. Although most people would have agreed that the saints were physically 'dead', some considered them still subject to the usual—even trivial—sensations of life. 'Saint' William of Norwich appeared to a man in a dream or vision to complain that pilgrims soiled his tomb with spittle, on another occasion he told a young Norwich girl in a vision that his neck was giving him pain as he lay in his coffin. St. Edmund Rich reported in a dream that he could work no miracles since the earth crushed his body and kept him from raising his hands to assist suppliants, and Godric of Finchale confided to another sleeper that he had a distinct aversion to the stench of public latrines situated near his church, where he lay buried. Usually, saints were thought of as much more than captive cadavers: they were powerful spirits, ghosts who haunted their tombs. In their dreams and visions pilgrims saw the saint lift his coffin lid to get in and out and Godric's sepulchre even opened automatically as he approached it; one dreamer tried to snatch a piece of his clothing as the tomb closed over him.[29] A Canterbury cathedral window shows Becket floating out of his shrine to assist a suppliant, and other saints, such as Cuthbert, were also depicted this way in medieval manuscripts. Artistic and liturgical conventions could only stimulate or reinforce popular imagination and encourage the literal interpretation which is so characteristic of folk-beliefs. For example, a sleeping pilgrim 'saw' the Virgin Mary float down from a window (which bore her image) and in another case a suppliant sleeping near a shrine decorated with small statues 'saw' a foot-high saint in his dream-vision; a third sleeper reported seeing certain saints 'standing' upon a rood-beam just where small caskets of their relics actually rested.[30]

These very literal, simple and straightforward images were only part of the story. Sleeping pilgrims also 'saw' the saints in heaven, usually elegantly dressed and seated among the angels in the vicinity of Christ or his mother; at other times saints were 'seen' walking about on earth, sometimes in the company of other saints. Because saints could easily escape from their graves it was commonly believed that it was not necessary for men to have access to a relic to invoke them, or even to be punished by them. On this point theology agreed with popular beliefs. It was most unwise to deride saints' powers as, for example, a certain Aliza learned to her dismay. When she heard that a woman who had gone to Becket's tomb lost her sight, she

> burst out laughing, saying, 'Others, whom the Martyr receives in sickness, he sends back healed: you, however, went there well, and now return blinded'. While dissolved in laughter, Aliza was suddenly blinded, and eventually only partially cured.[31]

Saints were also quick to punish a disregarded vow or promise (especially a vow of pilgrimage to their shrines); indeed, any promise to them was ignored at great peril:

> After a knight vowed a pilgrimage to Becket's tomb his son was cured,

but the promise was forgotten. Another son sickened and died, and the knight himself and his wife fell ill. To prevent further calamities they decided on an immediate pilgrimage. Though they had great discomfort because of their illness, at last they reached the tomb and discharged their vow.

A twelfth-century English monk summed up the vindictive aspects of the saints in this way: 'The more mighty and worshipful they are, the more caution is needed lest they be offended.'[32] Their wrath was clearly to be feared, but most often medieval folk preferred to attribute to their ghostly heroes beneficent rather than malevolent actions. In this they were at one with the biographers of the saints, the hagiographers.

In the primitive Church the *acta*, or records of the trials with the valiant statements of Christians who fell under persecution, were cherished by the Christian communities scattered around the Mediterranean; hagiography, the writing of saints' lives, developed from such simple origins. We may take as one of the seminal works of Christian hagiography the *Life* of St. Martin of Tours (d. 397) by Sulpicius Severus, who died in the early fifth century. This work was repeatedly imitated by writers in the Middle Ages, when plagiarism was almost an act of piety. For instance, a twelfth-century English hagiographer claimed that a miracle he recounted had the authority of Severus; another English writer, Walter Daniel, unashamedly acknowledged Severus as the model for his *Life* of St. Ailred, while a third English cleric described Hugh of Lincoln's corpse as 'like Martin's, clearer than glass, whiter than milk', words lifted from Severus. The same expression was also pirated from the same source by Walter Daniel.[33] Severus was not the only early hagiographer useful to the English, for wherever there were books in medieval England there was Bede, whose *Ecclesiastical History* and *Life of Cuthbert* provided dozens of motifs for later saints' lives. Sometimes whole sentences from Bede reappeared unaltered in the writings of later hagiographers, just as Bede himself had used the works and occasionally the words of even earlier biographers of saints. One of the imitative hagiographers mentioned above found Bede at least as helpful as Severus: after discussing a case of an amorous demon he suggested that incredulous readers should turn to the commentary on Luke by the irreproachable Bede for an even stranger tale.[34]

Hagiographers busied themselves in extolling the wonderful penances and frightful austerities of their subjects, their charity, chastity and charisma, their extreme piety, feats of healing, and so on. They did not produce what one could call an impartial biography—if such a thing has ever existed—but on the contrary they often went in for highly embellished accounts of the lives and miracles of their saints.

Although some writers were more objective than others, hyperbole found its way even into the 'official' canonization documents of the later Middle Ages.

By the thirteenth century the papal *fiat* was essential to canonization, as it is today. This had not always been so. In the earlier medieval period translations or other official recognitions of sanctity were often associated with Church synods. In a sense this was canonization by counsel and consent, in which individual bishops often played a prominent part. As the papacy grew more self-assured, individual popes began to claim the right to designate those who should be honoured as a saint by the universal Church. The first extant papal canonization comes from the tenth century and expresses the rationale followed ever since, that martyrs and confessors are honoured as saints in order that glory redound to the Lord, whose servants they are.[35] By the twelfth century the papal (rather than episcopal or conciliar) right to canonize after proof of virtuous life and posthumous miracles (no definite number required) was generally acknowledged in the West, thanks primarily to Pope Alexander III. The very first saint he canonized, in 1161, was Edward the Confessor, the first English saint to be so honoured by a Supreme Pontiff. The energetic popes of the thirteenth century, trained in canon law and jealous of their plenitude of power, spoke with unquestionable authority in such matters. Innocent III sent commissioners out to take testimony from sworn witnesses and to return their notarized depositions, even the witnesses themselves, to the papal curia for further examination. The sole right to canonize was claimed for the papacy by Gregory IX in the Decretals of 1234, but, naturally, popes could delegate this authority: in the twelfth century Alexander III had given Becket a free hand to canonize Anselm after proper examination, though in fact Thomas never did so.

The canonical inquiry or inquisition into a prospective saint's life, morals and miracles increased in complexity and formality from the thirteenth century. Procedures were laid down at Rome and then Avignon for the careful sifting of testimony, interrogation of witnesses and elimination of hearsay wherever possible. The technical niceties of Thomas Cantilupe's inquisition, for example, would have brought a nasty twinkle to the eye of many a Dickensian lawyer; it took place in 1307, when the hearings were becoming very formal. By the end of the Middle Ages it was certainly as, perhaps even more, expensive and time-consuming to make saints as it was to resolve any other important ecclesiastical suit, especially as one drew nearer the papal curia. Everyone had to be paid, from the very least of scribes in the notary's employ working at a standard rate per sheet of parchment copied, all the way up to the agents and cardinals at the curia who brought the case to the attention of the right people and ultimately to the pope. These expensive procedures, which could take many years—even centuries—required a small army of notaries, proctors, commissioner-judges, and witnesses, who generated volume after volume of evidence. This is still true: in 1973, after eight years of investigation into the canonization of Pope John XXIII, oral testimony alone was said to fill twenty-five volumes, each of 300 to 400 pages.

The high cost explains why, usually, only the members of religious orders, royal families, or bishops of larger sees found their way into the universal calendar of medieval saints and why the canonized peasant saint was a rarity. Only the well-established could afford to support candidates decade after decade. Yet sometimes the fees were still unpaid long after the application for canonization. In Hereford, for instance, the cathedral canons argued for years over the cost of Cantilupe's process and in 1313 the bishop, unable to contribute to the royal funds for the Scottish wars, offered as a partial excuse the expensive attempts to canonize Cantilupe. These were not always empty pleas. At one point in the following century a schedule of tariffs for the formal Mass of canonization included:[36]

To the pope in gold or silver	100 Ducats
To the three commissioners of canonization	190 Ducats
For constructing a 'parco' in the church	100 Ducats
Notaries who record the process	20 Ducats
Clerks of the ceremonies	12 Ducats
Papal chamberlains	20 Ducats
Fiscal procurator	4 Ducats
For bulls	60 Ducats
For images of arms, shields and spears to be hung up	15 Ducats

The time required for a complete process was quite variable. Becket died in 1170 and was canonized in 1173, a speedy elevation. Sometimes even relatively unknown individuals were quickly recognized as saints, like a certain Lombard merchant named Homobonus who died while quietly attending Mass and was canonized two years later by Innocent III in 1199. Usually, however, popes added the dead—even those well-known—to the calendar only after repeated nudges from sponsors. Eventually, for one reason or another—often lack of money and interest after so many years with no apparent progress—many attempted canonizations were written off by their sponsors as bad ventures. For every successful candidate, hundreds failed; the archives of the Vatican include thousands of dossiers on would-be saints.

An example of a long-delayed but finally successful process is that of

St. Osmund. He died as bishop of Salisbury in 1099 and the campaign to canonize him was waged through the twelfth century. After a papal order for an examination of his purported miracles in 1228, further commissions followed—with little result—as one pope died to be replaced by another who had probably never heard of Osmund. He was enrolled at last among the saints in 1467, over three centuries after his death and after the expenditure of at least £700 at the papal curia, quite a sum even in the inflationary fifteenth century. Perhaps the record for procrastination, however, involved St. Anselm who, ironically, probably deserved to be honoured as a saint more than most prelates of his or any succeeding age. He died in 1109 but was not officially canonized until A.D. 1720.

The Church tried, then, to control the veneration of saints and their relics from the early to the central Middle Ages. These tendencies—to regulate, determine and prohibit—grew more marked as the Church attained a commanding position, but at the same time the tensions generated by this situation also increased. The hierarchy could neither deny the sanctity of relics and the intermediation of saints, nor condone the excesses committed not only by the lay public but even by some of its own clergy, in their dealings with these very saints and relics. It was a conflict between the ideal and the real, between what the Church prescribed and what ordinary Christians actually did. Relics should be honourably preserved as vestiges of great and holy people, but they were used in ways we can only call magical; self-sacrifice and great piety should be rewarded by the Church as a matter of course, but the people honoured whomsoever they wished, often for reasons entirely divorced from piety. In any case in the big business of saint-making, money and a promotion campaign were often more effective than holiness. These contradictions were criticized with growing vehemence in the fourteenth and fifteenth centuries by churchmen as well as by many among the laity. Meanwhile, this uncomfortable situation also affected attitudes toward pilgrimage and 'miracles'.

Chapter 3

Pilgrims' Progress and Wonder Tales

I do not believe in miracles. I have seen too many.

Oscar Wilde

The conviction that the saints, who inhabited both the earthly and the celestial realms, were especially responsive to prayers uttered in the vicinity of their relics was one of the dominant themes of popular religion in the Middle Ages. There were many corollaries to this, among which the most important were the belief in the efficacy of pilgrimage to a saint's shrine or tomb, and the expectation of posthumous miracles at these holy places.

Pilgrimage is one of civilized man's oldest habits. Egyptians, fierce Hittites and mysterious Hourrites, Babylonians and the wisest of Greeks undertook *peregrinatio*: then as now Hindus, followers of Buddha and of Mohammad set out along their own dusty holy ways with staff and begging bowl or wallet. Hebrews had known centuries of perpetual pilgrimage: when Christ was twelve years old his family went on pilgrimage 'as usual' to Jerusalem, itself to become a city of Christian pilgrimage by the third century. Written accounts of routes to the Holy Land were in circulation before the end of the fourth century and by the seventh the holy journey to Rome was so common a practice that it was considered customary for Frankish nobles, and among the English one could already arrange to expiate a vow of Roman pilgrimage without ever leaving England.[1] Then during the ninth century a third major shrine, that of St. James (Santiago) of Compostella in northern Spain, was launched on a successful career. Becket's death at Canterbury in 1170 initiated yet another pan-European cult. These famous holy places were only a few of literally thousands of European shrines, each attracting its 'own' pilgrims. Pilgrimage accelerated with the pace of life until it was ingrained tradition by the twelfth century, and it remains one of the hallmarks of the Middle Ages, like the fairs of Champagne, the Bayeaux tapestry, the Quest for the Grail, the Black Prince.

The motives for pilgrimage were very varied: people went simply to express piety; to show opposition to kings by honouring their slain enemies; to have a sight-seeing holiday away from the farmyard drudgery; to carry out a penance; to collect free alms and food from monasteries and wealthier travellers, even to rob them; to ask for some special favour from the saints (or to thank them for favours received) such as male heirs, or business success, or overall protection. Many went to shrines to be cured of physical or mental afflictions.

Beginning with the rather frivolous reasons, it is evident that many people took advantage of the freedom pilgrimage offered, the chance to escape the knowing eyes of neighbours, for decidedly unspiritual ends. The moral dangers of wandering about the countryside were well-recognized. Even in the eighth century an English missionary in Germany asked the Archbishop of Canterbury to prohibit matrons and nuns from pilgrimaging to the continent since many died *en route* and 'few keep their virtue. There are many towns in Lombardy and Gaul where there is not a courtesan or a harlot but is of English stock.' Some of these unfortunates had probably run out of money and in despair had fallen from pilgrimage to prostitution. Casual sexual opportunities were no doubt more likely on pilgrimage, and some may have used the journey to facilitate their adultery, as was rumoured of two Canterbury pilgrims; in a poem an English servant, impregnated by a cleric, coyly mused, 'I shall say to man and page/ That I have been on pilgrimage'.[2]

Though the hope of sexual adventure may have lured some, many other wanderers took to the high roads of springtime England when 'longen folk to goon on pilgrimages', as Chaucer says, out of simple curiosity and the wish to get away from their villages, perhaps for the first time in months or years. Anyone who has experienced a particularly wet and cold English autumn and winter can fully appreciate Chaucer's words. It is not difficult to imagine their mood, with the April sun warming their huts and the trees beginning to revive; naturally they wished to get away from sodden cottages reeking with human and animal smells. Journeys to fairs or shrines were excellent excuses to see new places and people, to be entertained. The gaiety of fairs was not altogether absent from shrines, where musicians sometimes performed near sacred precincts and occasionally buffoons amused pilgrims as they queued at a holy tomb. The entertainment may have been inappropriately jocund at times; in the twelfth century a man was struck mad after staging a somewhat ribald interlude at an English shrine.[3]

Some pilgrims were snobs. When they came home they would proudly display their pilgrim badges purchased at various shrines, for then as now travel was supposed in some mysterious way to improve people. This was a favourite theme for the satirists of the later medieval period, as we shall see when we examine some of the literature of fourteenth- and fifteenth-century England. Although ordinary laymen were relatively free to come and go as they pleased on these jaunts, the movements of members of religious orders and the secular clergy could in theory be controlled. Wandering clerics, particularly monks, were sometimes criticized for neglecting their stations and a twelfth-century English bishop complained that too many monks were meandering about the country 'on the pretext of a pilgrimage'.[4] The Church, however, could hardly deny the value of pilgrimage undertaken in the proper spirit. For example, in a Hereford customal of about 1200 the right to go on these holy excursions was carefully quantified. Provided that a canon had resided at the cathedral for a year, he was allowed a three-week pilgrimage within England and in addition once in his life he might cross the sea on pilgrimage. He was given seven weeks for a visit to St. Denis in Paris, sixteen weeks for Rome or Compostella and if he went to Jerusalem for his once-in-a-lifetime journey the chapter allowed one year's leave. But no matter what his destination he had first to obtain permission from the Hereford chapter.[5]

Some pilgrims, especially clerics, obtained a licence from their bishops before setting out, and royal letters of protection—primitive passports—were available to pilgrims for long-distance journeys: 'Henry [III] to all who may inspect the present letters, greetings. Know that we have given licence to our beloved and faithful Roger la Zouch for going as a pilgrim to Saint James [etc.], Oxford, 1220.' Pilgrim-ships departed from specified English ports year after year and it was possible to mingle mundane with sacred affairs. French ships with wine for Ireland, for instance, returned with holds full of Gaelic pilgrims bound for Santiago.[6]

The greater the distance traversed, the greater the risks:

> Some pilgrims to Compostella, engulfed in a storm, were saved after calling on Becket and vowing offerings at his shrine. They landed at Sandwich, and several of the crosses which according to the English custom they had intended for St. James, they gave to St. Thomas, their liberator.

An often-fanciful late medieval chronicler claimed that some pilgrims returning from Jerusalem lost their way and spent the night in the trees of an English forest out of reach of wild beasts. St. Hugh of Lincoln's early thirteenth-century biographer called attention to the castles of pilgrim-robbers in France, as did Joinville a century later.[7] Archangel Raphael was believed to extend special protection to pilgrims, but they—like merchants—often travelled prudently in bands to minimize the dangers. There was even a spiritual insurance policy or pilgrim blessing. In the Salisbury rite, for example, after confession intending pilgrims went to the altar where their wallets and staffs were solemnly blessed; pilgrims to Jerusalem had further special blessings. Variant rites were customary at York, Hereford and other English cathedrals.[8] Certain French historian-sociologists have suggested that these liturgical activities were rites of separation from the usual social milieu, and dedication—to the holy journey. Be that as it may, in most of these rituals the wallet is called the 'sign of the pilgrim'. There were also signs for returning pilgrims, the emblems or badges (often of lead) purchased at shrines, which some pilgrims collected just as modern tourists collect the insignia of the countries they visit, and for the same reasons. Many medieval examples of pilgrim tokens survive; so do some of the moulds in which they were cast. Certain families or ecclesiastical bodies held exclusive rights of manufacture and sale of these items. Modern versions are still sold at Walsingham and Canterbury and at many European centres of pilgrimage; in India at the shrine of St. Francis Xavier one can even purchase miniature caskets containing a plastic representation of the saint's body.

Most medieval pilgrims undertook the journey of their own accord but some were unwilling penitents set upon the high road by their confessors in expiation of their sins. (This was not peculiar to Christianity; fourteenth-century Moslems were said to feel deeply shamed when undertaking pilgrimage to Mecca to atone for their misdeeds.)[9] Depending upon the instructions of their confessors, some penitential pilgrims visited the shrines of Europe on a carefully-organized itinerary, others wandered aimlessly from shrine to shrine. If they had wounded or killed a person the weapons they had used might be turned into metal bands worn, usually on the arms, until they rusted off or the time assigned for the penance expired. The harshness of the punishment suffered by penitential pilgrims sometimes matched the heinousness of their crimes. A certain Christian, captured by Moslems, was forced by starvation to kill and eat his own daughter and then to kill his wife for the same purpose, though he could not bring himself to do it. As penance for his 'sin', enjoined by Pope Innocent III himself, he was never to eat meat again, must fast through the week, never remarry, and must say the Lord's Prayer a hundred times daily. He was also ordered

> to go about unshod, in a woollen tunic with a very short scapular, carrying a penitent's staff a cubit in length. He is to accept no more food . . . than suffices for a day, and he is never to spend above two nights in the same place unless driven by necessity . . . In this way let him visit the shrines of the saints for three years.[10]

Bishops or clergy assigned lighter penitential pilgrimages for minor offences, as in the case of an English chaplain who was ordered to undertake

> one pilgrimage to St. Thomas of Hereford, where he is to offer forty

pence, and one . . . to St. Thomas of Canterbury, where he is to offer one-half mark [nearly seven shillings]. These are to be carried out barefoot before Whitsun, and the chaplain is to obtain certificates from the sacristans at each shrine to prove that he had performed this penance.

These certificates generally followed a standard form:

To bishop or archdeacon, greetings. Lord O. de C. came to us humbly and devoutly on pilgrimage, and reverently fulfilled, in the monastery of St. Edmund, the penance imposed by you for his actions. In witness whereof, etc.

By the later Middle Ages pilgrimages were being meted out by secular magistrates as punishments for 'crimes' rather than 'sins'. In one case two poachers drew up a contract with the lady of the land on which they had trespassed, promising to go on an expiatory pilgrimage by way of compensation.[11]

For a fee one could obtain a certificate of pilgrimage without being a penitent, just as one can at Lourdes today. The following is from Canterbury:

To all let it be known by the presents that, on the fourth day of the month of November, . . . 1312, N. de L. came to the church of Canterbury on pilgrimage, as he said, and personally visited the shrines of the Blessed Thomas the Martyr and other sanctuaries of the said church.[12]

Perhaps such a pilgrim, returning to his manor-house or thatched cottage, proudly displayed his parchment to all and sundry as proof of his piety and as a souvenir of his holiday in Kent.

Some pilgrimages were actually protest marches, demonstrations of anti-royalist sentiment. When an enemy of the king was killed, especially by royal command, the corpse easily became a natural focus for rebellious subjects, as in the case of Thomas of Lancaster and Simon de Montfort; such cults were usually prohibited by royal authority. (It is interesting, for the sake of comparison, to note that the body of the Czech Jan Palach—who killed himself in protest against the 1967 Soviet occupation—was secretly removed by police in 1973 to discourage public commemorations. It has only recently been restored.)

The indigent visited holy places for charity, especially at Easter and Christmas, a custom which seems to have irritated the Evesham chronicler who wrote that

every year, four or five days before Christmas, and again after Palm Sunday for the whole week before Easter, paupers and pilgrims arrived as a huge army

for alms and gifts of clothing.[13] Monasteries played a considerable part in supporting the poor, and famous shrines only increased this charitable role by attracting more poor, as well as rich, pilgrims. Beggars usually took up stations at church doors or, if allowed, within the church itself. But perhaps it is misleading to call these beggars 'pilgrims'. Another type of wayfarer deserves the name even less—those who went to shrines to steal. Since the offerings belonged to the saint, it was sacrilege—in the strict sense—to take them away. One of the more ingenious *modus operandi*, mentioned by several medieval writers, had actually been established before the end of the fourth century. From a very early description of pilgrimage to the Holy Land we learn that the True Cross was venerated in the midst of a guard posted round the piece of wood because an enthusiastic pilgrim once took a bite out of it when bending to 'kiss' it, and carried away the precious bit in his mouth. In the Middle Ages, however, pilgrims were usually more interested in cash: a sly suppliant would kneel at a shrine as if to kiss it, and with a flick of the tongue pick up the small coins lying there and carry them away in his mouth;[14] saintly retribution could be swift and certain. In the twelfth century the Laon canons who came through England with their holy relics on a fund-raising campaign lodged in a certain town. Two locals decided to patronize their tavern but discovered they had no money, and to remedy this one of them went into the church where

> pretending that he wished to show his reverence for [the relics] by kissing them, he put his mouth against them with his lips open and sucked up some coins that had been offered.

With his companion he went off to their ale-house where, as Guibert de Nogent says, 'they almost drank the sun down into the ocean'. But that night—at least in Guibert's version—the sacrilegious culprit hanged himself in a nearby forest.[15]

A more serious menace was the cutpurse, who milled about with pilgrims at a shrine and was lost in the crowd after removing the purse from an unsuspecting visitor's belt. Since the better-off pilgrims usually carried money for travelling costs, shrine offerings and alms, these purses might well repay the risk. One man on his way to Compostella stopped to visit Frideswide's shrine in Oxford where, in the press of pilgrims, a thief relieved him of his purse with its five shillings. Fortunately the saint, so the tale goes, momentarily blinded the thief who began to walk into walls and hit his head against the pillars. In another case a Worcester husband and wife team arranged things so that he would cut away purses and immediately pass them off to her as she walked out of the church.[16]

Another reason for pilgrimage was the search for indulgences—remissions of temporal punishment for past sins—offered by popes and local prelates to those who visited specified shrines. Indulgences brought income to the shrine through pilgrim offerings but abuses of the custom of selling them to laymen became a standard issue of the Reformation. A random selection from just some of the indulgences issued for visitors to Thomas Cantilupe's tomb at Hereford gives some idea of their variety. Before Thomas was canonized the Bishop of Salisbury in 1289 offered an indulgence of twenty days for a visit to the tomb and a contribution to the cathedral fabric fund. Other indulgences were granted by the Bishop of Ossory in 1291, in 1318 by the Archbishop of Dublin, and after the canonization of 1320 by the Bishops of Hereford, Salisbury, Bath and Wells, and Chichester. The pope's bull of canonization itself provided an indulgence of two years and two forty-day periods for pilgrims present on the feast of 2 October, and one hundred days for anyone arriving within the octave of the feast, that is, during the week following 2 October. Indulgences did not cease with the canonization. The Archbishop of York provided a further indulgence in 1321, as did the Bishop of Clonfert in 1324 and the Bishop of Exeter in 1328.[17]

Clearly the indulgence was as flexible as it was profitable. Contributions in lieu of pilgrimage were prefectly acceptable and if one chose instead to go on pilgrimage an offering was expected on arrival at the shrine. As Cantilupe's indulgence catalogue reveals, the saint need not even be officially canonized to attract these incentives: the Bishop of Glasgow granted the usual forty days for a visit to John Dalderby's tomb although John (Bishop of Lincoln, d. 1320) never was canonized. An example of what one historian has called 'the indulgence inflation' comes from the cult of John of Bridlington. When canonizing this last medieval saint of England in 1401 (Osmund and Anselm were canonized later, but had died centuries before John of Bridlington), the pope provided seven years and seven forty-day periods of remission for visits on the saint's feastday.[18] Indulgences, which were not only associated with saints' cults, were in demand to the very end of the Middle Ages. One of the earliest printed documents from Gutenberg's press (in 1454, before the appearance of the famous Bible) was a Letter of Indulgence.

Shrines were also visited by those about to be knighted or to undergo judicial ordeals or other combat. Edward I prayed before St. Edmund's shrine at Bury before he gave battle to the Scots, and as he was leaving he looked back and bowed to the blessed martyr:

> after a few days he sent back his standard to the prior and convent, entreating him in an urgent letter that the Mass for St. Edmund should be celebrated over this emblem, and then finally that it should be touched by all the relics at Bury.[19]

Probably the most common underlying motive for pilgrimage was a pious desire to honour the saint, though piety is never simple and seldom entirely unselfish. For most people pilgrimage was an opportunity to show reverence to a saint *and* to ask a personal favour, even a very general one of physical and spiritual protection; a desire to gain some benefit in this world as well as the next. In this wish to obtain or give thanks for saintly assistance medieval folk are indistinguishable from their modern Indian or Italian counterparts who visit shrines, or from the pilgrims of Homeric Greece or for that matter those of present-day Ghana who offer a bottle of rum at their local oracle-shrine every year. All ask for prosperity and happiness or, as Erasmus put it in the sixteenth century, for the 'Health of my family and the increase of my Fortune':[20] in a nutshell, they seek good luck. Medieval society recognized and appreciated the protection of good and strong lords; saints were looked upon as even better and stronger protectors. It was even possible for an individual to consider himself literally the vassal of a saint, and to bind himself as a lifetime servant at a shrine.[21] Beyond the secondary motives, mentioned above, most pilgrims probably looked upon shrines as sources of help—*auxilium*—in the present life and as yet another bit of security against that final day, *Dies Irae*, when the world would come to an end. Without this belief in the virtues of the saints and their powers, and the efficacy of honouring them, pilgrimage would indeed have been mere tourism.

Though the urge to bridge the two worlds by visiting the shrine was of capital importance, records of posthumous miracles say very little about this. The ordinary folk who came to shrines, prayed, left an offering and walked back into their private humble lives are lost forever. Even so, in what is recorded about the special pilgrims who experienced and reported what they called miracles, there are various details which must have applied to all pilgrims regardless of their motivation. They all, for example, had to face the practical problem of actually getting to the shrines.

No doubt the most comfortable way to carry out a pilgrimage was to pay someone else to go. Pilgrimage by proxy was far from rare, and not uncommonly money was provided in wills to pay for this service—when it would be most needed. In the fifteenth century Margaret Est bequeathed money to Thomas Thurkeld for pilgrimages to St. Thomas of Canterbury and other specified shrines 'yf my goodys wyll stretch so ferr for his costs'.[22] Professional pilgrims, known as 'palmers', were available to discharge other peoples' vows or simply to bring back bits of the Holy Land or Rome; they might take someone's ring along and touch it to famous shrines in distant places. Unless they went on Crusade—ever less likely as the Middle Ages drew to a close—a journey to Jerusalem or even to Spain or Italy was probably beyond the means of most English folk, although it is surprising to see how readily some took up the mendicant life for the sake of foreign pilgrimage. Generally speaking, though pilgrim ships continued to depart until the early sixteenth century, for most English people domestic shrines had to suffice. Even here the problem of expenses could not be avoided.

A vowed pilgrimage was sometimes delayed until enough money could be saved to cover it. Obviously expenses varied with the destination, means of transport and—very important—the pilgrim's social status. The sub-prior of St. Augustine's, Canterbury, was allowed the rather large sum of five shillings for a mere fifty-mile journey in the twelfth century. A few years later the Oxford theft mentioned above occurred, and *that* pilgrim was bound for distant Compostella with the same amount—five shillings—in his wallet. The poorer pilgrim turned to various expedients to finance his journey:

> Ralph and his wife wished to visit Becket's shrine, but lacked the money to do so. They decided to brew up some beer, from the sale of which they hoped to earn enough to cover the cost of the journey.[23]

The rich put up at abbeys as honoured guests or at inns where, as one traveller commented, one should take care 'for love of the fleas, that they may not leap on your legs, for there is a peck of them lying in the dust under the rushes . . .'[24]

Monasteries provided hospitality and charity for poor pilgrims who could not afford inns; this charitable work was an accepted routine as well at hospitals, episcopal households and other ecclesiastical establishments. These institutions of the Church were reinforced by the Christian virtue of charity practised by many laymen. One well-off family put up twenty of Becket's pilgrims at a time, a Norwich tanner supported a blind man in his house along with many others too poor to fend for themselves and a baker at Canterbury cared for poor and sick pilgrims for the sake of Christ. Wealthy Lincoln citizens supported destitute pilgrims and when one was cured at St. Hugh's shrine his benefactors were fetched to witness the cure of their protégé. Not all private charity was voluntary: when her washerwoman became crippled the lady of a village near Arundel Castle ordered some of her peasants to shelter and care for her. Private charity might not go on indefinitely: Samson cared for a paralysed man for a year but when he could no longer afford to support him he had him taken to the city gate—at Old Sarum, which can be a bitterly cold and windy place during the winter—where the ill usually lay; here the sick man remained another year until St. Osmund cured him.[25]

Charity was a virtue dear to the pilgrims whose ventures would have been impossible without it, for a great many seem to have relied wholly on alms for sustenance. These were not the indigent who went to shrines to beg what they could, but poor pilgrims who could go to the selected shrine only by begging.

It was thought right and proper, a meritorious act, to give alms to begging pilgrims, though the coin donated to many poor wayfarers bound for Canterbury in the twelfth century was usually only a farthing. The better-off pilgrims provided themselves with sufficient small change for almsgiving before taking to the road, and there are several accounts of miraculous multiplications of money in the wallets of these charitable travellers. Besides small sums of money, poor pilgrims received gifts of food and drink from charitable folk both clerical and lay. In most cases, that is; sometimes they ran into people like the parsimonious lady near Abingdon who, exasperated by importunate pilgrims, ranted that she would give a drink to no one,

> Not for the sake of Thomas, nor the Lord, nor the Blessed Virgin Mary, or any saint whatsoever. Not today; go away, you beggars.[26]

Poor or rich, pilgrims first had to make plans for their journey, since they could not stride out on pilgrimage whenever the fancy took them, no matter how common the activity may now seem to us. Major pilgrimages required considerable preparation. Even pilgrimage to local shrines involved at least a minimum of planning. These journeys demanded the right opportunity, sufficient means as an alternative to begging, and the right season—obviously farming peasants could not wander off at critical periods in the agricultural cycle. The 'pilgrimage season' in England was thought to include the feasts of Christmas, Easter, Whitsun, and St. Michael's (29 September) or, alternatively, the Easter week, Whitsun, and 'after the harvest (*autumpnum*) because then men—having a holiday from their labours—can go on pilgrimage more freely'.[27]

The cost of pilgrimage seemed even heavier when the journey was not one's own. One man complained of the expense of taking his stepson round to shrines and a husband who grumbled about his wife's pilgrimages finally claimed he had no further means to finance her travels. In some cases the cost of going to a particular shrine was found to be so great that an alternative holy place was selected.[28] Poorer folk usually walked since possession or even hire of horses—there was a standard rate along the Southwark-Rochester-Canterbury route—was beyond them. Even the rich usually dismounted to walk the last few miles of their journey, as an act of piety. At the shrine pilgrims often underwent ritual purification, perhaps involving fasting (though this might have already begun at home) and confession; one of the collectors of miracles who sat at Becket's shrine in the twelfth century claimed—somewhat rhetorically—that the incoming pilgrims were 're-baptized in the font of confession and their own tears'.[29] Some removed their shoes as they actually approached the tomb, customary from Biblical times for those entering upon holy ground.

After these preliminary rites they knelt by the shrine and prayed, sometimes aloud, in the midst of bystanders awaiting their turn. At this point the suppliant normally presented his offering, usually a coin or candle. Candles and wax were sometimes on sale at the church, and the income could be considerable; at Hereford cathedral there were years of dispute between the treasurer and the other canons over sharing the wax proceeds. Many pilgrims offered their own home-made candles and on one occasion a woman even came to the church with her personal candle-making kit:

> A woman took pity on a poor girl who had nothing to offer at Becket's tomb, and from her pocket took a lump of wax and some thread, which she doubled into a wick, and coated with the wax to make a candle for the girl to offer.[30]

After presenting his offering and uttering a final prayer and request the ordinary pilgrim left the church, but if his visit coincided with a feast-day he would probably also hear a Mass or join in a procession before leaving. For those who had come to the tomb hoping for a cure a different routine was followed. They settled down in the church, kneeling, sitting or lying on cold pavement before the tomb where shadows danced in flickering candlelight. There they remained until impatience conquered hope, or hope was rewarded with a cure, a miracle. The magic word which drew the first pilgrims, the vanguard of armies of devotees, was miracle; the sweetest promise a pilgrim could hear was *miracula magna videbis*, 'you will see great miracles'. Soon after the discovery of St. Milburga's bones in twelfth-century Shropshire a messenger arrived to find out whether any miracles had occurred. If so, he explained, his master would come to pay his devotions with his family. If not, presumably his master would stay at home.[31]

If according to Faust the 'dearest child of faith is miracle', it was a child of very mixed parentage. Although Biblical miracles echoed down through the literature of the Middle Ages the word itself—*miraculum*—is not even found in the Vulgate New Testament. It appears in the Old Testament nine times but there it means 'terror', 'fear' and 'horror'. In the New Testament the words for cures and similar marvels, in the Latin memorized by generations of medieval clerics, were *signum, virtus, prodigium*, never *miraculum*. But perhaps this is of little significance, for there is no denying that the idea was there whatever words were used. Most of the signs and wonders are recorded in Mark's gospel, such as quelling storms, curing lepers, cripples, the deaf and dumb or paralysed, demoniacs, feverish patients and those suffering flux, blindness or epilepsy, as well as raising the dead.[32] Not one of these cures involved holy bones or relics in the later, medieval sense. There is in fact only a single miracle associated with such carnal relics in the whole of the Bible, in the Old Testament, and even then it seems almost accidental:

> Year by year Moabite raiders used to invade the land. Once some men were burying a dead man when they caught sight of the raiders; they threw the body into the grave of Elisha and made off; when the body touched the prophet's bones, the man came to life and rose to his feet.[33]

The great future which was in store for holy bones was evident in neither the Old nor the New Testaments. Nevertheless, by the Middle Ages theologians looked to the word of God and the works of Christ as set forth in the Bible, when discussing the relic-wonders of their own day.

The influence of the Bible on the clerical subconscious was incalculable. Often deliberate mimicry was evident: the words of *Acts* 3:6 are *in nomine Iesu Christi Nazareni, surge et ambula*. When Godric of Finchale (d. 1170) cured a cripple his words were believed to have been, *in Nomine Domini Iesu Christi Nazareni, surge et ambula*. In the printed edition of Becket's miracles nine hidden references to Scripture occur in the first eighteen lines of the first page, which emphasizes how much the writings of the time were 'made of the scriptures', a truth acknowledged even then. John of Salisbury, a leading twelfth-century intellectual, described a leader of twelfth-century piety, Bernard of Clairvaux, as

> so saturated in the Holy Scriptures that he could fully expound every subject in the words of the prophets and apostles. For he had made their speech his own, and could hardly converse or preach or write a letter except in the language of scripture.

When to 'learn to read' meant to 'say the Psalms', the words of the Bible must have coloured the ideas of even semi-literate novices.[34] Ideas about miracles were also inherited from other writers in the same way that earlier biographical anecdotes about the saints were constantly refashioned. There is evidence that even cures at pagan shrines, particularly Greek, influenced early Christian *literati*, though a far greater fund was the work of earlier Christians and the Bible. In one revealing sentence Gregory the Great (d. 604) wrote 'We have new miracles, then, in imitation of the old', and seven centuries later the novice in Caesarius of Heisterbach's *Dialogue on Miracles* echoed this: 'Ancient miracles are renewed again in our time.'[35]

Most hagiographers were eager to record any marvellous event no matter how unlikely, or *outré*. While Hugh of Lincoln's corpse was being embalmed in the presence of his clergy, for instance, his biographer Adam inspected the holy intestines and claimed that they were exceptionally clean—a miracle. He querulously added that certain bystanders, who 'made light of the miracle', replied that the physical condition of the body was due as much to Hugh's dysentery and his pious abstinence as to any miracle.[36] Monastic chroniclers were sometimes as uncritical as hagiographers. The distinction should not be stressed since many men composed both chronicles and saints' lives, such as the twelfth-century historian William of Malmesbury who recorded hundreds of miracles including a few he himself had witnessed.[37] Of course hagiographers strenuously defended their subjects' thaumaturgic powers: Walter Daniel was outraged when asked to name witnesses to Ailred's miracles, as if, he complained, proof of crime and of virtue were on the same level.[38] It was not long, however, before papal commissioners and episcopal tribunals, in the routine course of their saint-investigations, were asking the very questions which upset Walter.

This more rigorous attitude toward miracles was an outgrowth of theological and philosophical attempts to define the term itself, a problem that seemed to have been resolved by the end of the thirteenth century—the golden age of scholasticism. Caesarius of Heisterbach, a German Cistercian who died about 1250, had much to say about this subject in his highly entertaining *Dialogue on Miracles*. He mingled anecdotes and *exempla* (light tales designed to point out a moral) with attempts to define miracle theologically, and though his theology is not altogether successful, his book is amusing and instructive reading. For Caesarius, miracle is anything contrary to the course of nature at which we marvel, something ultimately performed by God but proximately through saints or evil spirits. This last point was not original with Caesarius—indeed, very little was—but reflected the ancient Christian belief that demons, devils or magicians could perform miracles, which lay behind the thirteenth-century rule that proof of miracles was not enough in the process of canonizing a saint. Since evil beings could deceive, by virtue of their miraculous abilities, a candidate must also present a virtuous life: in canonizing Gilbert of Sempringham in 1202 Pope Innocent III wrote, 'the evidence of miracles . . . is on occasions misleading and deceptive, as in the case of magicians'. The same confusion arose over dreams and visions, sent either by God or by the Devil. Caesarius goes on to explain that miracles happen so that God may show his power, wisdom, or mercy, and they occur in men, the four elements, birds, fish, beasts and reptiles.[39] The garrulous Cistercian provides several examples for each of these subdivisions as well as a discussion about eucharistic miracles, the wonders of the Virgin Mary and visions of the other world. His book is a treasure-chest of medieval folklore. Thomas Aquinas approached the question of miracle from a more philosophical point of view. Aquinas (d. 1274), the archetypal thirteenth-century theologian, defined miracle as whatever God did outside or beyond the order commonly determined or observed in nature.[40]

References to nature, found in other writings on miracles such as the works of St. Augustine, John of Salisbury and William of Auvergne, were laudable in themselves, but medieval philosophers and theologians were severely limited in what they could observe of the 'natural' universe. The medieval mind had not yet worked out in neat practical terms the idea of nature versus supernature, a dichotomy which was so self-evident to the scientists and philosophers of two or three generations ago. Even when 'experimentation' or simple observation is mentioned the results are sometimes surprising. St. Augustine convinced himself by 'his own' observations that the flesh of the peacock did not rot and he accepted the belief that a diamond counteracted the effects of a magnet; Roger Bacon wrote that a new mirror would be stained with a bloody mist if a menstruating woman looked into it, first because Aristotle had said so and second because *experience* taught that it was so.

Though they could not define miracle in a 'technical' sense without leaving some loose ends, and though the medieval Church never ceased to struggle with a coherent, universally-acceptable theological explanation of miracle, at least the philosopher-theologians drew attention to an objective approach, to the need for definition. That same need was recognized in the practical sphere—in the Church pastoral rather than the Church theological—when it came to attributing holiness to particular relics or to individuals with whom miracles were associated. We have seen that in the first half-millennium of Christianity miracles were useful aids to conversion and evangelization but, as with relics, saints and pilgrimages, by the central Middle Ages the Church was trying to control the popular impulses it had once encouraged. Miracles (like relics, easily faked) were closely examined at the appropriate ecclesiastical levels in the central Middle Ages. In the thirteenth century, for instance, Peter Quivel, Bishop of Exeter, called for greater objectivity when dealing with miracles, and in the fourteenth century Archbishop Fitzralph of Armagh warned his flock against 'false and fabricated miracles'. About the same time another English prelate, John Grandisson, would not accept any reputed miracle unless he could interrogate the persons involved and inquire into the 'nature and length of the disease' reputedly cured, and elicit other particulars. Sometimes more strenuous action was taken. In 1290 Oliver Sutton, Bishop of Lincoln, prohibited pilgrimage to St. Edmund's well at Oxford, where miracles were reputed to be happening. He heard in April 1296 that pilgrims were going to a chapel at Hambleden because of reputed miracles of healing (*miracula sanitatum*) there. He ordered this pilgrimage stopped for the time being since it was improper that people should acknowledge miracles not approved by the Church (*que non sunt ab ecclesia approbata*). By August he relented somewhat since fewer were coming on account of the 'miracles' (*cessante . . . concursu*) and finally in March of 1297 he removed his prohibitions provided that no pilgrims were coming there in expectation of miracles (*dum tamen confluencia populi intuitu simulationis miraculorum illic cessaverit omnino*). In 1298 Sutton sent someone to investigate unauthorized pilgrimages encouraged by reputed miracles at Great Crawley and in 1299 he prohibited pilgrimage to a holy well at Linslade, using practically the same terms as in his earlier mandate of 1296. Again the reputed healing miracles (*miracula sanitatum*) were not to be accepted since they were not approved by the Church (*ab ecclesia approbata*).[41] Such prohibitions were frequently brought up in English Church councils from the thirteenth century to the end of the Middle Ages.

On the one hand, then, bishops complained of crude and too-avid beliefs in unauthorized and unexamined wonders and miracles, while on the other theologians (possibly also these same bishops) tried to come to terms with the matter. Although they attempted to define miracle by appeals to universal natural law, such definitions were not entirely successful, and in specific, individual cases, common sense was a better guide than medieval cosmology. When papal commissioners sat down to hear testimony about Thomas Cantilupe's miracles at London and Hereford in 1307 they had in front of them a schedule of things to ask about such wondrous events: they wanted to know, for example, how the witness came to learn of the miracle, what words were used by those who prayed for the miracle, whether any herbs, stones, other natural or medicinal preparations or incantations had accompanied the miracle; the witness was expected to say something about the age and social situation of the person experiencing the miracle, where he came from and of what family; whether the witness knew the subject before as well as after the miracle, what illness was involved, how many days he had seen the ill person before the cure; whether the cure was complete and how long it took for completion. Of course witnesses were also asked in what year, month, day, place and in whose presence, the wonderful event itself occurred.[42]

This inquisitorial procedure was elaborated at the papal court, assuming that the candidate ever reached this stage in the process. For instance, in the case of St. Louis of France, seven witnesses interrogated about one particular miracle were asked *inter alia* if the cured woman had made a vow to Louis, whether in their region it was commonly thought Louis was a saint, if they had been prompted beforehand or were testifying from hope of reward or fear of punishment (also asked of witnesses in the Cantilupe inquisition). Then the pope and some of his cardinals met in consistory and compared the depositions of the seven witnesses detail by detail.

> And thus these two witnesses seem to disagree about the day of the cure,
> since witness number one says that she was cured six or seven days after
> arrival, but witness number four says that it was eight days later. Also
> these two witnesses . . . say that the hour of the cure was after the meal,
> but the second witness says . . . (etc.)

Physical as well as verbal evidence was offered, as in the case of the man who came before the pope claiming to have been cured of leprosy by St. Edmund Rich. He had to remove his shirt to prove that he was of a uniform colour, which was supposed to allay any suspicions of cosmetic treatment of his skin.[43] On occasion 'cured' people were asked to perform various exercises in front of the examining board at canonization hearings, basic tests which even shrine-keepers sometimes applied to pilgrims before recording their miracles.

By the end of the Middle Ages the Church was moving toward that rigidity in definition which culminated in the eighteenth-century work of Prospero Lambertini (later Pope Benedict XIV), *De Servorum Dei Beatificatione et Beatorum Canonizatione*, a veritable encyclopedia of conditions and characteristics of sanctity and miracles. An example of this complexity comes from a fifteenth-century English archbishop's register in which a miracle is described as follows: it must (1) proceed from God not the Devil or human fraud (2) be *contra naturam* (3) be an evident result of individual virtue and not an indistinguishable result of words alone (4) corroborate the Catholic faith. Without the third condition, any priest who whispered the sacred words of consecration at the Eucharistic sacrifice of the Mass could claim to have worked a miracle, that of transubstantiation. Accordingly, the central rite of the Mass was not, by these criteria, a miracle (*non est miraculum*).[44]

Even with this growing sophistication in dealing with miracles medieval churchmen and intellectuals were sometimes less consistent than might be expected. With one part of his brain Caesarius of Heisterbach set up standards for testing miracles, with another he indulged his *penchant* for story-telling, and while entertaining himself and his readers with miscellaneous marvels he repeatedly violated the very conditions he had established. Roger Bacon, sometimes taken as a prototype scientist, in one place in his writings expressed the tradi-tional academic contempt for wonder-tales told by rustics but then immediately offered his readers two miracles concerning the eucharist which, he proudly remarked, had never been reported before. John of Salisbury, one of the leaders of the twelfth century Renaissance, was pleased to write that he had personally assisted in the miraculous cure of a blind man at Chartres.[45] The tension and the paradox which we noted when discussing relics, saints and pilgrimage, is here, too, in miracles; this religious schizophrenia became an even greater problem in the fourteenth and fifteenth centuries.

Most people who experienced miracles were neither theologians nor hagiographers. They were the simple folk who came from the great bulk of medieval England's population who could neither read nor write. The popular, uncritical acceptance of wonders and miracles stemmed partially from ignorance of the natural world and partially from an overwhelming need, created by the conditions of medieval life, to believe in miracles. The Church was responsible, too: instructed by gullible clerics and sometimes entertained by sermons featuring famous miracles and visions of the other world[46] the laity went away prepared to accept as a miracle the wildest coincidence and most far-fetched tale. These illiterate masses, when they thought about it at all, explained miracles as wonders performed by hallowed ghosts who flitted in and out of their graves, the tombs and shrines containing magic relics. It was sometimes acknowledged—if only in passing—that God was the ultimate source of miracles. But theological *dicta* really had no place here. For most people, the important thing was not the theory evolved by the Church to explain miracles and saints, it was what those saints did for them and especially the faith-healing, the curative miracles, that sometimes went on at their shrines.

Part Two

English Shrines and Pilgrims

Chapter 4

Faith-Healing: Medicine and Miracle

> They passed the long night in weeping and singing
> psalms. When morning dawned and all was ready for
> the funeral office, the corpse began to move. . . . He
> rose from the bier, feeling no ill effects from the illness
> which he had suffered.
>
> *Gregory of Tours*

When a villager heard that miracles were occurring at some shrine or
other, probably his first thought was that a cripple had been cured, or
perhaps some old blind woman or a 'leper', and he would not be far
wrong. Analysis of the surviving miracle reports from English and
European shrines between the twelfth and the fifteenth centuries
indicates that over nine-tenths of the wonders were cures of human
illnesses. In modern terms, shrines were faith-healing centres. Those
who now set out for Lourdes specifically in search of health have
usually tried all other available avenues first; so it was for many earlier
pilgrims.

At the very least, ten out of every hundred recorded medieval
English pilgrims who arrived at a shrine to seek or report a miraculous
cure had already sought some sort of medical assistance. They started
with other possibilities in what medical men call 'the hierarchy of
resort', but these alternative therapies had not cured them. Disappointed by the doctors or medicines that had failed, pilgrims found
eager listeners in the registrars at the shrines to whom they described
the indignities inflicted upon them by would-be healers at great expense, all to no avail. These registrars, hardly objective listeners, were
interested in collecting reports of miracles as evidence of the powers of
their saints; few of them had any respect or liking for the competition
of profane healing. Though this quite understandable attitude is biased
and unsympathetic there is enough patchy evidence left in the miraculous matrix to glimpse the way *medici, physici, sirurgici,* monk-
physicians, wandering barber-surgeons, village wizards and cunning
women, even grandmother's favourite herbs, were enlisted in the battle

against illness. In this way we can learn something about medieval medicine in practical terms going beyond the theories of medieval medical manuscripts.

What were the available therapies? It is well known that flebotomy or bleeding was one of the most widely-used prophylactic and therapeutic practices, and several examples of this treatment are found in the miracles. The operation was performed by cupping, leeching, scarification (scratching incisions), or venesection (usually in the lower arm). The medieval doctor was guided by 'flebotomy-men' illustrations in his medical texts, showing the proper places at which to bleed the patient for particular illnesses. By homeostatic theory blood was thought to accumulate in limbs and organs and since an imbalance was held to be one of the causes of illness certain amounts had to be drained off from time to time. Flebotomy was a regular institution for monks of certain orders—four times a year for the Cistercians—who took their *minutio* or periodic bleeding sessions in much the same spirit that we take holidays; indeed it had similar functions, since monastic regulations were relaxed during *minutio*.

It is curious that the habit of blood-letting should have continued into the twentieth century since the shortcomings and positive dangers of flebotomy were evident even to the Anglo-Saxons. It could have been easy enough for patients to bleed to death—this nearly happened in a recorded twelfth-century case—but the techniques were so well established that this risk was usually easily avoided. The main deleterious effect was infection, which shows up repeatedly in the miracles: little imagination is required to foresee the effects of slicing into limbs with improperly sterilized knives, and infection following flebotomy, recognized even in Bede's day, was also mentioned more than once in Becket's twelfth-century miracles. Hugh of Lincoln's 'discomfort increased so much' and his health deteriorated so rapidly after the operation, that it probably hastened his death in 1200. In one instance flebotomy resulted in temporary insanity, in another a knight's arm was swollen and red the third day after a blood-letting session, and a woman also claimed to have had a swollen and red arm from flebotomy (*brachium habuit inflatum et rubicundum ex fleobotomia*) for more than a month but was cured when she bathed it with water which had washed Gilbert of Sempringham's corpse. Disregarding the indications that the operation could be harmful, in their desperate ignorance medieval folk went on submitting to it, believing that it aided the memory, warmed the marrow, checked tears, removed nausea, helped digestion, moved the bowels and enriched sleep besides curing specific illnesses.[1] It is characteristic of such systems of belief that they are closed, self-contained: 'The objective properties of things and natural causation of events may be known, but are not socially emphasized or are denied because they conflict with some social dogma.'[2] Men argued that, since there was nothing wrong with the basic principle, if flebotomy caused infection the operation must have been carried out during the wrong phase of the moon or on one of the forbidden 'Egyptian Days'. Unfortunately there was disagreement about precisely which days were, and which were not, Egyptian. The same hermetic quality is evident when monks explained why some visitors to shrines were not cured: the pilgrim was unworthy, he had some hidden sin—one he might not even know about—he lacked sufficient belief in the saint, he did not carry out his vow properly, he had consulted human doctors or used human medicines, and so on. Some modern Nigerians will explain the failure of their traditional medicine in much the same way.[3]

A similar situation arises with another remedy, very popular in the Middle Ages however 'irrational' it might seem to us. Cauterization may have been beneficial in some cases, to close a wound for example, but it is difficult to see how branding a patient with a hot iron rod below the left armpit could have relieved his headache. Even internal organs might be cauterized for particular ailments. As in the case of flebotomy, many medical manuscripts contain 'cautery men' with lines running to points on the skin—which were related to particular illnesses—where the hot iron was to be applied; there were ten points of cautery, for instance, for treating asthma. The whole business is reminiscent of acupuncture. No matter how refined may have been the theories behind it cauterization often had evil effects, as some of Godric's pilgrims learned to their regret. One had a tumour which, he claimed, became worse after the burning, another's blindness was in no way relieved when her skull was branded and the knee of a third was not healed by the cautery iron, though in one case the remedy seems to have had a round-about beneficial result: a man was cauterized on the back but felt no relief; as he knelt down at Godric's tomb the cautery scars burst open, infectious matter flowed forth, and he was 'cured'.[4]

Besides wielding the cautery rod and flebotomy knife, medieval doctors and surgeons recommended the application of plasters, fomentations and 'very bitter' medicines. They prescribed diuretics, controlled diets, administered traction, used roots and herbs even on themselves, doled out pills and potions, and sewed up incisions with silk sutures.[5] In the twelfth century the waters of Bath were resorted to by a Reading monk with leprosy and it is reported in the *Gesta Stephani* a generation or so earlier that sick people came 'from all over England to wash in the healing waters' of Bath.[6] Presumably some of these had gone on their doctors' advice. Other remedies included purgatives, decoctions and unguents, like the preparation used by a Gilbertine nun to treat another nun with leprosy, and clysters—enemas—which St. Thomas Cantilupe had to suffer just before his death. Setons too were used, threads sewn into and intended to irritate the skin according to theories similar to those used to 'explain' cauterization.[7] Post-Conquest *medici* were not really as clever as they may seem since practically all of their skills, tools and *materia medica* had been known to their Anglo-Saxon predecessors, as they were to the Greeks and Romans, too.

Before applying a particular remedy a diagnosis was in order. The *medicus* usually took the patient's pulse, sometimes combined with a urine inspection. Besides the manuscript diagrams used as guides for flebotomy and cautery another diagrammatic aid was a colour chart showing twenty or twenty-two hues of urine, neatly arranged from light to dark yellows and browns with appropriate diagnostic comments. There is no record of the diagnosis suggested for the Canterbury monk caught mixing beer with his urine in order to fool the doctor.[8] By these and other diagnostic means, application to astrological tables for instance, medieval medical men considered themselves—with the help of the standard Greek and Arabic medical treatises—capable of distinguishing three or four varieties of epilepsy, dropsy and leprosy. Even so, in one case three different doctors provided three different diagnoses and in another case one medical expert diagnosed as gout what his colleague considered an attack of 'evil spirit', However questionable these distinctions between illnesses were, the miracles do sometimes supply valuable information about the physical appearance of individuals suffering particular ailments, such as the victim of leprosy whose repellent aspect was carefully described in a Wulfstan cure, or the unfortunate girl who presented symptoms of plague in the later fifteenth century.[9]

Medieval folk called upon local healers and providers of 'home remedies' in addition to learned members of the healing profession. The miracles are especially useful here since even though the monks who guarded shrines had little sympathy for such healers and charmers, their comments reveal something about the peasants who actually healed and charmed. They were not always lay folk. The priest of Ramsholt in Suffolk tried to cure his daughter with 'charms and medicines' before appealing to the spirit of Becket. Such charms were freely used along with herbs and semi-precious stones, sometimes self-applied or tied round the neck of the sufferer—often by a parent. Herbal lore was brought to bear in nearly every affliction by both the folk-healers and the professionals. There were lay herbalists of both sexes and various social classes; in one of the miracles of King Henry VI the patient sought out a herbalist who was a 'weaver, not a surgeon or a physician'. Other folk-practices are mentioned such as tying a red scarf or band round a girl's swollen throat to 'draw off' the affliction, 'as the common people wrongly believed', added the scribe. An old woman tried to help a cripple with what appears to be a perfectly reasonable proposal, immersion in a hot bath, while another miracle suggests that it was customary to chant rhymes while dripping relic-water into the patient's mouth.[10] To this repertoire we should add the chanting of nine Paters by five widows gathered around a victim of drowning, or nine Paters recited by a pilgrim as he knelt with his afflicted hand thrust into one of the apertures in Hugh of Lincoln's tomb. Such cases confirm the general impression that Paternosters accompanied 'every conceivable' healing process.[11] Usually more vigorous action was taken in drowning cases, such as hanging the victim upside-down or placing him by a fire and forcing toast dipped in warm beer down his throat. Some even tried to apply to themselves more complex treatment, which they supposed physicians would have suggested: a leper's attempt to flebotomize himself, however, only resulted in infection.[12]

There was sometimes only a very fine line between folk-remedies, some of which the Church branded as 'superstitious', and ecclesiastically-approved therapies. Although it was 'superstitious' to place a magical stone around a swollen throat, it was thought an act of piety to use a phial of relic-water for the same purpose. Some charms condemned by the Church as a form of 'magic' were written down and then placed on the patient's body; some miracles were written on parchment bound to the ailing victim. A similar practice has been recorded in twentieth-century France, where toothache was supposed to be relieved by touching the sore gum with a piece of paper on which a prayer was written.[13] The fourth book of the *Iliad* used to be placed under the pillow to cure ague, but in twelfth-century England it was the Gospel of John or a relic. A third-century Roman doctor recommended writing *abracadabra* repeatedly on parchment and applying this to the body of an ague victim; in the archives of Canterbury cathedral a medieval parchment, which was folded up and carried around in the pocket of a good Christian—the fold-lines are quite clear—contains the *abracadabra* paradigm along with several symbols and prayers useful in getting out of tight spots. The Church, or at least Thomas Aquinas, was dubious about the legitimacy of casting lots, but it was occasionally practised by pilgrims to find out to which saint they should turn in their hour of need.[14] Theological distinctions aside, and looking only at procedure, there was often very little difference between sacred and secular healing techniques at the non-professional level.

The miracles, then, provide examples of everyday medical practices, but a negative attitude, a condemnation of human healing in any form, is far more obvious. The monks or canons or whoever was responsible for setting down the records of miracles will naturally be suspected as the principal source of this prejudice, but many uncured patients who became 'cured' pilgrims added to the general chorus of derogation. It is all rather unfair, because any successes the *medici* might have claimed would *ipso facto* not be recorded, at least not in collections of miracles which consistently emphasized the superiority of sacred to profane healing. It was often said to be foolish and vain to seek the help of human doctors in the first place. This attitude, common to the shrine-registrars, was also evident in some of the dreams reported by pilgrims. One pilgrim described how Becket came to him in sleep and directed him to go on pilgrimage rather than seek medical help, in another the pilgrim was especially warned *not* to seek medical care (*curam medicorum*). A learned *magister* had an elaborate dream or vision in which a magical parchment, shown to him by an angelic courier, was decorated with rows of knights stitched in silk, and above them a message directing him to place his hope in 'saint' Simon de Montfort, not in medical preparations (*nulla praeparatione*). The registrars hinted in *obiter dicta* inserted in the pilgrims' stories that it was unwise to spend money on doctors in whom—as one commented—there was nothing salutary; the expression *inaniter* (vainly, uselessly) often appears in connection with pilgrims who spent good money on doctors. Other passages mention the 'useless' care of doctors who often left patients in worse condition than before and the 'fact' that the sick might suffer a relapse if they turned to human medical aids after being cured by the saints.[15] Such aspersions, liberally scattered through the miracle collections, arose not only from a sense of rivalry in those who composed the records, but also from the natural disappointment felt by pilgrims who had consulted doctors whom they thought had failed them.

The Church could conveniently be called in to justify the registrars' denunciations of doctors. For instance, both in the Fourth Lateran Council of 1215 and in repeated diocesan legislation in thirteenth-century England the faithful were reminded that their spiritual welfare was more important than their physical, and that the priest had preference over the physician. The shrine-scribes hardly needed theological fortification: their self-interest had the same tendency, which is underlined by their implied criticisms of other saints' shrines. In some miracles it was said that pilgrims had first travelled to other saints' tombs (often Becket's) but no cure followed until they came to *this*—the registrar's—shrine and in a few cases a pilgrim was even said to have been punished for going to the 'wrong' shrine. There is little indication of the more orthodox ecclesiastically-approved healing rites such as the priests' blessing of sufferers from eye trouble or curing with blessed bread or oil. Although this last rite was dying out it was still occasionally mentioned in the central medieval period.[16]

A common but rather more specific complaint was the high cost of medical care. Every miracle collection contains a variant of St. Luke's story of the woman who spent much on doctors, all in vain, a refrain that echoes through collections whether they were composed in northern England, southern France or western Poland. Given this criticism of fees it is unfortunate that information regarding the actual incomes of medieval doctors is scattered and usually limited to *medici* of exalted status who received yearly pensions, lands and robes for their services. What is lacking is an overall view of the cost of medical care rendered by the ordinary doctor to the everyday patient. It would be helpful to know, for instance, whether a thirteenth-century complaint about fees charged by Oxford doctors was justified.[17]

Some examples of very high fees demanded by famous doctors in medieval England have been uncovered and it is known that many of the clergy received their benefices through their medical work (in which case individual charges cannot of course be ascertained). In a Becket miracle the patient's father, Roger, Earl of Clare (Hertford), offered forty marks and more to any physician or surgeon who would undertake the cure, and in another version of the same miracle this is called a great sum of money, *multam pecuniam*. No one would take on the job without permission to operate, which the parents refused. This suggests that forty marks or nearly £27 was considered a large fee in the last decades of the twelfth century. Other indications of individual charges involve much lower figures, such as a few shillings. In a Cantilupe miracle a surgeon who charged four shillings left his patient worse off than before, and in some interesting litigation from about the same time a patient sued his doctor who had gone away leaving him to find and pay a second doctor. The first had been promised two, and the second received four, shillings. In another example from this period the Bishop of Hereford paid his physician six shillings and eight pence for his ministrations. The dates of these sums vary by about a dozen years either side of 1300. Establishment of a scale of fees is defeated not only by the lack of enough evidence but also by the suggestion that doctors usually charged what they thought their patients could afford, and for the poor sometimes the work was carried out for nothing. Criticisms about fees were heard not only at curative shrines: both Langland and Chaucer denounced doctors too much in love with gold, and at about the same time across the Channel Froissart was complaining that 'this is the aim which doctors always pursue, to get large payments and profits from the lords and ladies they attend'.[18]

Among the healers briefly mentioned above was the surgeon, usually a layman since the Church tried to keep the clergy out of this branch of the healing arts because of the prohibition against the shedding of blood by a clergyman. Surgeons, too, were roundly denounced by the miracle registrars. Their services ranged through amputations and bone-setting to cranial repair work—usually begun with a cross-shaped incision—and surgery for stone, fistula, abdominal operations, treatment of wounds and administration of flebotomy. The great complaint, raised presumably by pilgrims but no doubt encouraged by the monkish scribes, was of the pain they inflicted. Like the complaint about fees this charge had a long pedigree. St. Augustine of Hippo noted that in most bodily illness 'the cures and remedies are themselves tortures', and he then told the story of a pathetic sufferer from fistula whose fear of the knife is vividly and oppressively described. Fear remained as potent in medieval England as in fifth-century north Africa. We have already encountered the Earl and Countess of Clare refusing to permit surgery on their son. Other parents shared their views. Grown men were just as reluctant to allow surgeons to approach them. There was the Franciscan who would not let the surgeons operate for stone and the Frenchman who declared himself quite ready to die rather than permit the amputation of his toes, and there was even a knight who refused surgery. Surgical operations, it was claimed probably with good reason, brought one to the brink of death. After a bungled operation to remove bladder stones from a young boy, a twelfth-century Oxford surgeon simply left a 'corpse' bound to the 'operating table' in its parents' home and fled the city. The child, however, was revived by St. Frideswide and grew up to become Mayor of Oxford.[19] Perhaps his father was partly to blame for offering a large fee to the surgeon to undertake the job. In another miracle it was reported that a woman had suffered incontinence for seven years as a result of surgery for stone.[20] Some surgeons seem perhaps to have been unusually eager to wield the knife. One advised the removal of a sprained foot, another recommended cutting off a broken arm, a third thought a woman who had run a spindle through her hand should have it amputated. These seemingly drastic measures must be set against the probability of septicimia in simple, uncomplicated wounds; even Anglo-Saxon medical men were aware that amputation into sound tissue might save a life.[21]

Condemnation of doctors and surgeons was common to all the miracle collections. Reading between the lines, however, we can discern a certain degree of professional ethics among medieval medical practitioners. Sometimes doctors, perhaps as much to protect themselves as for any other reason, are said to have refused cases which they judged incurable, even when fat fees were offered. Unfortunately a natural bias would lead the miracle-scribes to declare, if they could, *every* case incurable by human means, so that their saint's power would seem more manifest. In one case a royal physician who had declared a knight beyond hope was astonished to see him cured after visiting a shrine; he convinced himself of the cure by inspection of the patient's urine.[22] Further incidental information emerges from the miracles helping to make medieval doctors more human, such as their quarrels over fees. It would be lacking in charity not to end this brief review of attitudes toward doctors, necessarily distorted considering the sources, by mentioning Gilbert the London surgeon who 'for the love of God and in piety' gave free treatment to a pauper with a twisted and ulcerated foot.[23] There must have been many like him.

Collections of posthumous miracles emphasize one special kind of healing, but it is clear that in practice most sick people called on both the powers of saints and of trained physicians. This was as true at the very top of the social ladder as at the bottom; as true for laymen as for clerics. Regardless of papal edicts and episcopal pronouncements, prelates and canons, priests and monks called in their doctors whenever they felt illness coming on—and many of the doctors were themselves monks and priests, canons and prelates some of whom became quite wealthy through their medical practice. At the same time, doctors who could do nothing for them sent their patients along to curative shrines, miracles were worked even on ailing doctors (or in one case on a doctor's wife) and doctors could be found giving testimony and miracles at canonization hearings. In their quest for health, or at least non-illness, many medieval folk clerical and lay, doctor and patient alike, moved ceaselessly back and forth between sacred and profane healing. In one miracle—which sums up this attitude—a girl's father led her about among doctors *and* holy places (*per medicos et per loca sancta*) in search of health.[24]

The miracles illustrate the intermingling of sacred and profane healing in yet other ways. *Medicus* was a word also used for God and the saints, as in the St. Richard Wych collection when God is called the 'greatest doctor of all doctors (*medicorum*)'. A certain Roger of Middleton dreamed that Becket and St. Edmund of Bury, announced to him as *medici duo*, chided him for using ordinary *potionibus et medicamentis* more than he needed. Some of the small metal phials or ampoules in which Becket's curative water was carried to the ends of Christendom were stamped with a legend naming Thomas as the 'best physician', and when the dead St. Edmund Rich began to perform miracles he was called the new doctor, *novus medicus*. In the middle of the fourteenth century a well-known vernacular religious work, *Livre de Seyntz Medicines*, presented Christ as physician, with symbolic ointments, lotions, bandages, and so on. The sick came to churches and shrines where the saint resided as a sublimated *medicus*. The bleeding accident victims rushed to shrines or the 'dead' newborn infants carried in the midwives' arms directly to holy tombs make it easier to see the shrine as a hospital, even as a casualty ward.[25]

Perhaps the best illustration of an unconscious fusion of roles, however, is provided by dreams and visions which portray saints as doctors in action carrying out operations or prescribing medicines as if they were quite 'human' healers. St. Thomas Cantilupe appeared and cured one dreamer by thrusting his hand into the patient's side causing such pain that he awoke shaken but healed. Saints might prescribe quite mundane remedies in visions, such as a poultice of warm wax for a dropsical foot, or a herbal cure. Simon de Montfort appeared in a dream to a Winchcombe monk and proposed some minor surgery, but when the monk disagreed the saint grasped and struck his foot; the patient awoke to find his bed soaked with putrid liquid but the ailment gone. Even the Blessed Virgin figured as a quasi-earthly healer when she appeared to a mute, thrust her fingers into his mouth and pulled out the reluctant tongue.[26] Two of the more striking visions or dreams come from Becket's collection. In one a knight suffering an internal affliction dreamed that he saw the Blessed Virgin, St. Leonard and St. Edmund of Bury come to his bedside and scrape his bowels clean. It seems that the job had not been well done, for Becket arrived and placed two toes into the patient's viscera to remove what the others had missed (*duobus articulis pedis sui visceribus meis immissis, quod residuum erat infirmitatis amovit*); the knight himself told King Henry II about this miracle when the king came to Canterbury on pilgrimage. The final example is illuminating because the dreamer, named Peter, was a well-known French *medicus*. In a vision which included the Virgin Mary he was approached by SS. Becket, Cosmus and Alexander 'the Physician'. Becket ordered them to take Peter out of his bed and stretch him over a chest, cut open his belly, take out his liver, wash it, replace it and sew him up. In the pain of the stitching he awoke or returned from his ecstasy—the registrar could not say which—and found the very stitches.[27]

In practice the distinctions between what is now called 'folk-remedy', faith-healing, and 'proper' medical attention are inappropriate to the Middle Ages. The sick drew upon all at the same time or went from one to another. This is not an exclusively medieval reaction to illness. About the mid-second century A.D. a loquacious denizen of the Empire wandered into Rome, ill, seeking medical help. After submitting to purges, cupping and other remedies he failed to respond, and his doctors gave up. He next tried one of the best-known curative measures of his day, pilgrimage and prayer at a temple of the healing god AEsculapius, and there Aelius Aristides, author of *Sacred Discourses,* was cured. He had fallen ill while sojourning in Greece. In a modern Greek village it has been observed that when illness strikes it is not unusual for one of the women of the family—the patient's grandmother perhaps—to 'make sure that the ikons of St. Cosmos and St. Damianos, the healing ones who take no pay, hang in the bedroom over the pillow of the sick person'. A priest is called in, silver votives (similar to those dug up from pre-Christian strata at Athens) are offered in church, and perhaps herbs are administered. As a last resort the old woman is likely to 'make the pilgrimage to Tenos' to pray for the recovery of the victim and on her way back she may take a scraping from an ikon in the village church to mix in a healing tea.[28] Though the names have changed from AEsculapius to the Virgin of Tenos the responses to illness are not dissimilar.

The sick would try all available remedies. One of Langland's characters had a fever

> lasting a whole year. And then I begin to despise the Christian doctors, and resort to witches; and I say quite openly that no trained doctor, not even Christ himself, can cure diseases as well as the old cobbler-woman of Southwark, or Dame Emma of Shoreditch.[29]

This blasphemous outburst was a piece of fiction, but the following advice comes from the writings of one of the intellectuals of the thirteenth century, Michael Scot: in certain cases

> where medicine fails, the physician should advise the patient to go to diviners and enchantresses, although this may seem wrong (*inhonestum et nephas*) or contrary to the Christian faith, but true nevertheless.[30]

For most people their 'illness behaviour'—an expression coined by the new breed of medical anthropologists—depended upon a multitude of things such as their social status and wealth, availability of doctors or shrines, type of illness involved and their attitudes toward saints and surgeons or *medici*. The sufferer might use both sacred and profane remedies since for him the end and not the means was of greatest importance: 'In a culture where there are several independent systems available . . . one does well, in seeking a cure, to cover one's bets.'[31] For some the shrine of a saint was the first place to turn for help in sickness; for others it was literally the last resort.

The records of posthumous miracles, then, can throw some light on alternative forms of therapy available in medieval England. But their main burden, obviously, is to describe the cures reported by people who prayed to particular saints or went on pilgrimage to supplicate them through their relics, the enshrined bones. Since about nine-tenths of the registered miracles were cures, by asking what the pilgrims meant by 'cure' we are also asking what the majority of them meant by 'miracle'. For the present the small proportion of miracles which were not cures will be disregarded. About half the 3,000-odd English and French posthumous miracles examined in the nine major and the other, minor, cults, were said to have occurred in the patients' homes, the other half at the shrines of the saints. In both groups the vast majority of patients or pilgrims only gradually became aware of an improvement in their health, which they called a miraculous cure. The instantaneous faith-healing miracle was rare. Before examining the circumstances of the purported cures, however, a matter of some importance must be dealt with, the possibility of fraud on the part of the pilgrims.

No doubt some people feigned illness to gain more sympathy and alms than they would as plain and simple paupers. Others faked miraculous cures for the momentary attention they would enjoy and for whatever advantages they could gain from their notoriety. There were in a few cases substantial advantages. In the early fourteenth century a toddler named Roger fell into the ditch outside the walls of Conway Castle in north Wales. The coroners came and, apparently convinced that he was dead, began writing up their report, but the boy revived after a bystander made a vow to St. Thomas Cantilupe. In 1307 the case came before the commissioners investigating Cantilupe's claim to canonization and in 1311 the Bishop of London (a member of the 1307 commission) wrote to an abbot to make sure that a pension would be paid for the boy, then being schooled under the bishop's care. Evidently the boy had attracted the bishop's interest.[32] There is little reason to suspect fraud in this case, which is cited to illustrate why some people might enjoy being considered *miraculé*, i.e. miraculously cured by a saint.

To reduce the possibility of fraud, registrars at shrines usually asked for witnesses to the suffering pilgrim's earlier condition or subsequent 'cure'; on occasion unsupported testimony was refused. The greatest worry was the *ignotus*, or stranger. Unless he were of high social standing or of the clergy he would probably have to bring witnesses along, or a letter from his priest. Given such primitive safeguards, and admitting that many registrars must themselves have been tempted to record unverified cures now and then, fraudulent activities undoubtedly accounted for some of the so-called miraculous cures. A thirteenth-century specialist in this sort of confidence trick was in Oxford when he heard that a revered Franciscan had recently been buried there. He engaged one of the Franciscan friars in conversation and told him that the convent could make a great deal of money if they wished. Asked how, he said that since the dead brother was so highly praised, if miracles were worked at his tomb much money (as pilgrim offerings) would follow. The innocent Franciscan suggested that miracles were in God's hands, to which the schemer replied that he had twenty-four people in various parts of England under his control, who would undergo miracles anywhere in any way he wished. The Franciscan threw him out.[33]

The same source records that a Scottish lady supported a 'paralysed' man until she discovered that he was a fraud. He then confessed that he used to go to a certain cross in Scotland where many pilgrims congregated and had pretended to be miraculously healed there. A boy who feigned loss of speech was recognized by someone who had already seen him 'cured'; a blow on the back restored his tongue. A blind man 'cured' at Becket's tomb about 1290 showed up at Cantilupe's tomb shortly afterward and underwent another 'cure', but a Franciscan happened to recognize him.[34] In questionable cases mutes were asked to open their mouths and if they had tongues their dumbness was presumed to be fraudulent. Blind people who claimed to be cured were sometimes asked to identify things. This got one fraud into trouble with Humphrey Duke of Gloucester, as told by Thomas More and retold by Shakespeare: hearing shouts of 'miracle', the duke had the cured man brought to him. He claimed that he had been blind from birth but miraculously cured. He was asked what colours the Duke was then wearing, and when he named them correctly Humphrey remarked, 'Sight may distinguish of colours, but suddenly to nominate them all, it is impossible' for one blind all his life. And so the man—and his wife—were whipped home to Berwick.[35]

Traditionally medieval cures have been attributed to this sort of fraud (sometimes blamed on the monks themselves) or to the delusions of people who were never 'really' ill to begin with. No doubt fraud explains some of the recorded cases, but it is unlikely that the majority of them can be accounted for in this way. The fundamental difficulty which inhibits modern comprehension of how medieval cures could have been attributed to saints is our preference for defining health, illness and cure in terms which have little relationship to medieval circumstances. We need to look at the idea of a 'cure' not from the modern but from the medieval point of view.

For most people in medieval England life was a constant battle to get enough food, fuel and shelter to sustain existence from one year to the next. Insanitary living conditions and little if any personal hygiene were unavoidable facts of life. Even the greatest lords in the land could not escape the evil effects of their environment, in which infant mortality was high, life expectancy low, illness and early death commonplace. Malnutrition was aggravated by seasonal fluctuations in crop yields, sometimes even by local famines, and primitive sewage disposal especially in towns probably rendered water unfit to drink. The cramped hovels of the peasantry—many of whom shared their quarters with their animals—were excellent breeding-grounds for communicable diseases. During the winter, the inclement weather that kept folk indoors would only have further weakened resistance to disease, at the same time as the quality of their food declined. Many, especially the peasantry, probably ended the winter nearly scorbutic; what was sometimes known as 'winter sickness' may well have been scurvy. Disease thrives in the midst of squalor and ignorance, and medieval medicine has provided ample evidence of the latter. Considering some of the 'remedies' offered by medieval doctors, patients were probably better off without the medical 'science' of their day. Even less can be said for contemporary ideas on the causes of disease.

Of course the *medici* were quite prepared to offer their opinions: an imbalance of the humours, perhaps, brought on by eating moist foods when one should have eaten dry; the unlucky conjunction of the stars; evil-smelling 'airs'. All of these ideas were common in Greek and Roman medical treatises and were passed down vitually unchanged and unexamined to medieval practitioners. The uneducated had their own ways of explaining the onset of illness. It was believed, for instance, that one could become ill by wandering about or sleeping out in the open, and not merely as a result of exposure to the elements. This could happen day or night, even while merely walking for a short time out of doors. It was not unusual for pilgrims to report simply that they fell asleep in good health and awoke seriously ill, like the Oxfordshire boy who 'went to sleep well and awoke mute' in a field and remained dumb for five years.[36] These reports may originally have contained further information, perhaps that during sleep the victim was accosted by field or forest spirits which dwelt in the region, though there are few references in the English posthumous miracles to attacks by such beings. One instance comes from Wulfstan's collection, where three forest fairies interrupted a cleric's journey through a dark wood. Perhaps the registrars either disregarded the prattle about sprites and fauns or put them into more acceptable forms as various manifestations of the Evil One or ordinary demons.[37] It is sometimes claimed that in the Middle Ages demons were thought to be mainly responsible for illness. On the contrary, if the evidence of some 3,000 cases is anything to go by, the intrusion of demons was quite limited. They were normally only associated with mental aberrations, when the victim was said to have become possessed, and they seldom appeared in other forms of illness. Sin is nearly as rare as a *stated* cause of illness. When mentioned at all, it was most often associated with leprosy. The sin might be that of the victim or even his parents, an Old Testament idea. In learned circles presumably greater weight was given to Pope Innocent III's pronouncement that 'bodily infirmity is sometimes caused by sin', and in a medieval medical treatise the physician was enjoined to encourage confession for his patient because 'many ill-nesses originate on account of sin'.[38] But most people did not regard sin as an important cause of illness.

In most cases the miracle records say nothing at all about the causes of illness. There are occasional attempts to provide some sort of reason besides demons and sin, sleeping outdoors, or the will of God. Poison was sometimes mentioned, especially if one had enemies and fell ill for no 'apparent' reason. Toad flesh was thought to swell inside anyone unfortunate enough to swallow it, causing the victim to swell up as well. One woman claimed that she was 'swollen' for fourteen years, which would have made her 'poison' very tenacious stuff. The breath of a viper (the classical basilisk) was also something to avoid: after Gaufrid was hissed upon with the 'sulphurous vapour' of a large snake he claimed that he began to 'puff, swell, and grow black'. Other 'causes' of illness were suggested by the pilgrims and registrars, such as divine punishment for working on Church feastdays and Sundays, the phase of the moon (an ancient belief), failure to carry out a vow to a saint, or a curse uttered by an enemy or even a parent in a moment of anger. Witches make only rare appearances as bringers of illness; their day would come after the Middle Ages had drawn to a close. Finally, as we have seen, illness or even death could be 'caused' by a saint whom the victim had slighted.[39]

The great bulk of medieval Englishmen, then, lived in squalid, unhealthy conditions in which disease and early death were all too common; relatively few individuals, or at least few families, escaped the consequences. With sufficient food and adequate shelter some might pull through with less difficulty, but a great many people were sometimes lacking even these basic necessities. In addition, so little was known about the body and disease that practically nothing—certainly in twentieth-century western 'scientific' terms—could be done for the ill. It is difficult to imagine this state of affairs, prior to the revolutionary nineteenth-century developments in anatomy and physiology and advances in understanding microbial infection, prior even to Harvey's seventeenth-century discoveries about the circulation of the blood. An indication of what it may have been like comes from certain modern Greek villages, where 'practically no one could state the function of the liver, the blood, or the heart'.[40] In the Middle Ages perception of the illness or healthiness of a given individual was practically a social generalization, whether someone was 'cured' little better than a consensus of opinion. Sometimes it was even found difficult to decide whether a person was dead or alive. Though this problem still occasionally arises, it was far more common in even the relatively recent past.

During the Victorian era when swoons and trances were in fashion, fear of live burial (taphephobia) reached such a pitch that a woman left instructions in her will 'requiring my throat to be cut before I am put underground', choosing absolutely to die rather than to risk waking up in a coffin after the mourners had gone home. A twentieth-century Suffolk gravedigger recalled that 'bodies used to be kept in the house for twelve days . . . They were afraid that the corpse might still be alive'.[41] In the Middle Ages the inability to tell the dead from the living obviously had much to do with miraculous 'revivals from death'. In a macabre tale of a girl who 'died' of the mysterious late-medieval sweating sickness, one of the women sewing her into her shroud detected a heartbeat; they at once fell to praying to King Henry VI and eventually the girl recovered. Those revived were often infants or children, just as accident-prone seven or eight centuries ago as they are today; the case of Roger who fell into the castle ditch at Conway and appeared 'dead' even to the experienced coroners who examined him has already been mentioned. A child who fell into Summergil Brook in Herefordshire was revived by one Hugh who held him upside-down, took him in by a fire, gave what sounds like the kiss of life (*applicuit os suum et genas suas ad os* [*sic*] *dicti Willelmi*) and kept thrusting a finger down his throat; when the finger was bitten, Hugh knew that life remained. He sensed the child breathing and, placing a hand on his chest, felt a heartbeat. Because the neighbourhood crowd had meanwhile been praying to St. Thomas Cantilupe the eventual resuscitation of the boy 'from the dead' was recorded as another miracle performed by that saint.[42] It may seem unfair to Hugh, yet many saints were given credit for a 'miracle' in very similar circumstances.

Part of the reason for the uncertainty about death was a reliance on superficial indications such as body temperature, rigidity, skin colour and respiration, the usual expressions being *pallidus, frigidus* and *rigidus*. The pulse was sometimes considered as well. Alternatively, on one occasion doctors declared a patient dead because he had lost his reason, sight, hearing, speech and breath.[43] Arguments sometimes developed on this crucial issue. A Welsh rebel executed at Swansea was taken to a chapel where there was a dispute as to whether he was alive or dead; out in the Ely marshes in 1144 a debate took place around the prone form of a certain Lewin, whether to begin the funeral or not. Fortunately for Lewin they 'decided that he ought to be kept until they could be more certain upon the point' and agreed to put things off for three days, by which time he had regained consciousness. In the Becket miracles, consultations were often necessary when deciding whether someone was alive or dead. Now and then medieval registrars assure the reader of the miracles that the victim under discussion had 'really' been dead and not merely suffering deep trance, but the unexceptional nature of many 'revivals' is ironically spelled out by William of Canterbury, one of Becket's shrine-guardians. He claimed that revivals from the dead after two or three days were not uncommon in England though a revival after seven days was, as he admits, somewhat unusual.[44] Miraculous resuscitation 'from death', therefore, was hardly as unusual in the Middle Ages as it would be in the twentieth century. On the other hand it is anyone's guess how many people in those past centuries were actually buried alive.

If we would hardly consider a 'miracle' the case of the drowned boy resuscitated by Hugh (and attributed to Cantilupe), we would perhaps be even less inclined to call many other recorded events miracles, although medieval people ascribed them to a saints's intervention. A prior who claimed to be 'nearly dead' prayed to Simon de Montfort and during the night awoke, belched, vomited and was 'cured'; and Simon was also said to have miraculously healed a woman to the extent that she could make the sign of the cross over herself before she died. At Old Sarum a woman with toothache prayed to St. Osmund and went to his shrine where the tooth 'miraculously' fell out.[45] These incidents were all grist for the registrar's mill and were recorded as miracles.

Partial recoveries were also thought to be miraculous cures. In one case a woman received her sight through the merits of Becket, but not completely (*tamen perfecte non recepit*). A mute was only partially cured after a vow to Edmund Rich, and a cripple 'cured' at Cantilupe's shrine in Hereford still needed a walking-stick to get about (*cum baculo claudicando*). A blind man from Northampton considered himself cured by Simon de Montfort when he regained sight—in one eye; another pilgrim felt so 'cured' after a vigil by Simon's tomb that she only required one stick to help her walk. William of York's relics cured a dumb woman so that she could speak *somewhat* better (*in loquela aliqualiter meliorata est*) and a blind Gloucester girl was cured at Wulfstan's shrine at Worcester although vestiges of the ailment remained in one eye. After a cure of dropsy there were marks left in the pilgrim's legs and feet 'as in many other cases' adds the registrar, as reminders of God's mercy. Blind Agnes of Dun's Tew went to Frideswide's shrine at Oxford for a cure and was healed in one eye; but why the other was not cured too, only God knew. On a few occasions the registrars hesitated before accepting a cure, but all of the instances cited above were recorded as 'true' miraculous cures and there were many other similar 'cures'.[46] What we would call only parital or incomplete improvements were attributed to the saints as complete 'miracles'.

Sometimes the ill were said to have been partially cured at one shrine, wholly at another. One deformed pilgrim had some of the affliction removed at Becket's tomb, went on to a shrine in Scotland where nothing happened, and finally regained full health at Finchale. One of a pilgrim's infected ears was healed at Canterbury, the other at St. Frideswide's shrine.[47] These examples also illustrate another characteristic of medieval miraculous healing, the fact that some cures might take time. In Prospero Lambertini's eighteenth-century work on canonization, already mentioned, one of the conditions of miraculous cures was their instantaneity.[48] But most medieval miracles were not sudden, and if we expected to find as a daily occurrence cripples flinging away their crutches or mute pilgrims breaking out in a *Te*

Deum, we would be disappointed. Certainly a few cures were sudden, taking place as soon as the suppliant approached the holy dead, but these were not typical. The medieval collector of St. Wulfstan's posthumous miracles was surprised to witness such a cure, noting that it happened all at once and not, 'like others', after a certain delay (*per intervalla et certas interpolationes temporum*). The modern editors of Henry VI's posthumous miracles have observed that few of them were instantaneous. More characteristic was the woman who felt some mitigation at the shrine of William of Norwich, went home, and in a little while was cured, or the dropsical suppliant who left the same shrine 'much more nimbly' than he had arrived and whose neighbours later claimed that he was cured. These would have been considered miraculous cures that occurred as a result of pilgrimage to the saint's shrine. A woman went to Gilbert of Sempringham's tomb, prayed, and went home still blind, where she improved day by day (*de die in diem*) until her sight was restored, and St. Gilbert got the credit for another miracle.[49]

Reference to the 'ill lying about the church waiting for a cure' is made in many of the collections; sometimes these recumbent folk got in the way of other incoming worshippers. Generally speaking, they were accommodated until they were cured (or their patience ran out), like the insane girl who lay raging fifteen days at Wulfstan's tomb before her sanity returned, or another who stayed there for different reasons for three weeks. One pilgrim had to wait two weeks at Becket's tomb, another waited a month by the shrine of Hugh of Lincoln, a third waited by Frideswide's bones for an unstated period, *interjecto tempore*. A two- to three-day wait was not uncommon, and examples can be found in any miracle collection. Some pilgrims, after waiting for some time at a shrine went home but came back later on, hoping for better results on their second visit. A woman who made two trips to Frideswide's shrine was finally healed on the fourth day of her second pilgrimage. A 'leper' visited Becket's bones twice before a cure, another 'leper' made four or more journeys to Canterbury, while a girl who had the same symptoms and whose new step-father had turned her out, had to go to the bones of Godric at Finchale three times before she was cured.[50] Obviously, time was not of the essence in medieval miracles. According to the eighteenth-century criteria set by Lambertini this was no longer true, but in the Middle Ages a miracle might take weeks or, in some cases, months.[51] No matter—in the end the saint still received credit, another miracle was recorded.

Besides partial cures and delayed cures there were temporary 'cures' which were still—for the most part—recorded as miracles. There were cases of relapse following other forms of therapy as well, after bathing in the Jordan river, for instance, or after receiving traditional medical treatment from the physicians. One teenage girl relapsed after a 'cure' effected by the Royal Touch administered by King Henry II. As for temporary cures at saints' shrine, there was the boy with a curved spine who was cured at William of Norwich's tomb, for example. He went home but 'after some days, by what chance or accident I know not, the old weakness and trouble returned'. Like many other victims of relapse, he was cured again after another vow or visit to the saint in question (or another saint). On a few occasions the registrars claimed that the relapse was permanent: one of Becket's pilgrims went home cured of skin disease but was again attacked by the same affliction. He was not recured, 'I know not by what judgment of God', confessed the registrar.[52] In two or three cases the pilgrim was even said to have ended up in worse condition than before his pilgrimage.

Among the explanations offered for relapses the most common were the pilgrim's neglect of a vow, even one made fifteen years earlier, or his turning to human medicines and doctors as added insurance after a saintly cure.[53] These reasons were offered by the people closely involved, and one or two others might be suggested. From the psychological point of view, it may be significant that some pilgrims improved only while actually at a shrine. On occasion the registrars themselves seem to have had doubts about the permanence of some of the cures. In a Wulfstan miracle, a pilgrim was told to come back in three months to prove that the illness had not returned—but such caution on the part of the shrine-keepers was rare. A few pilgrims seem to have had their own misgivings. A foreign cleric remained at Becket's tomb for two years, afraid to leave in case his epilepsy returned (*timens repatriare ne post convalescentiam in morbum suum recidiverat*).[54] Psychological dependence upon a shrine is suggested in such cases but another reason for relapse was very likely physiological, in self-limiting or remissive ailments, to be considered more fully below.

Finally, very little is said in the collections about the out-and-out failures, the pilgrims who went to shrines, prayed for a cure for two days or two weeks but in the end went home perhaps even more depressed and ill. Naturally, the most likely place to find examples would be in the records of 'rival' shrines. Registrars had no qualms about publishing the failures of other saintly remains, so in the Frideswide miracle collection we are told of a pilgrim praying in vain at Becket's shrine for two weeks, and the story of a mute whom Becket failed to cure even after two pilgrimages appears among the posthumous miracles of Godric of Finchale.[55] There are one or two cases of near-failures which succeeded in the end. A mute girl waited with her mother for four or five days at Frideswide's shrine but nothing happened and at last the mother, bored with waiting, made ready to go home—with the theologically correct but in this case not very comforting observation that God's power was the same everywhere. At this the girl collapsed, slept, and on waking up began to speak. In a Wulfstan miracle a Welsh woman and her blind daughter waited for a cure at the tomb in Worcester for three days. When nothing happened the mother—for her race are easily moved to wrath, notes the scribe, presumably not Welsh himself—left the shrine in anger. On arriving home her unsuspecting husband asked why she was in a temper, at which she burst out, 'If what they said about St. Wulfstan were true, he would have cured my daughter.' The girl was never cured, and the only reason the tale was recorded was to show how the mother had been punished for her blasphemy: her son also became blind but after she saw the error of her ways and ran down the road screaming 'Mercy, St. Wulfstan, mercy, St. Wulfstan' the boy was healed.[56]

From these cases it is apparent that the slightest improvement or partial and even temporary recovery was considered a miraculous cure and that the medieval concept of 'cure' was very flexible. Since the recovery need not be permanent many recurrent illnesses would apparently be affected by the holy aura of a shrine. As summed up by one sixteenth-century observer, pilgrims with headaches who claimed be miraculously cured at a certain shrine went home 'and then their heads should ache no more *till the next time*'.[57] Certainly in those centuries when survivors of the perils of infancy were constantly threatened with disease, when the slightest infection might lead to death or the simplest ailment (which we shrug off with an antibiotic) leave permanent damage behind, even slight recovery must have been—subjectively—a tremendous relief. The saints also took credit for delayed cures so that a pilgrim who felt no better at a shrine but improved a week later while at home in bed could claim miraculous healing, and the registrar—thanks to this retroactive attribution—could add another example to his list.

Just as there was no time-limit in which a saint must effect a cure, there was no way to determine the *degree* of regained health, the extent of the cure. We have cited cases of relapse which came to the attention of the registrar only because the patient was cured again by a saint. How many relapsed pilgrims never improved or never re-visited a shrine, it is impossible to say. The very fact that a pilgrim was cured by a particular saint's relics but later relapsed might suggest to him the futility of returning to the same shrine. The registrar would only note the original cure and describe the pilgrim happily setting out on the homeward journey, or he might summarize a letter sent from home when the cure was thought to have been completed. In the vast majority of cases we know nothing of the cured person's subsequent fate since there was no medical 'follow-up'. He might have died a few months later from the very same illness. This is precisely what happened to the first person 'cured' by St. Thomas Cantilupe's relics in the late thirteenth century.[58]

Though the illnesses themselves may be put into any number of categories, a modern anthropological study of folk medicine helps to simplify the general picture. In adults who have developed immunity to common pathogens, many illnesses are short and self-limiting, that is, they will get better on their own. Another type of ailment is made up of complaints which are chronic but temporarily reversible. These go on from year to year, sometimes seeming to get a little better, sometimes relapsing, such as rheumatic conditions. The 'remaining category is a very large one. It includes all those illnesses in which psychological or neurotic elements are involved'.[59] We may summarize these as (1) self-limiting (2) chronic but subject to remission and (3) psychogenic. In all three faith-healing is a distinct possibility. Many medieval 'miracles' belonged to the first group, the minor afflictions which in time got better on their own, such as severe indigestion, headache, constipation, bone fractures which mended and bad teeth which fell out 'miraculously'; all of these are found in the collections. Trivial though they may seem, to the people who suffered and found relief after calling on a saint or visiting his shrine they were miracles, recorded as such by the registrars. The same is true for the second group, the chronically ill whose periods of remission they associated not with environmental, physiological and psychological changes which they could not understand, but with the power emanating from a shrine, which they could. Rheumatoid arthritis is one of those diseases in which remission may account for many of the 'cures' of cripples. Recurrence may in fact be characteristic of an illness, built in as it were. We may well wonder how many reputed cures by the medieval saints of Pisa were permanent and how many 'the tricks of a malaria infection'.[60] Seasonal changes could be beneficial as well as detrimental to health. For instance, certain eye diseases brought on by vitamin-deficient diets would probably clear up as the quality and variety of food improved in spring and summer—the prilgrimage season. But to contemporaries, the shrines they visited, not nutritional improvements, brought about the miraculous healings of blindness.

Finally, there is the third group of illnesses, the psychogenic. A steadily-rising flood of literature has been pouring from hospitals and clinical laboratories ever since the days of Mesmer, Charcot, Pierre Janet, Joseph Breuer and Freud, all to prove what Socrates once casually remarked to Charmides: 'And therefore if the head and body are to be well, you must begin by curing the soul; that is the first thing.' These days expressions like psychosomatic and conversion reaction convey the idea that the mind and body cannot function—or mal-function—independently. Conversion reaction used to be known simply as 'hysteria', but by whatever name, it was and is a 'real' illness, producing 'real' paralysis, blindness, convulsions, deafness and pain, to mention only the more common motor and sensory areas involved, even though there is no organic pathology, nothing 'physically wrong'. Most of the patients suffering conversion hysteria tend to be women around forty, or so they were in studies reported in the 1960s.[61] Since the symptoms change with time and place—as we have noted, in the Victorian era the great faint was a common manifestation—this says very little about what may have been happening in medieval England. It is probable, at least, that many ill pilgrims were suffering what is known today as conversion hysteria and that the build-up to their pilgrimage and especially the emotional environment at the shrine itself may in some cases have shocked them into health.

The association between miracles of healing and illness which originates in the mind was recognized, for instance, by Paley in 1727 when he drew up a questionnaire to test certain miracles claimed by the Jansenists: were any of the cures, he wished to know, merely of a nervous complaint? The Medical Bureau at Lourdes, with responsibility for passing scientific judgment on miraculous cures, refuses to consider 'hysterical or neurotic' cases. On the Confidential Medical Certificate for present-day English pilgrims to Lourdes the doctor is to answer the question 'Is there any underlying neuroses? or psychiatric disorder etc.?' Presumably an affirmative answer would lessen the chances of any cure being proclaimed a miracle by the Bureau, a rather old-fashioned approach which has aroused some criticism.[62] We may assume, in any case, that some medieval pilgrims suffering hysterical blindness or paralysis and so on were so affected that their health returned if only for the time being. When they went home perhaps the old anxieties and frustrations of family life caused the illness to recur but, in a sense which the Lourdes Medical Bureau would not appreciate, they had been healed.

A great many of the recorded cases of miraculous healing at the medieval shrines belonged to one of these three categories, the self-limiting, remissive, or psychogenic.

> Now, whether the patient is on the National Health Service in Britain, . . . or whether he lives in a village in Africa and visits the herbalist, if he is in fact suffering from one of these three types of disturbance, the prescribed treatment will be credited with the 'cure'.[63]

Whatever alternative therapy is applied, including visits to saints' shrines, the particular treatment for these categories of illness makes little empirical difference, be it modern encounter groups, magical drawings in coloured sand, flebotomy by a medieval doctor, application of charms or pilgrimage to a holy tomb. In the twelfth century a young man cried out in his illness for curative Canterbury water. Knowing that they had none, one of his friends ran and fetched some ordinary water and gave it to him saying that it was the desired Becket-water, a medieval placebo. The patient was cured, of course, by his faith. The force which caused healing at shrines or through vows to saints was expectant faith. Even in illness which only partially cured itself or which took a month to heal, the faithful imputed a miracle to the holy dead because that was what they had expected of the holy dead. 'Every year', wrote Bede, describing a church in Lincoln, 'some miraculous cures are wrought in that place, for the benefit of those who have faith to seek the same.' The opposite was true, too, for when Jesus went back to his home town 'he did not work many miracles there, such was their want of faith'.[64]

The expectation of miracles was so built-in that on occasion it was reduced to the rather unexciting terms of a liturgical rite. In an *Ordinale* of the nuns of Barking written about 1400 there are explicit directions for processions and prayers *whenever* a miracle happened in the church. Expectation has also been noted in modern Lourdes pilgrims, though this is probably a pale reflection of medieval faith.[65] It is interesting to see, however, how such expectation might be built up. A young woman named Edeltraud Fulda was suffering from Addison's disease.[66] In 1945 she read a book called *Our Lady of Lourdes*, in 1946 another entitled *Lourdes in the Glory of its Miracles*; the following year she wrote in her diary, 'I've received some longed-for Lourdes water!' In 1949 she sent a letter of supplication to the Blessed Virgin at Lourdes. By 1950 she had arranged for her pilgrimage and arrived in August, well-provided with three medical certificates as proof of her illness. Around the middle of the month she experienced the beginnings of her cure and eventually—in 1955—the Church proclaimed the miracle, citing *inter alia* the conditions laid down by Lambertini in the eighteenth century. This modern pilgrim had at least five years' rumination before her trip to Lourdes, sufficient to generate more than usual enthusiasm, one would think. At modern shrines as in medieval England the therapy resides to a great extent in the preparation for the trip, the journey itself, the anticipation of seeing for the first time the place where faith worked miracles.

In considering the posthumous miracles attributed to medieval saints, then, it is necessary to recognize that pilgrimage in search of cures at shrines was a fully-formed tradition received from earlier centuries and legitimized if not encouraged by the Church. At the same time the expectant faith which motivated such a journey and the hope placed in saintly *auxilium* were in themselves therapeutically beneficial. Pilgrimage also provided a less costly, simpler alternative therapy to that offered by the *medici*. The single success outweighed a hundred failures since 'failure' was not imputed to the holy dead but to the poor state of the pilgrim's soul and the shallowness of his belief in the saint's curative powers. Environmental conditions were such that dirt and disease, malnutrition and poverty drew the general level of health down, and ignorance of causes and cures rendered one thereapy as effective as any other.

Three types of illness were especially susceptible to 'cure' by any treatment, the self-limiting, the chronic but remissive, and the psychogenic, provided patients had faith in the chosen therapy. In addition, the medieval concept of 'cure' itself was so flexible as to embrace partial, temporary, and delayed improvement. We have noted that half of the miraculous cures happened in the unhurried atmosphere of the patients' homes and that the majority of all cures, wherever they took place, were gradual. Considered from these points of view the shrine-miracles to be examined, far from being 'the most ridiculous and disgusting portions of the belief of the middle ages' are for the most part 'true accounts of occurrences some of which are ordinary, others unusual in themselves, but which without exception do not constitute marvels in our senses'.[67]

Chapter 5

Saintly Therapy in Action: Shrine-cures and Home-cures

The medical journals of the time were collections of
miracles, *libri miraculorum*, written in the centres of
pilgrimage.

A. Luchaire

For every individual involved in a medieval miracle perhaps a hundred
or even a thousand ordinary pilgrims came and went unnoticed by the
registrar. Though some 800,000 people visited an American priest's
grave in 1929 only about 100 claimed some sort of cure; out of millions
of Lourdes pilgrims roughly 5,000 have reported cures during the past
120 years, and the Church has officially accepted fewer than 100 as
miracles. About 2,500 pilgrims visited certain Ashanti shrines in Ghana
in 1955 but only a fifth of them went for reasons connected with
health and illness.[1] There is no way even to guess how many 'other'
medieval pilgrims were represented by each one of the recorded
miracle-touched or *miraculé* visitors. Given these limitations, the fact
remains that the records of posthumous miracles provide virtually the
only evidence of day to day events at saints' shrines in the Middle Ages.

Nothing succeeded like success in the miracle world. Most pilgrims,
like the lame Canterbury girl cured at Becket's tomb, were 'stirred up
by the renown of the miracles' before setting off for a thaumaturgic
shrine in an expectant, receptive state.[2] The most common reason for
choosing to go to a recently-established shrine was the rumour of
posthumous miracles and, probably to a lesser extent, the decedent's
'living' reputation and circumstances of his death or translation. Sometimes friends, parents or spouses prompted people to visit shrines. The
expression 'advised by the neighbours' prefaces many miracles and
pilgrimages, and returning villagers who praised a shrine stimulated
many to try their luck at the same place. Some went to particular
shrines after being advised to do so in dreams or visions.

Vivid dreams were usually freely discussed among friends and
family. Sometimes the local clergy might join in to help to identify the
'visitor' who had come at night to stand by the bed and deliver his

message. The grandfather of William of Norwich, for instance, was a priest skilled in the interpretation of dreams. In addition to identifying precisely who had appeared in dreams, priests sometimes helped with the other images which had vividly impressed their parishioners in the middle of the night. Some used a 'dream-book', an alphabetical list of objects with appropriate 'significations'. Dream-books were known in antiquity and seem to have become common in the West some time before the tenth century. Unfortunately for dreamers, they sometimes disagreed in 'significations'. Taking two such dream-books at random, it appears that to see a dove signified damnation in one, peace in the other; to walk in an orchard, either happiness or anguish.[3]

The distinction between dreams and visions was thought to be important in the Middle Ages. A vision was usually accepted as a 'real' message from the other world which was to be heeded, whereas a dream was less significant, perhaps—as some medieval writers claimed—only a result of overeating before retiring. If the experience was especially vivid, this might in itself convince the recipient that he had had a vision. Alternatively it was generally believed that dreams which recurred three times were visionary; one lady was graced with a six-fold repetition. The saints who appeared in dreams or visions could be most accommodating: one addressed a mute in sign-language, 'the language of the fingers' (*digitorum lingua*); the Virgin Mary was kind enough to address a recumbent Hereford canon in French and the dead Becket spoke to a sleeping Irishman in his native Gaelic.[4]

Whenever pilgrims, perhaps influenced by the registrars at shrines, wished to emphasize the 'truth' of a nocturnal message they declared that they had had a vision, not a dream—*visionem non somnium*. Some people went back to sleep in the hope that the event would be repeated, thus determining whether it were a dream or revelation (*sompnia an revelatio*), others deliberately induced it:

> He afflicted his body with fasting, his mind with watching and tears; he slept on the bare ground and would accept no consolation until he received some answer from the Lord.

After a night vision the biographer of William of Norwich 'greatly set my heart upon a second and a third revelation'. With that sort of determination, and constantly expecting to 'see' in his sleep what he so desired while awake, it is not surprising that he received his two revelations, at two-week intervals. As Gibbon put it when describing a near-contemporary of the Norwich biographer, 'whatever he wished, he believed, whatever he believed, he *saw* in dreams and revelations'.[5] Medieval sceptics ridiculed visionary messages long before Gibbon, especially dreams reported by illiterate peasants. Sometimes a person's own family remained unconvinced: when a blind Gloucester girl told her mother and brothers about her vision of the Blessed Virgin Mary who recommended pilgrimage to St. Wulfstan's tomb, they laughingly commented, 'as you wished, so you dreamed', *sicut concupisti; ita sompniasti.*[6] This sceptical attitude may in fact have been far more common than would appear from the stories collected at shrines. Naturally, the monks who composed the miracle collections could allow themselves only occasional doubts as to the authenticity of visionary appearances of 'their' saints.

Many pilgrims, then, decided to go to a particular shrine because they heard about its reputation from neighbours or from others passing through their villages or because they had received dream-admonitions. Others, however, wandered from one shrine to another in search of health, until they felt sufficiently cured.[7] Many English pilgrims went first to Becket's tomb, an indication of his popularity. Sometimes these perambulations in search of health took pilgrims well beyond the coasts of England. An Attenborough man went to Compostella in early 1201 for a cure. He felt some relief while there but after his return in mid-May his condition deteriorated and he spent the next few months 'shrine-hopping'. Things grew worse until someone recommended Sempringham, where on 29 September he was cured by the relics of St. Gilbert. Another example is the priest who was paralysed while singing Mass. He visited shrines for the next three years begging for health from the saints, *a sanctis sanitatem mendicans*, until at last he was cured at Worcester, some sixty miles from his home. Though they may have agreed that God's power was the same everywhere, the ill—especially the chronically ill—went right on with their quest for health, trudging or riding from shrine to shrine. Perhaps the record is held by the man who visited eighty-seven holy places. While these people moved about (in one case for fourteen years) it was likely that eventually *some* shrine would receive credit for their 'cure';[8] on the other hand, perhaps they felt better at *every* new shrine they visited. Some pilgrims 'chose' their shrine by casting lots: three saints were selected, and the sticks or whatever were thrown or drawn three times. Since God controlled all things it was not 'luck' but His will which operated on the lots to pick out a particular shrine. In parts of France early in the present century lots were cast to discover which saint had inflicted an illness and should be placated.[9] But lots are seldom mentioned in the medieval miracles.

Having decided where they wanted to go, the would-be pilgrims next had to arrange the trip which they hoped would bring relief from illness. All the ordinary obstacles were heightened because many of them were invalids barely able to walk or ride, for whom any journey was a major undertaking; they could certainly expect some discomfort and possibly even death as a result of the rigours of their journey. One prudent man was reluctant to escort his wife to a shrine, fearing that she might die *en route* to leave him suspected of a skilfully-contrived murder. In a few cases even the ill themselves were hesitant, like the French lady who turned down a trip to Canterbury, saying, 'It is unsuitable to start what I shall be unable to finish, because I am an old woman, because I am ill, because the sea is dangerous.' She chose a Becket shrine closer to home.[10] Most pilgrims, however, were glad of the opportunity as they set out by one means or another; the sheer physical struggle may even have been therapeutic in itself.

Lame pilgrims used walking-sticks or crutches; a Lincoln priest presented a boy with a pair of padded crutches so that his skin would not be harmed. Obviously this particular disability hindered progress, as in the case of the old woman who could hobble no more than half a mile a day. Some medieval pilgrims who had lost the use of their legs pulled themselves along with hand-trestles, dragging their lower limbs behind, or they used a wheeled platform and pushed themselves about. The blind were led to shrines usually by friends or family. These guides required great patience, but on one occasion a wife's forbearance simply ran out: she became so exasperated with her husband's peregrinations that she told him, 'I'm leading you nowhere else except to St. Laurence', the shrine of the Archbishop of Dublin (d. 1180).[11] Some pilgrims hired litters for short distances. Anyone strolling about the nave of Hereford cathedral about 1290 would have seen several litters on the floor and in them the ill who had paid a penny or more to be carried from nearby villages. The wheelbarrow was yet another form of transport for the disabled. A Londoner was pushed all the way to Evesham in a barrow 'with one wheel and two feet' as the writer helpfully explains. About 1300 an even longer wheelbarrow-assisted pilgrimage took place, from London to Hereford. Some rode to shrines, but here, too, they might require special treatment, like the sick woman lifted by her family on to a feather-cushioned saddle. Even poor people who were ill might take to horse; one was placed 'like a sack' across the animal's back by a charitable priest who led her round the shrines. That ubiquitous and multipurpose farmyard fixture, the cart, was another common conveyance adding to the confusion outside a shrine-church.[12]

Some twentieth-century English travellers in Italy who went out one Sunday morning to visit a curative shrine could well have been describing medieval English pilgrims:

> We could hear strange cries and shouts ahead, and then saw lying in the centre of the road a poor cripple sufficiently uncovered to show his terrible deformity, while a young man, apparently in charge of the cripple, gesticulated and uttered loud cries and appeals for help.

Before reaching the church they saw 'at least twenty of these poor deformed creatures, each lying in the centre of the road', each with a helper.[13]

Some medieval pilgrims were cured in the course of their journey, but continued on to give thanks at the shrine. A few were cured at the church doors, like the blind woman who received her sight at the entrance to St. Frideswide's in Oxford and went unassisted to the shrine to give thanks. Miracles occurred outside some churches, however, because further entry was prohibited. In the early years of St. Edmund Rich's cult in the mid-thirteenth century, women were not allowed within the Cistercian house of Pontigny where his bones rested, so relics were carried out to them at the gates. On one occasion a pilgrim woman was singing the praises of St. Edmund so enthusiastically outside that the clergy had to send someone to ask her to quiet down. In twelfth-century Durham St. Cuthbert was supposed to be a feared misogynist who, it was believed, punished females who dared to enter his church and approach his shrine. Another division of the sexes seems to have been at least partially enforced at the tomb of Gilbert of Sempringham.[14] But usually pilgrims of both sexes were welcome at the shrines, where they offered a coin or placed a candle on or by the tomb and settled down to wait for a cure.

Occasionally, as noted above, this came easily, as it did for the cripple taken to Canterbury who knelt in prayer, arose and relinquished her crutches. Most sick pilgrims, however, stood, knelt, sat or slept in the church waiting for something to happen. Sometimes they had to have permission to spend the night, *licentiam vigilandi*. They usually had plenty of company, and shrine-keepers often went round rousing these suppliants early in the morning. To return to the twentieth-century English travellers in Italy:

> On entering the church we found the floor covered with the recumbent figures of persons who had been there through the night, and we could only reach the High Altar and the shrine . . . by slowly and carefully making our way through a side aisle where the crowd was less thick and the sleepers had begun to move away.[15]

Some medieval reports claimed that there were such crowds of visitors, especially on holy days, that the ill were unable to approach the relics. Hysterical fervour sometimes gripped medieval pilgrims when relics were exhibited and in such circumstances it could be dangerous for the weak or the sick to mingle with others who had come to pray to the holy dead; a pregnant woman lost her child after being pressed in the throng at a shrine.[16] (*Mutatis mutandis*, a more recent case is at hand: in April 1976 twenty-one people including cripples were trampled to death in the rush to greet a faith-healer in a Brazilian church.)

Some of the infirm sleeping or dozing through the night were visited in a vision/dream. Our modern travellers in Italy 'asked two women if they had dreamt in the church, but they said it had been impossible to sleep on account of the number of folk in the church'.[17] Sleeping pilgrims were not only visited but also cured by saints as they lay round and about the holy tombs. This occasionally produced reactions—of varying degrees of violence—in the pilgrims as they awoke. At Wulfstan's shrine a blind girl who woke up mumbling something about a candle was bluntly told to keep quiet, *increparent eam ut taceret*; in the end it was found that she had been cured. Even for medieval shrine-goers, outbursts by devotees grew tiresome now and then: when a blind man who was suspected as a fraud kept shouting 'I see, I see' the people at Edmund Rich's tomb thought him a nuisance and told him to quiet down.[18]

Most suppliants who were cured at shrines were conscious when this happened. The curative moment was sometimes preceded by great pain and then even unconsciousness. Screams, tears and groans might accompany this agony; a Weobley girl filled the church with shouting, *clamore horrifico*, during her cure at Wulfstan's tomb in Worcester cathedral. These scenes must have been dramatic:

> A blind woman at Becket's shrine felt a great disturbance in her head, as if she were engulfed in a raging furnace. Ripping away her veil and clawing at the garments at her breast she fell to the floor and lay there for the space of an hour, after which, opening her eyes and picking herself up she burst out, 'I can see'.[19]

Although half of the recorded miracles happened in the pilgrims' homes (after which they went on a thanksgiving pilgrimage) these violently emotional reactions or hysterical fits, with very few exceptions, occurred only at the shrines. It is not unlikely that they were brought on by the emotional environment at the shrines in highly excitable individuals probably suffering from psychogenic illness. The falling, writhing and screaming of pilgrims who arose healed after semi-consciousness or sleep was no surprise to veteran shrine-keepers, who claimed to have seen some cures heralded by great discomfort, *magno dolore*. One registrar thought it the usual signal that a miracle was about to begin: 'We saw many similarly tormented before the cure', wrote Wulfstan's scribe. In fact most of the cures at shrines were *not* preceded by these fits, although when they did happen they naturally left a strong impression on the minds of the registrars.[20] An inquisitive twelfth-century monk asked a pilgrim to describe his attack: 'He remembered feeling his body being contracted, and the impression that the church had become very narrow, as many others have described to us.'[21]

Some of the fits took rather unpleasant forms, with effusion of blood or putrid matter. Again, these were relatively uncommon when set against all of the recorded cures. Some of them appear to have marked crises in the usual course of an illness which coincided with the visit to the shrine. We must bear in mind the fact that sick pilgrims were accustomed to waiting at shrines for several days, weeks or even months, during which acute inflammations, for example, could rupture—and be considered a miraculous cure.

> A girl from Eynsham, blind for some time, wished to go to St. Frideswide's for a cure; taken to the shrine, she slept at the sepulchre. In the morning, after shedding many tears bloody pus flowed from her eyes and she recovered her sight.

A deaf woman felt twigs snapping in her head; while she screamed from the pain a great deal of bloody matter flowed from her ears, after which she could hear. This took place in the crypt in Canterbury cathedral.[22] We shall leave these unpleasant scenes with the reminder that they were not typical of the cures at shrines, most of which occurred quietly, undramatically, and often only after trying the patience of the suppliants:

> A cripple was carried in a litter to Cantilupe's shrine on a Tuesday, remained there through Wednesday, and on Thursday about sunrise was seen to stand up and walk from the litter to the tomb saying 'Saint Thomas, Saint Thomas, thank you'.[23]

Following medieval logic, the closer one was to the relics, the greater the chances for a cure. Many people experienced relief simply by viewing the shrine or touching it, but more determined pilgrims slept— or tried to—on the tomb itself. When a blind French physician objected that he would be unable to get to sleep on St. Louis of Toulouse's tomb his wife suggested that he drink enough undiluted wine to cause him to sleep 'wish to or not'. An adventuresome or perhaps demented devotee was supposed to have squeezed in through the holes in the outer shell of Becket's tomb and become trapped; he was only released, so the monks claimed, after miraculous intervention which allowed him to slip out. The monks were so taken by this that they ordered a slender youth to try the same feat, without success.[24] The usual procedure was merely to introduce the affected limb or head into these apertures or, in the later designs, the larger niches, and pray for health or whatever else the pilgrim sought. There were other techniques:

> Henry, paralysed in the right side and carrying his arm in a sling, came to Simon de Montfort's tomb and took dust from it, which he rubbed on his arm. He was healed at once, before many witnesses.

Another who sprinkled holy tomb dust on his wounds was healed but marked for life since the scars incorporated the curative powder.[25]

A widely-used healing substance was water which had absorbed the virtues of a relic, for example by washing a saint's corpse. One of the most common agents of cure among Becket's followers was water containing—in theory—a tincture of the blood shed at his martyrdom (constantly diluted ever since to make up supplies to sell to pilgrims). Metal phials or *ampullae* of 'Becket water' or 'Canterbury water' became the symbol of the archbishop, as the shell was of St. James. These ampoules, often worn round the neck, could be re-used, and one was even refilled from a curative well 'belonging' to another saint. Water taken from a well or spring associated with a saint was another common therapeutic agent. Several pilgrimage-centres manufactured ampoules for their curative water, similar to those from Canterbury.[26] (Even today, one of the most common souvenirs of a Lourdes pilgrimage is a bottle of the famous water from the spring near the shrine. The suppliers of 'Lourdes water lozenges' use grotto water and sugar, with peppermint, lemon and aniseed flavours; an image of the Lady of Lourdes is stamped on the sweet.)[27] Although this sanctified water was often used as a home remedy, it was also drunk at shrines. In a few cases an unfortunate side-effect was the induction of vomiting, possibly due to the emotional build-up preceding the administration of the water to people already primed to react in some manner or other, though vomiting sometimes happened spontaneously with no administration of relic-water. Some of the ill were no doubt already susceptible to attacks of nausea, which would be aggravated by the general excitement around them. Whatever caused the vomiting, and whatever the mess looked like—even 'worms' or, as it was claimed in the case of one ailing lady, cherry stones, plum pits and sprouting acorns—the whole thing must have been unpleasant for nearby pilgrims.[28] A 'poisoned' woman went to Norwich cathedral on a feastday when many pilgrims were present, and kissed William's shrine:

> [She] forthwith vomited all that poisonous discharge on the pavement. I can only describe it by saying that it was horrible—nay, unbearable, that there was enough of it to fill a vessel of the largest size, that the bystanders were constrained to leave the place, and the sacrists to cleanse the spot and strew it with fragrant herbs.

The embarrassed woman fled and finished her vomiting outside the church.[29]

Cures of cripples at shrines occasionally presented striking features. Most of them quietly hobbled in on crutches or crawled with hand-trestles and, perhaps feeling better for their efforts, just as quietly hobbled and crawled home again. A few experienced spectacular cures at the shrines:

> A man crippled from birth got about by dragging himself along with hand-trestles. His thumb, too, was bent back, the nail nearly through the palm. While huddled at Godric's tomb crying and moaning he straightened his legs and began to extend them. During this many heard a

crackling noise of bones and ligaments stretching. At dawn he arose and walked up to present the trestles as an offering; his hand was healed, only a red spot remaining in the palm.[30]

Crackling noises were noticed in a similar cure reported for St. Louis of Toulouse, where the sound was like 'brittle wood'. Mormon healers in nineteenth-century America said these noises resembled the 'crunching of an old basket' and more recently when a thirty-year-old woman's spinal deformity was cured in faith healing 'her body suddenly cracked as it assumed a normal posture'. The crackles are often heard by modern physiotherapists as they manipulate and straighten the limbs of unconscious patients.[31] In the late nineteenth century a routine manipulation had interesting results, as remembered by a young doctor by the name of Sigmund Freud:

A very intelligent man was present while his brother was anaesthetized and his ankylosed [stiffened] hip stretched. At the moment when the joint yielded and cracked, he perceived severe pain in his own hip, which continued for almost a year.[32]

In some cases of hysterical paralysis it has been observed that tissues accommodate so that the limb actually becomes immobile or twisted. Perhaps under special conditions this accommodation could be reversed: under strong auto-suggestion encouraged by the peculiar atmosphere at holy tombs and condoned by example and belief, pilgrims suffering certain psychogenic crippling ailments may have been unable to resist forcing their own limbs back into position. Whatever the mechanism, the phenomenon was reported by several registrars.

A crippled Lincoln boy, with one leg shorter than the other, went to St. Frideswide's church. There he was cured while his sinews were heard to crackle, and both legs became equal.[33]

Although the circumstances of most cures at shrines were neither as curious as crackling limbs nor so repugnant as vomiting visitors, one class must have been dramatic whenever it occurred, the healing of demoniacs. Mildly neurotic individuals usually pass unnoticed or are fully accepted by most societies, but when there is violent and dangerous behaviour appropriate action is taken. Demoniacs were tied up and taken to medieval shrines and kept there for days or even weeks, until their rage subsided, though it was difficult to carry on the liturgy with much decorum during their screaming 'fits'. They sometimes even brought the great cycle of prayer to a halt:

A girl was rapt into a frenzy and brought bound to Hugh's tomb; she remained there until the feast of All Souls, and that night her screaming was more violent than usual, disturbing the choir and whole church, so that they could not celebrate Mass at the altar of John the Baptist, near the tomb. Finally she fell asleep; when a crowd of worshippers woke her up she was well again.

Demoniacs sometimes disrupted the flow of shrine-goers as well. In Norwich cathedral a mad woman was dragged away from the shrine where she had been deposited so that 'the people who assembled at the tomb with their offerings might not be hindered by her presence'. Occasionally the cure was as dramatic as the frenzy. After a madman chased everyone from St. Frideswide's church one May day about 1180 one of the canons brought him to his senses by flinging holy water in his face.[34]

Most pilgrims who experienced their curative transformations at shrines did so inconspicuously, without screaming, rolling about, vomiting or bleeding on the church fixtures. Registrars, therefore, usually asked for witnesses to their earlier debility and subsequent return to health. This was standard procedure when receiving pilgrims who claimed that they had been healed at home. Before continuing the description of what went on at the shrines, then, let us consider the other half of the recorded pilgrims, those who came to shrines to give thanks and to report the wonderful event *after* experiencing their miracle.

Obviously many miracles could not occur in churches, such as rescues at sea, escapes from captivity, and so on, but most of the 'external' miracles, like those at shrines, involved the cure of physical infirmities. Curative techniques tended to be different in such cases. When illness or some other calamity struck, one of the most common home remedies was a vow or promise made to a saint, with certain concomitant rituals. Even benighted 'pagans' respected vows to their demigods: just before the hemlock silenced him forever Socrates remembered a promise to the healing god—'I owe a cock to Asculapius'. Vows were made by medieval Englishmen under all manner of duress, but especially when they lay gasping on what they thought to be their death-beds. The idea of a bargain with a saint carried with it the possibility of the saint's non-performance, which would invalidate the contract. Occasionally already-vowed pilgrimages or offerings could be switched to whatever saint was successful, as in the case of Henry, who went blind

> and his parents prayed and vowed a penny to Becket; no cure followed. They then went to Finchale, where he was healed at Godric's tomb, after which the coin intended for Becket was offered to Godric.[35]

Sometimes saintly failures were anticipated: a man made a vow to Cantilupe on behalf of his daughter; after doing so, he made a second vow, dedicating the girl to St. Giles in case Cantilupe failed to cure her. As one woman expressed it when vowing an offering to St. Louis in exchange for a cure, 'If he does not do it, he will not have it.' The promised *quid pro quo* was usually a pilgrimage and offering at the shrine. There were many other possibilities, such as the vow to undergo an annual fast, become a life-long supporter of the saint, pay a penny per year or refrain from certain foods. Sometimes these promises sound very much like threats; two women even vowed to kill themselves if the saint (Edmund Rich) failed to cure a child.[36]

Vows could also be made on behalf of someone else, even though the saint still held the sufferer personally responsible.

> Robert (a priest) was near death, and some pious women made a vow to Becket; a cure followed. The saint later appeared to Robert to ask why the vow was not fulfilled. He protested that he had not made it; Becket replied, 'Certainly you did not vow; but, since others made the vow on your behalf, payment lies upon you'.[37]

Vicarious vows are commonly encountered when illness struck small children and infants incapable of making promises or when the victim was unconscious or unable to speak. A mute boy, for instance, made signs to bystanders to make a vow for him. In a few cases these vows were also approved by the affected person:

> A man's swollen tongue nearly suffocated him and rendered him mute. His friends thought him near death and vowed one of his cows to Cantilupe in exchange for a cure. They led the cow to him and he ratified the vow as best he could; the tumour burst, evil matter flowed out, and in a few days he was well. The cow was duly offered.[38]

One vicarious promise was cast in the first person as if the ill individual were himself speaking: a girl made a vow for her insane brother, saying 'I promise St. Louis that, if by next Wednesday, he shall cure me of this infirmity and restore sanity, I personally shall visit his body and I shall light a candle.' All the while her brother continued as he had done for a week, singing silly songs and mumbling stupidly.[39] The power was in the words themselves, as in other charms and incantations, rather than in the motives of the individual uttering them.

One could promise almost any action or object besides or in addition to pilgrimage. Sometimes there were technical problems. One particular individual suffering from fever and an eye affliction vowed a wax image for fever; when he realized the omission, a second vow included wax eyes as well. Saints sometimes accepted objects of equal worth, such as a calf or its market price, a cow or its value, coins in lieu of a silver ship. Even here, though, one could not always anticipate saintly moods. After a woman vowed a candle and her husband offered two pence in its place, the saint appeared one night and ordered her to follow the *exact* terms of her vow.[40]

Besides the promise made at the sickbed by or for the frightened patient, relic-water could be administered, usually drunk or rubbed on the appropriate parts of the body while a vow was pronounced. Though pilgrims used it at shrines, much more often they took it home and set it aside for emergency use. Another panacea used by Christians from at least the fifth century consisted of dust, dirt or particles of stone from the tomb mixed in water or wine. These magic scrapings were also saved for future needs. One noble pilgrim took not just shavings but a chunk of William of Norwich's tomb, which she used to prepare medicines for her family as needed. Such curative elixirs were almost as sought-after as relics and, like relics, they were sold and stolen and treated as sacraments *sui generis*, for example by the priest who demanded a two- or three-day fast of those who wished to use 'his' Canterbury water. Pilgrims to Becket's tomb might bring along the empty *ampullae* of their neighbours for a refill.[41]

Another common sickbed rite was the bending of a penny, a small, thin silver disc, to set it apart from other coins—*ut eum dinoscere posset*—in confirmation of a vow—*ad voti confirmationem*. This reflects a common medieval attitude: one must offer *this* coin only or present *that* candle and no other; a preference for the literal and concrete over the figurative and abstract. The saint must be given *precisely* the candle or coin indicated when a vow was made. In one case a woman made several candles, each for a particular saint. She accidentally used the 'wrong' one which began, or so she claimed in a fit of imagination, to bleed in protest. Coin-bending could take place in diverse conditions, in a storm at sea, for example, when some cried out to St. Nicholas, others to Becket, some to this and others to that saint until finally a man who had visited Worcester bent a penny, saying 'I vow myself and this penny to my lord Saint Wulfstan.' Then everyone else did the same, and the storm passed.[42] A blind horse was cured after someone vowed and bent a coin for it, and even flames were said to have been turned back when a certain Geoffrey had the presence of mind to hold up a coin and bend it in Cantilupe's name. During King Edward I's reign pennies were bent once a year for his hawks and the royal chargers.[43] Most often coins were bent while held above reclining human patients or over those parts of their bodies which seemed to be the source of their illness:

> Alice injured her foot and the disability became chronic, with suppuration. Her father vowed to visit Cantilupe's shrine, and invoking his name and saying prayers he bent a penny over her (*plicavit unum denarium super caput ipsius Aliciae*), after which they went to Hereford.[44]

Some of the pennies were gilded and more than one might be vowed. On the other hand a woman was told in a vision to take two farthings and one halfpenny and convert them into a single coin. Apparently the saints disliked small change.[45] Coin-bending was called 'the English custom' by the commission investigating Cantilupe's canonization in 1307 but more European cults would have to be investigated before it could be said that it was found only in this country; it seems unlikely.

Bending pennies may or may not have been an English rather than a European tradition, but another custom associated with home cures was most definitely a universal one in the Middle Ages. From at least the sixth century the ill were measured with a piece of thread or string which was then incorporated in a candle that was taken to a shrine. Measurement was practically a spontaneous response to illness or danger. After a girl was pulled dripping from a well at Ifield near Canterbury her first words were 'Measure me to St. Thomas; measure me to St. Thomas', so that, the registrar explained, 'a candle could be made to the measure of the length of her body' to offer to Becket. A fifteenth-century plague victim recovered and exclaimed 'Have me measured . . . whence a wax candle may be made to King Henry's honour.' The measuring-thread usually became the wick of a candle. Most miracle collections contain examples of this practice; one could even measure oneself and make a candle with the length of thread.[46]

Since large candles were often used in churches, if the subject were four feet tall then a four-foot candle might be presented at a shrine, and when an ailing limb or head or hand was measured the size of the resultant candle would not be great. This applies as well to small animals and children or birds such as the peacock whose health was restored after it was measured 'from the tip of his beak to the end of his tail' and the thread, coated with wax, was sent to burn on an altar. But what are we to say when we find people measuring the boundaries of a piece of land (a total of about '500 arm-lengths'), the perimeter of a house, sick cattle—individually and by the herd—or a ship in a storm at sea? To take only the first instance, a candle over 1,000 feet long is out of the question. The solution was to fold the thread or wick back upon itself several times or twist it before coating it with wax or alternatively to roll it into a coil or 'trindle' in English, *rotula* in Latin.[47] The space-saving principle is set out clearly in a Wulfstan miracle: 'and as quickly as possible a candle was twisted (*contorqueretur*) to the measure of the ill person (*ad mensuram egrotantis*), and sent with him to Worcester' where it was offered at Wulfstan's shrine. It was essential that the length of the wick was right—the candle had to 'contain' the person's height and sometimes width, usually from one outstretched hand to the other. It was thought wonderful if a string broke at just the proper length while measuring, or if a candle purchased from the monks turned out to be the exact length of an ill child left at home.[48] These flickering candles, stuck on the tombs or the floor around them, may have represented the suppliants absorbing the beneficent aura of the holy bones, just as the people of ancient Sumer used to leave little clay statues of themselves standing in reverent prayer before the altars of their gods. Certainly pilgrims gave ordinary candles as routine offerings and the Church had accepted this 'pagan' custom as early as the fourth century.[49] But in measuring objects and living creatures and transforming them into candles we are dealing with white magic which has very little to do with neat distinctions between 'pagan' and 'Christian'. It is even possible that disease, transferred via the thread into a candle, was supposed to 'die' as the wax melted away under the watchful eye of the holy dead. In twentieth-century eastern Europe the process is reversed:

> The people take a wax candle to the church to be blessed. The candle they wrap round with wool and cotton thread. When they return home they measure the wrists and necks of the children with these threads.

Here the protective virtues of the candle are transferred by the thread to the children. This observer of Slavic customs concluded, 'In several instances I noticed that the mere act of measuring was considered to be healthy or stimulating.'[50]

Whether they experienced their miraculous cures before, during or after their pilgrimage, the beneficiaries usually brought or sent votives to the shrines. The most common offerings were coins and candles, less often jewellery. Although the variety of oblations was overwhelming, they can be arbitrarily divided into four groups, which we shall call animate, inanimate, exuvial and replicative votives.

Strictly speaking animate offerings included the people who dedicated themselves to service at a shrine. This was sometimes done indirectly, as in the case of the lady who released all her rights in one of her serfs to St. Edmund Rich. Most live offerings, however, were animals or birds, such as the goose eaten with great gusto by the twelfth-century Canterbury monks.[51] Inanimate votives were objects which had actually played a part in a miracle, like the halter used to 'hang' a man who was said to have been miraculously revived, or a portion of a ship's cargo saved in a storm. Crutches were very common, as at modern shrines, and other objects were a belt, weapons, carts, chains from miraculously-freed prisoners, peacock feathers, and a boot by which a drowning boy was pulled from the water.[52]

Some exuvial offerings were rather macabre, like the burnt crown of a boy's scalp sloughed off in the healing process, offered by a grateful parent at the Windsor shrine of Henry VI. Similar bits and pieces of humanity dangled over other tombs: an arm-bone, human hair, a diseased bone which a child's mother had cherished for a year, a bone dislodged from someone's throat, a piece of the head of a wounded boy and stones ejected from the urinary system, some mounted in attractive silver settings. At times cured pilgrims were too fond of their own *disjecta* to present them to a shrine. One, for instance, refused to give a sneezed-up cherry stone to the Canterbury monks for their collection.[53]

The most common votives after candles and coins were the replicative gifts, 'images' or replicas—occasionally life-size but usually miniature—of the part cured or the object(s) involved in a miracle. Sometimes wax images of afflicted parts were sold by local dealers at established shrines, as at Marseilles where pilgrims to the tomb of Louis of Toulouse bought wax teeth and eyes at convenient shops nearby.[54] In the nature of things, most replicative offerings were human organs or limbs, and countless miniature men, women, children, eyes, arms, hands, legs, hearts, breasts, heads, were suspended above the shrines. But there were also wax images of animals, anchors, birds, ships, carts or wagons, a little wax man swinging from gallows of wax, *furcas cereas cum ymagine hominis cerea in eisdem furcas suspensa*,[55] a head with an arrow thrust in, a head and arms with the victim's wounds depicted, a horse and rider, even a wax sardine. Pilgrims also brought silver and gilt images of the same sort of objects.

Some votives caused slight problems. One pilgrim offered the hired litter in which she had been carried to the shrine, an appropriate gesture had it not been for the owner of the litter who demanded its return; after a wax image was dedicated to King Henry VI that monarch appeared in a vision to request a more elaborate version than the one offered.[56] Whatever the details, the custom of offering such objects was as widespread as it was ancient. Votives from the Egyptian temple of Isis were shaped like human organs and similar finds are well known to archaeologists of both the Old and the New World. By the early fifth century Christians were donating such objects to their saints, some offering the 'figures of eyes, some of feet, some of hands, made either of gold or of silver'.[57] Although votives still adorn the altars of continental churches, in England such artefacts are with a few exceptions now relegated to museum cases. In the church of Our Lady of Warwick Street, a few minutes' walk from the secular chaos of Piccadilly Circus, are glass display-cases of scores of silver hearts and other twentieth-century offerings. As for extant medieval votives, a chance find at Exeter Cathedral during alterations in 1943 revealed, on a ledge over the tomb of Bishop Edmund Lacey (d. 1455), arms, legs, hands, fingers, feet, and fragments of animals all of hollow wax made from moulds, some with strings in them by which they had been suspended above the bishop's holy bones. Perhaps the most interesting figure was a wax woman eight inches tall whose 'wide-open eyes have looked into the future for . . . 500 years'.[58]

Many contemporary accounts of the offerings in coin have survived, but medieval inventories of other votives at shrines were usually composed decades, even centuries, after the excitement had died down, when the saint no longer worked miracles and pilgrims had ceased to bring their wax and silver images. Fortunately, a list of offerings was drawn up just twenty years after the first miracles were reported at the curative shrine of Thomas Cantilupe. Midway between his death (1282) and canonization (1320), papal commissioners went to Hereford where, early on Tuesday, 29 August 1307, they examined the dead bishop's shrine and found

170 silver ships
41 wax ships
129 silver images, whole and of diverse human limbs
436 whole images of men, wax
1,200 wax images of parts of the body and limbs
77 figures of horses, animals and birds
an uncountable quantity of eyes, breasts, teeth, ears [presumably
    of wax]
95 silk and linen children's shifts
108 walking-sticks for cripples
three carts
one wax cart
10 large square candles
38 cloths of silk and gold
many belts [or 'girdles']
many ladies' jewels including
    450 gold rings
    70 silver rings
    65 gold brooches and pins
    31 silver brooches and pins
    diverse precious stones
iron chains offered by prisoners
anchors of ships
lances, spears, swords, knives

At the end of the hearings in mid-November a recount was made. There were one more wax and two more silver ships, another silver image of a man, eighty-five more wax images of men or limbs and two more shifts belonging to children said to have been aided by Cantilupe; and 'we saw candles brought in beyond number by pilgrims every one of the seventy-eight days we remained at Hereford'.[59] They did not take account of oblations of coins, which were probably far more common than images. Hereford was somewhat removed from centres of population, Cantilupe a rather colourless prelate of conventional piety; the offerings at Becket's shrine, the most famous in England, must have been tremendous.

Precious metal votives were eventually melted down, candles were used by the churches in the ordinary course of things for practical and liturgical purposes, most of the wax images were remelted or simply consumed with age. Some, however, were deliberately preserved at shrines to advertise the powers of the holy dead whose tombs they decorated. Sometimes the very existence of such objects was, by circuitous logic, 'proof' of the sanctity, the miraculous powers, of a dead individual. It was suggested in the fourteenth century that Cantilupe was a saint because pilgrims brought offerings to his tomb as they did to other, recognized, saints' shrines, and in the papal bull canonizing John of Bridlington in the fifteenth century it was claimed that the images and votives at his tomb confirmed the truth of the miracles.[60]

Shrines rose and then fell in public estimation as curative centres; the tumult came and went leaving behind it strings of wax or metal figures to dangle above the tomb, mute evidence that people had once seized upon the reputed saint as a new source of healing, a new therapy. They felt themselves cured—and they were, by the standards of the day—and brought their oblations as rewards for their ghostly benefactors. Yet before their cures were recorded in the great book of miracles kept at the shrine, the registrar must be convinced. He might gladly accept any votive offering, but sometimes even he, partial though he was, required a modicum of proof.

Chapter 6

Recording and Sorting Posthumous Miracles

*The miracles were even attested before the courts by a
whole host of witnesses who had almost seen them,
since they had come there in the hope of doing so.*

Voltaire

Some cures occurred in front of the registrars themselves, or quickly
attracted their attention. Thomas of Monmouth, hearing a commotion
which he thought indicated a miracle, 'ran up and inquired diligently
into the facts' at William's shrine in Norwich Cathedral.[1] Simple tests
were tried out in these cases and if the results were satisfactory the
miracle was enrolled. These examinations, sometimes carried out by
visiting dignitaries, for example by three English bishops paying their
respects at Edmund Rich's shrine in Pontigny, were not particularly
thorough. Those who had once been blind identified things, an egg or a
coin, or named colours or followed lighted candles. Cripples were asked
to walk about; after screaming, twisting and moaning in the Canterbury
crypt a sixteen-year-old girl breathlessly announced her cure, but just
to make certain the monks made her pace up and down. One cured
woman overcame the registrar's doubts by obligingly lying down and
getting up from the ground, with great agility. Not everyone passed
these tests, such as the old woman who walked into a thorn bush while
trying to demonstrate her miraculously-returned eyesight. Canonization commissioners also verified cures at formal hearings by similar
'experiments' or tests (*experimentis*).[2]

Some physical examinations were rather delicate undertakings. In a
case also reported in contemporary legal records a certain Thomas,
after losing a trial by battle, was deprived of his eyes and testicles. He
later claimed to have been healed by St. Wulfstan. Benedict, Bishop of
Rochester (d. 1226), heard of this wonder while he was in Worcester
and decided to verify it. The healing of the eyes was evident, and as to
the other he ordered his monk-chaplain to touch the genitals and
ascertain how things were. Doing so with some embarrassment the
monk 'exclaimed that it was just as had been reported'; then Bishop

Benedict also satisfied himself on this point, praised God, and rode away. A question of delicacy also arose in the case of the woman healed of incontinence whose improved condition was verified by respectable matrons who described their findings to the registrar. At other times shrine-keepers were given more evidence than they may have desired, as in the healing of the man with haemorrhoids and ulcers who flaunted his scars before the very eyes of the monk-scribe, *cicatrices oculis nostris ostendit*, or the Londoner cured by Becket of ghastly abdominal fistulas who was so pleased that he walked the fifty miles to Canterbury in one day, so the registrar wrote, to strip, show himself cured, and challenge all comers to a foot-race.[3]

Pilgrims awaiting cures were only rarely 'pre-tested' for illness, like the woman whose closed fists the Lincoln Cathedral subdean tried to pry open.[4] Because of this, it was easy to exaggerate the seriousness of the disability or sickness after it had been 'cured'. Witnesses were required in most cases since the majority of cures and other marvels occurred outside the immediate cognizance of the registrars. Pilgrims and their witnesses testified on oath or on a Bible to prior circumstances, the miracle itself, and subsequent developments. Anyone with a miracle to report usually arrived with friends and family to back up his story and answer the registrar's questions, occasionally through an interpreter. These witnesses, often simple villagers (listed by name in many of the collections) sometimes brought along their priest to add weight to their testimony. Unsupported sworn statements about their own miracles by the clergy and upper ranks usually sufficed, though many of them brought witnesses anyway. In doubtful or important cases some registrars sent for witnesses or had them interviewed by local clergy. A Beverley woman seemed cured after a month-long stay at Hugh's tomb in Lincoln. After the *custos tumbae* ascertained her identity and origin the Lincoln chapter sent messengers forty-five miles north to Beverley to ask about her. The Beverley chapter in turn convoked the trustworthy men of three neighbouring villages, took their testimony (sworn on the relics of St. John of Beverley or the Bible) and then wrote a letter with their findings to Lincoln, where at last the miracle was publicly proclaimed and celebrated.[5] Some registrars themselves went out and verified their facts; Thomas of Monmouth travelled from Norwich to Canterbury on one occasion to examine the circumstances of a cure attributed to little William.[6] Many bishops and other clergy sent testimonials about local wonders on their own initiative, and so there are hundreds of English and foreign letters scattered throughout the Becket miracle collections, for example, some of them carried to Canterbury by the cured pilgrims themselves. To be safe, a pilgrim brought both witnesses and letters when he could obtain written verification, because the written usually carried more weight than spoken declarations.

Registrars sometimes hesitated or refused to record a miracle, usually because the lower-class people who reported them arrived without witnesses, or because the evidence was too slender—even for them. One of the Becket registrars confessed that in some cases 'inasmuch as these have not produced witnesses, and the truth has not been perfectly sifted by us, we let their stories pass out of our ears as fast as we let them come in.'[7] In one ear and out the other. His cautious attitude made him quite unpopular with one female pilgrim who

> gave me bad words, calling me hardhearted, wicked and unbelieving,
> unfit and unworthy to attend at the tomb . . . inasmuch as I envied his
> [Becket's] glory and detracted from his miracles in my excessive anxiety
> to track out the truth.[8]

If the miracle were accepted it was recorded either by type—usually illness cured—or chronologically; sometimes both systems were mixed and in a few collections no particular order is evident. Occasionally duplicates crept into the records, when for example a pilgrim's verbal tale was recorded and then later substantiated by letter, which would also be copied by the registrar; or several letters about a notorious miracle might be sent to a shrine and copied into the list. These duplications sometimes illustrate how an ordinary mishap might later on be blown up into a wonderful miracle. In one report a boy who fell into a well was cured—presumably of exhaustion—by Simon de Montfort; then in a second version the child, 'held for half a day in the chains of death', was recalled 'from death' after being measured to Simon.[9]

Some scribes had other systems of recording miracles: although William of Canterbury claimed to follow 'truth' not sequence he quite deliberately grouped Becket's miracles by type of illness and social class of pilgrim, collecting them in rough notes and later transcribing them.[10] The miracles at Cantilupe's tomb were recorded in chronological order and later a 'topical' re-arrangement was made, duplicating a great many miracles. Both documents were taken in evidence by the papal canonization commissioners. Manuscripts of miracle collections are often annotated with a word or two describing each event for quick reference. These lists of miracles were kept at shrines, like votives, for advertising purposes—in one case even into the seventeenth century—and copies were sent abroad to be re-copied for further distribution. By one method or another miracle lists were built up over the years, even over the centuries.[11] Obviously the registrars' prejudices affected their judgment, which influenced what they chose both to record and to ignore. Sometimes the prejudices are conveniently evident as with William of Canterbury, who assumed that beggars were liars, and that the nobility always told the truth.[12] In such cases certain allowances can be made, and it is probable that most registrars would have stressed participation by the upper classes and clergy whenever possible.

In the course of describing how sick pilgrims got to shrines and underwent their cures or what they did at home to achieve the same results we have mentioned various types of illness (or cure). In order to understand the relationships between miracles and the pilgrims who claimed to have experienced them we must be able to describe these miracles more accurately; some system of classification is needed. In William Hutton's scheme of 1903, miracles were catalogued in this way: directly imitative (of the Bible), dreams, coincidences, or 'natural causes'. As an alternative Hutton suggested that they be divided into those performed by the living saint, by his relics, and in answer to prayer alone. In 1930 another writer distinguished miracles of justice (punishment and reward) from the imitative, coincidental, natural and whimsical—such as animal cures.[13] These systems seem to ignore the medieval outlook. For example, whether or not a miracle is 'whimsical' probably depends upon the modern observer's sense of humour—certainly the medieval peasant who called upon the saints to protect his emaciated cattle did not do so in a fit of whimsy. To say that miracles were 'coincidences' or due to 'natural causes' is explanation, not classification.

As noted, about nine-tenths of the posthumous miracles concerned illness, and some medieval registrars grouped the wonders by type of cured infirmity. This approach, also used in some modern analyses of medieval curative shrines,[14] is generally followed in the present study. It is difficult to ascertain what particular illness was indicated in most medieval cures since diagnosis after so many centuries, based upon imperfect descriptions is—to say the least—ambitious. Perhaps the best approach in these circumstances is to concentrate not on categories of diagnosed illness but on similarities in reported symptoms. We will follow the clues given by the registrars and pilgrims and classify ailments not by what we think they 'really' were, but according to the symptoms and signs as given in the miracle collections even if this only conveys a vague idea of the events going on at the shrines.

One type of cure or miracle (the order of illnesses as given here is of no significance) involved what will be called 'unqualified illness', which includes all ailments with very general symptoms: being bed-ridden and disabled, or simply 'paralysed' without further qualification or 'paralysed' on one side. This may well have been hemiplegia, but 'paralysis on one side' was often used in the medieval descriptions in a very loose sense. Cases of nonspecific 'pain' are also included and any combination of two or more different categories (which are set out below). Obviously this category, 'unqualified illness', is designed for those pilgrims whose ailments are described in vague terms, with very little specification of symptoms. All that can be known is that these pilgrims had been ill, generally disabled, usually bed-ridden. As an example, the report that Godric of Finchale cured a youth who was paralysed in all his limbs really says nothing whatsoever about the ailment except that he had lost the use of his legs and arms.[15] Why this was and to what extent he was actually disabled we cannot know. Sometimes pilgrims are merely said to have been suffering from a 'certain infirmity'—what that infirmity was, the registrar does not say.

A second type of miracle concerned the cure of afflictions in *specific* organs or areas of the body, symptoms involving internal organs, debility and pain associated with such words as stone, flux, dysentery, fever, toothache, insomnia, cough and so on. This category comes closest to an 'illness' but of course coughs and insomnia are only symptoms of hundreds of organic or functional problems. Though in modern medicine 'fever' is not a cause or type of illness, this was not so in medieval thought. Some periodic fevers might have been tertian malaria or ague, especially common in the East Anglian marshes, as Defoe noted in the eighteenth century. An example of this second type of miracle is the cure of Lady Margaret who was ill for a year with a 'grave infirmity which women call the flux', which may indicate menorrhagia (or dysentery in men). Some women were embarrassed to talk about this problem and one described her illnes to the registrar not without shame, *non absque pudore*.[16]

Another group of cures (or illnesses) involved impaired locomotion or articulation of the limbs, hands or fingers, those paralysed in *specific* areas, 'cripples' and the lame, deformed or contorted such as the woman, *contracta*, who was unable to move, raise her head or look at her own feet.[17] (The crackling limbs and snapping sinews noted by many medieval registrars came from this group.) It is pointless to try to guess what was troubling such pilgrims; it could have been anything from arthritis to hysterical paralysis.

A fourth category includes a general condition called *gutta*, sometimes translatable as 'gout', though qualifications added to *gutta* indicate distinct ailments which are classified accordingly, such as 'gutta called paralysis', *gutta caduca* or epilepsy, *gutta in renibus* or stone, and so on. A condition known as 'dropsy' (*ydropis*) is also included in this fourth category, like *gutta* a vague expression usually referring to a general swelling of the tissues. It is impossible to relate 'swelling', a complaint of many pilgrims, to any particular disease.

Another category included suppurative, open sores and localized swellings, tumours, ulcers, any abscess with flow of pus, fistula, quinsy, scrofula and 'leprosy':

> Matilda, a young girl, felt a swelling and pain in her right breast and then there was a discharge from nine openings in the afflicted part. After human medicines failed, she vowed some wax to William of Norwich and applied it to her breast; relief followed when she removed the wax. She went to the cathedral to offer the wax, and baring her breast applied it to the tomb, after which the disorder was completely cured.[18]

In this case her affliction seems to have been alleviated through application of a wax poultice.

We have placed the word 'leprosy' in quotes since even in Biblical times 'leprosy' covered a variety of conditions besides infection by *Mycobacterium leprae*. This confusion was common in the Middle Ages as well, and continues in the twentieth century. In 1964, for instance, a specialist noted that true leprosy was still confused with a number of other disorders such as ringworm, seborrheic dermatitis, psoriasis, even acne. Just as God commanded Moses to cast out lepers, so medieval popes and bishops promulgated rules and services for their exclusion. In one version of the ceremony of casting a leper out of society the leper was ritually buried after he had attended his own Requiem Mass.[19] He was socially dead: henceforth his relationships with non-lepers was carefully regulated, his usual associates were people thought to be suffering the same ailment. It was tacitly understood that sin might cause the affliction, even inherited sin, which might explain why some parents were ashamed to admit that any of their offspring was a 'leper'. Medieval leprosy has attracted much attention from historians of medicine, but little has been done to examine lepers sociologically, as an institutional minority; the sexual abandon sometimes imputed even today to minorities or 'out-groups', for example, was often also applied to medieval lepers. In any case, the casual use of the word does not mean that true leprosy was absent from medieval England, only that a contemporary allegation that someone was a leper may have been a statement about social conflict, not medical pathology.

The ailments so far listed in this grim catalogue attacked both sexes, but only women were involved in the next category, the complications of pregnancy and childbirth. As in many parts of the world today, in medieval England sterility was thought to be shameful. One pilgrim to Cantilupe's shrine stopped her neighbours' wagging tongues by producing twins after returning from Hereford. Why these women were afflicted, whether they and not their husbands were in fact sterile, we cannot say. One contributing factor may have been 'famine amenorrhoea' which inhibits ovulation during and after unusual physical or mental trauma, especially the stresses associated with famine. (In the blockades of the cities of the Netherlands during 1944 and 1945, 70% of the women ceased to menstruate.) Localized famines were a commonplace calamity in the Middle Ages, heralded by poor harvests or an interruption in already rudimentary transport, for example by warfare or rebellions. Life stresses were severe anyway, and any added problems might have rendered some women temporarily sterile.[20] As in the cases of many other transient physiological malfunctions these ailments were especially 'suited' to miraculous healing.

Though sterility may have been psychologically upsetting pregnancy brought its own dangers. This was especially true when the mother-to-be already suffered some physical ailment such as 'dropsy' or a twisted spine, to mention but two cases from the miracles. Some women carried a dead foetus long past its term. Conversely, premature births presented their own hazards: as one shrine-registrar commented, women who were delivered too early were at great risk. The midwives—normally more than one, in one delivery seven—gathered when the time for parturition arrived, the usual moment of miraculous intervention since the most common problem was difficult labour lasting from a few days to two weeks and more. On one occasion this was attributed to the girl's extreme youth, on another it was relieved by Caesarian delivery. Still-births were not uncommon. One woman was said to have been delivered of dead infants four times, another on seven occasions, while a third gave birth to triplets—all dead.[21]

A deformed infant, in the circumstances of medieval society, may have been better off dead. After giving birth to a crippled child a French woman moaned, 'Oh God, why was he not carried from my womb to a grave?' (*Ha Deus, cur non fuisset de utero translatus ad tumulum*).[22] Sometimes midwives even tried to hide the deformity or death from the parents, though this was futile. At the best of times a normal delivery was dangerous, given the conditions in which it occurred, and the risks were greater with awkward presentations:

> A woman was in difficult labour two nights and a day. The midwives expected to find the infant dead; early in the morning it came out, but inverting the normal order, with feet first, then one hand, and then the other—bent behind the back.

The instructions that were provided to midwives in cases of difficult births did not help matters. In one illustration, for example, the finger is to be inserted, the legs properly arranged, and the infant brought out by the feet. Some women were crippled by the birth trauma or by the after-effects of the crude surgery employed to assist delivery.[23]

Another major category of illness was blindness. The descriptions do not allow us to say much about what caused the blindness or its extent, though in some miracles a particular type of debility, a cataract, for example, seems to be indicated. Seasonal and chronic dietary deficiencies probably affected eyesight (seasonal ophthalmia was a problem even to the ancient Egyptians). Xerophthalmia, for example, may result when cereal diets are inadequately reinforced with green vegetables or animal foods (vitamin A), both of which were sometimes in short supply through the long winter season.[24] Trachoma, especially common in cramped and insanitary living conditions, would have found an ideal environment in many a medieval cottage. Whatever the causes, and the possibility of hysterical blindness was always present, we shall treat all cases of loss of sight as members of this category.

The healing of impaired hearing and of those who were mute or both deaf and dumb was not, in fact, a particularly common type of cure. Deafness was apparently something of an embarrassment to those afflicted—as it still is, for some people. Alditha of Norwich, for example, noticing her hearing grow weak, ceased to go out of doors; a nobleman's friends withdrew from his company when his deafness could no longer be ignored since they did not want to shame him, *ne pudorem inferrent ei.*[25] Because deafness or the inability to speak could easily be feigned, people suffering these ailments were often under suspicion, and in the case of mutes the lingual apparatus was sometimes examined, as we have seen.

The next type of miraculous cure involved overt mental affliction, which often erupted in violence. Medieval scribes seem to have distinguished at least three varieties: demoniacs, or those possessed by demons; 'visitations' by demons who disturbed their victims' minds or bodies but did not possess then; and those simply described as mad, *insania* or *furiosus*, without reference to demons. Contemporaries usually made no distinction between epilepsy and insanity.[26]

> A possessed boy was so violent that seven men bound him; he remained thus six days, neither eating nor sleeping. Taken to Norwich, as they approached the tomb he screamed 'What do you want with me? Where are you taking me? I won't go there, I won't go there'. Bursting his bonds he attacked his mother and threw her to the ground, sinking his teeth into her throat. Overpowered and taken to the shrine, he was soon cured.

There is a certain similarity between this medieval case and the following modern one:

> An eleven-year-old boy was seized with madness: 'Suddenly everyone became his enemy. His mother, approaching him to try to calm him down, was abruptly faced with a raging child who hurled himself on her, scratching and pummelling her face and arms.'

This last passage comes from an account of an epidemic of ergotism which swept the inhabitants of a French village to the verge of mass insanity in 1951, when other victims screamed 'Don't touch me; stand back' or 'Why are you bringing me here? why?'[27] It is possible that at least some medieval cases of 'possession' as well as communal outbursts of hysterical behaviour such as the so-called 'dancing mania' were caused by ergotism. This comes from eating ergot, produced when ears of rye are infected by the fungus *Claviceps purpurea*. When the rye is eaten the components of ergot, especially lysergic acid (the active agent in lysergic acid diethylamide, or LSD), affect the physiological and mental balance of the victims. The hard, dark, sinister-looking grains sprinkled about the ear of rye are psychotomimetic agents, substances which disturb the mental balance of otherwise 'normal' people. In the Middle Ages the number of attacks caused by ergotism was probably quite small in England, but since ergot also brings on strong uterine contractions whenever it is present, perhaps it had more significant effects upon the birth-rate, than the mental health, of medieval society.

Whatever brought about their attacks the violent ones were usually bound hand and foot and carried to shrines, where they lay with blood-shot eyes, foaming mouths, dishevelled hair, torn clothes—one man ripped off his clothing and ran naked and screaming through the church—and twisted features; their 'gnashing teeth' were a standard attribute. When he was a young boy the twelfth-century historian William of Malmesbury was terrified by a demoniac at a shrine who glared and spat at him. Well might he have been frightened: in their frenzy women attacked their own children, children assaulted parents; one deranged man fastened his teeth into his sister's breast. Some, in milder moments, were thought to see into the future and to speak languages previously unknown to them. Centuries earlier the Greek physician Hippocrates had queried the 'divine' element in madness and the ambiguity continued through the Middle Ages; even Erasmus in the sixteenth century thought there might have been 'something divine' about insanity. Medieval demoniacs shouted blasphemies—just as early-modern, even twentieth-century victims of possession were to do—and occasionally they were removed from churches until they had calmed down.[28] After a few hours or days at a shrine they fell into a deep sleep and awoke with a clear head and a good appetite.

Now and then demoniacs were chased from towns with sticks or whips, which was thought to be not only good medicine for the victim but also an effective way to remove a public nuisance from the streets, and sometimes their stay at a shrine was made uncomfortable by beatings administered by passers-by. In theory the resident demon, finding his lodging so unpleasantly treated, vacated the bruised and beaten body of his unwilling host; in medieval theology demons could possess only the bodies—not the souls—of their victims. There were less energetic ways to conquer demons, for example by traditional exorcisms performed by living priests or prelates. The contagious nature of possession was dramatically illustrated in a Becket miracle when a bystander in a crowd around an insane woman suddenly screamed that she too, was attacked by the demon.[29]

Some were affected in mind and body after being accosted (but not possessed) by demons. These phantoms might be the *incubi* or *succubi* who visited women and men by night for sexual pleasure or simply 'strangers' who came up to unsuspecting folk, struck them, and ran off leaving their victims crippled or mentally deranged. Demons were also thought to be able to take the guise of animals or birds, since shape-changing was regarded as one of their traits. It is difficult to fit 'demons' into either a purely hallucinatory or plainly imaginary and fictitious framework since the tendency to 'see' demons was so strong that, not uncommonly, medieval people seem to have considered quite ordinary individuals or harmless animals 'demonic'. A troublesome black dog was not merely a black dog, it was a demon in the form of a black dog; some 'demons' were so human that when captured and executed they screamed and bled and died just like a 'real' human. In short, the reality of demons was not merely 'in the mind' but was an objective social convention.[30] Further discussion of this aspect of medieval belief is beyond the scope of our study, and in any case these demons or imps appeared very infrequently in the miracles.

Commonplace causes of madness were acknowledged too. People in the Middle Ages went mad because of mental or physical trauma just as they do today. One woman lost her mind after her brother killed her lover, another because of excessive drinking, a third through anxiety about her ill daughter. A man was not right in the head for a month after suffering great losses in a war, and when her newborn baby died a woman fled to the forest and lived there like a crazed beast.[31]

Accidents, our next miracle category, also caused temporary insanity in some parents who lost their children through misadventure. One woman collapsed and nearly lost her mind when she learned that her son had fallen into a ditch and drowned, while another, deranged with grief, kept the body of her child for five days and refused to allow burial. Accidents claimed many more children than adults, and the violent grief of the mothers and fathers so often noted in the miracles reminds us that medieval parents were as capable of feeling anguish as modern.[32] Although drowning was the most common mishap to which children were liable, thirteenth-century English clergymen also warned mothers about the danger of suffocating their children while sleeping with them, or leaving them in cradles which might overturn, or too near a fire. 'Overlaying' was a problem arising from the habit of sleeping together for warmth. One night while an infant was being fed its grandmother noticed that for some time she heard neither the baby's whimpering nor the mother's voice, and when she went into the bed-room she saw that the mother had fallen asleep and suffocated the child; she screamed, 'Get up, get up daughter. Look: you have crushed your child.' Since so many accident victims were helpless children, sometimes there were suspicions of foul play, and it has been suggested that the fear of an accusation of homicide prompted those ecclesiastical warnings about smothering and so on.[33] Violent deaths were usually investigated by the coroners; the Cantilupe miracles show that, around A.D. 1300, ordinary Herefordshire villagers were keenly aware of their responsibilities to these royal agents.

Besides being drowned, smothered, burnt or injured in falls from trees and rooftops children were run over by carts and wheeled ploughs, rammed wooden sticks through the roof of their mouths, impaled themselves (or others) on farmyard implements, and choked on a badge from Becket's shrine. Adults too, careless or unfortunate, were dragged along by their stirrups as their horses ran wild, they fell down wells, were accidentally stabbed while (playfully) wrestling and were hurt in what might be called industrial accidents—especially on construction sites. Some accidents were spectacular, as in the case of Geoffrey who was blasted by lightning one afternoon when he was carting turf in a thunderstorm. Most were prosaic. For example, a clumsy Gilbertine nun tripped and sprained her ankle when running to answer a call from her prioress; in another convent a nun fell crashing through the floor to land on a stone tomb in the room below.[34]

The next type of miracle involved deliberate violence, the mutilations and woundings of tavern brawls, robberies with assault, ordeals by combat, attempted suicides, assaults on royal officers, attempted murders, all the usual atrocities of medieval warfare and domestic vengeance. Step-parents were standard villains here, many accused of poisoning stepsons and daughters or cutting out their tongues. Another kind of domestic discord centred on adultery. In one case a knight castrated a cleric he suspected of being overly fond of his wife but eventually, according to the Canterbury registrars, Becket restored the lover to his pristine condition, the Bishop of Coventry sent a letter confirming this to Canterbury, and the miracle was celebrated in somewhat bawdy verses composed by the wits of the day.[35]

Whether or not, as is sometimes claimed, violence 'permeated' medieval life—our own society is hardly pacific—there are plenty of illustrations of criminal assaults and murders:

> About 1293 a young man named William, a barber, living in London, took pity on a poor carpenter and invited him in to share his hospitality. During the night as William slept the carpenter arose, took the sharpest razor he could find, and slit the other's throat. He then took what he could and fled, leaving the body in its bloody bed, where it was found next day.

Obviously William's wound was not as bad as it seemed to those who found him in the morning, since he eventually recovered, except for a scar which remained on his neck as a sign of the miraculous assistance of St. Thomas Cantilupe.[36] Similar doleful tales of murder and mayhem are found in the coroners' and assize rolls of the period, except that in *these* records the dead remained quite dead. Judicial mutilation was another—perhaps even more repulsive—kind of violence, in which the gruesome details of the extraction of testicles and slicing of eyeballs were described with almost loving care in some of the miracles.[37] Hanging was a less abhorrent fate. A common hagiographical motif was the miraculous salvation of the hanged person (often an admittedly guilty criminal) in response to a last-minute prayer sent up by the victim. The saint 'arrived' at the moment of suspension and supported the victim, as the latter claimed, so that the rope did not strangle him. Medieval hanging was no more than gradual asphyxiation, and there is evidence that hangings were sometimes 'arranged' so that death would be deliberately delayed; the noose could be skilfully placed in a certain way 'above the apple of the throat', for example. In south Wales about 1300 any executioner who arranged his rope and knot so that the condemned did not die was himself well and truly hanged. When still-living victims were cut down too soon or the rope broke (another matter which might be 'arranged'), English custom called for a royal pardon in recognition of divine or saintly—at least miraculous—intervention. Just to be safe, one man who regained consciousness after being taken from the gallows wisely kept quiet until he was carried onto holy ground, that is, sanctuary.[38] Perhaps he knew that the custom of reprieve was not invariably followed and that some unfortunates were killed only after a second or even a third hanging.

We leave these bloody and violent scenes for more peaceful realms in the next type of miracle. As mentioned, many ill people went on pilgrimage because of a dream or turned to particular saints after a vision of the night. Those apparitions were associated with miraculous cures, but the saints also visited people merely to give fatherly advice or entrust messages, or even to reward the sleeping folk who had honoured their memory. Becket appeared in the dreams of a youth in Dover and told him where a gold coin might be found, a reward for the boy's prayers.[39] Though these visitations were neither very frequent nor strictly speaking 'miracles' as in the foregoing categories, they were nevertheless considered noteworthy by the registrars and so became part of the records of saintly concern for the living.

Finally, about one-tenth of all the recorded events involved neither visions nor cures; these may be termed 'nonhealing' miracles. They included escapes from captivity, recovery of lost or stolen objects, safety during war, the cures of animals, survival in storms at sea or the perils of flood, famine or fire. Nonhealing miracles also included transformations of substance, such as water to beer or milk and the spontaneous lighting or relighting of candles was another common nonhealing miracle. These were saintly interventions which had some physical, as opposed to purely spiritual, effect, but did not involve the healing of the body. Because of their very nature most of them occurred at places other than shrines, and often away from the homes of the affected individuals. It is among these nonhealing events that coincidence or inevitability are most evident. For example, in a storm at sea either the ship goes down or it does not, and if not, that saint whose name was uttered as the storm passed (as they all do, eventually), or as a safe port was reached, received credit for the miracle. The events may be 'natural' enough to us, but the interpretation, the perception of the event, is medieval.

Most of the miraculous events attributed to the powers of the holy dead will fit into one of the foregoing categories. But in addition we need to know who was reporting them, whether different classes of society patronized different shrines, and whether the sex or social status (or both) of pilgrims influenced the types of miracles they reported to the keepers of the wonder-working relics.

Chapter 7

Murders and Miracle-cults in Twelfth-century England

Many miracles done there brought renown . . . Let me pass over the ordinary healing of sickness and touch only on exceptional cases.

Guibert de Nogent

During his tour of Indian shrines in 1967-8 Surinder Bhardwaj managed to detain 5,454 Hindus in their holy perambulations long enough to ask them, among other things, where they came from, what their castes and professions were and why they had gone on pilgrimage.[1] Unfortunately such information cannot as easily be obtained from the records concerning medieval English pilgrims. The crowds of pilgrims at modern Christian shrines in France and Germany, all the little old ladies in black who mumble their beads at the holy places of Spain, Italy or Mexico, cannot help us here. But although times, societies and attitudes change, as may the social composition of the crowds at shrines, by examining the miracles of each of the major medieval saint's cults for indications of the social status of the pilgrims who were involved, and by assigning those pilgrims a place in a system of classification, we can obtain a social profile of at least a segment of the devotees at a given shrine. The purpose will be to distinguish the social classes involved in the miracles of different saints, and ultimately to determine whether there was any relationship between particular classes and types of miracle. In the end, we can discover whether and to what extent the miracles of Thomas Becket, for instance, were performed for the sake of haughty knights rather than for the simple and trusting lesser folk who made up the great bulk of English society, and whether the miracles of the two groups were similar or significantly different. These findings will tell us something about both the saint and the society.

The first matter to settle is the method of social classification. The sources describe the occupations of pilgrims as bakers, bishops, millers, peasants and so on. The problem is to equate these descriptions with a social status and end up with a manageable system into which everyone fits without too much overlap. Difficulties arise at this very first stage since the records very often say nothing whatsoever about an individual's social position, and there are debatable cases even when the records *do* shed some light on this point.[2] Modern historians may well disagree about the social class of particular individuals. Sometimes the matter can be cleared up by reference to contemporary records of a non-miraculous nature (such as charters, the Close or Patent or Hundred Rolls) where some of the cured pilgrims are found holding property, doing business, getting into trouble with the law, receiving gifts of land. There is usually no difficulty with the nobility, since registrars made it clear that they were the elite, the *nobilissimi*. Sometimes miracles involved different generations of the same noble family: about 1154 the granddaughter of William, Earl Warenne, was cured by William of Norwich, and some twenty years later another Earl Warenne, Hamelin (bastard brother of Henry II), was cured of an eye affliction by Becket.[3]

The lesser nobility and knighthood may be represented by Osbert Giffard, who was rather well-off for a knight, from a distinguished family which gave England archbishops, bishops and chancellors. Born about 1220, Osbert was at first a follower of Simon de Montfort but later switched to the royalist camp. After the battle of Evesham when de Montfort was killed (1265) Osbert seized 'rebel' lands in Bedfordshire, Buckinghamshire, and Oxfordshire. One night the shade of his slain enemy Simon appeared to him as he lay ill in bed. At Evesham, Simon's body had been stripped of its armour, and Osbert kept some of this booty at the foot of his bed. Simon's spirit advised him that, if he wished to be healed, he should put on some of that armour. Having done so, Osbert was cured of fever. He personally reported the miracle at Evesham. Another knight involved in the miracle world was Bartholomew de Creak, whose family—benefactors to various religious houses—held eight fees of the Earls of Norfolk. Bartholomew's little daughter was cured by William of Norwich and his half-cousin (of the Cheney line) was cured by the corpse of Becket.[4] Some of the miracles depict knights doing what the cinema would have us believe they did all day and every day. For instance, during the revolt of Rhys ap Maredudd, when the English attacked Dryslwyn Castle in south Wales in 1287, 'one of the defenders, shooting from the top of the castle, struck Ralph le Butler, knight, with an arrow, so that the point stuck in beneath one of his eyes.' His friends called on Cantilupe for saintly help and he was healed of his wound, though we are not told how long it took for the injury to mend.[5]

Less elevated than knights but still relatively well-off were those who would be known in later ages as the lesser gentry. William Child, for example, a local constable from a village near Peterborough, also had some land in Oxfordshire. His son 'died' but was revived after William measured the child and bent a penny to Simon de Montfort. Another of the same class also cured by Simon was Leticia Palmers, who held various properties in and around Oxford, some of which she exchanged or sold so that the Franciscans could put up their convent along the south city wall.[6]

A different social milieu is encountered among the artisans, craftsmen and merchants, carpenters, millers, smiths and masons, leatherworkers, bakers, chandlers, minters, and so on. A typical member of this group was Thurben, a fuller who lived in Holywell, immediately outside Oxford. One day as he was working some cloth he was afflicted in the head. Flebotomy only made him worse, so that he became mentally deranged and was taken to Frideswide's tomb, where he was eventually cured. Even the miller, that villain of medieval literature, was blessed with spiritual assistance: the son of Walter the miller of Hailes was 'drowned' in the abbey mill-pond but, as Walter reported in 1303, was revived after being measured to Cantilupe.[7]

Another social circle encompassed unskilled workers, herdsmen, labourers, fishermen, rustics and peasants *eo nomine*, servants, and sailors. These were the little people, simple village folk. Sailors' miracles illustrate the dangers of medieval commerce such as the constant threat of shipwreck, pirate attacks, strange landfalls where the locals might kill them for their cargo. The miracles of ordinary villagers were for the most part uncomplicated interruptions of their ancient and unchanging routines.

The next level is very nearly the lowest in this sociological survey, namely, pilgrims specifically designated 'paupers', those who slept rough by night and begged alms by day, or eked out a meagre living in some cramped hovel at the edge of the village. Their miracles often provide a glimpse of the misery and squalor of their surroundings. Disabled beggars were often subjected to various indignities to make certain of their infirmity before being given alms or shelter.

> An ill man, paralysed in the legs, was taken into the house of Samson, a leather-worker of Salisbury. First, though, Samson's wife tested the infirmity by thrusting a knife into the limbs, which he did not feel, nor did he feel the heat of a fire.[8]

Finally, nothing at all was mentioned about the social status of a great many individuals, and it is assumed that these unspecified pilgrims belonged to the lowest social levels, having much in common with paupers or perhaps the peasantry. Since no clues are given, they are relegated to the very bottom of the scale. It might be objected that this is an unwarranted assumption based on the perilous argument from silence. Perhaps it is. On the other hand there was a very strong medieval tendency to assign rank or social place whenever possible. If a person was given no rank whatever by the monks at the shrines, he will be classless in our eyes as well. To put it another way, pilgrims of any status would very likely have been given their due by the registrars, who wished to advance the reputation of their saints through their clientele. In addition to these lay participants there were many clerics among the pilgrims at curative shrines. For present purposes they can be split into two sections, an 'upper' and a 'lower'. In the smaller upper section were archbishops, bishops, abbots, some priors, cathedral dignitaries, some monastic officers and the *magistri* or university men (secular and regular) scattered through the professions. Two of the prelates miraculously healed by saints were Richard Swinfield, Bishop of Hereford (d. 1317) and Gilbert Foliot, Bishop of London (d. 1187), cured by Cantilupe and Becket respectively. How some of the miracles throw a tiny but very brilliant light into obscure corners of the Middle Ages is evident in a report involving a *magister* who, when still a law student at Orleans, used to wear gloves to hide the ugly warts on his hands:

> One day, when he was taking notes at a lecture, in order to write down the commentaries more quickly, he removed the gloves. At this, students sitting nearby at their benches jumped up and rushed forward to look at the deformity (*surgebant . . . ad circumspiciendum dictam deformitatem*). He was miraculously cured some time afterward, through a vow to Cantilupe.[9]

In the numerous lower section of the clergy were simple monks, chaplains, priests (often barely distinguishable from their parishioners in birth and learning), and their concubines and children.

> The Norwich convent acknowledge that Gunzelin a monk had a swollen arm, which pained him. He wrapped the limb in Becket's stole, waited a short time, and the entire infirmity was taken away.[10]

The social spread of the examples, from Gunzelin the monk of Norwich to Earl Warenne, represents in miniature the variations encountered among all the pilgrims affected by miracles. To comprehend the social pattern in general terms, however, a simplified system of classification is needed. To establish the precise social status of each of the pilgrims, some of whom lived eight centuries ago, is an unattainable ideal. In these circumstances it seems advisable to adopt broad rather than narrow categories. We will divide the pilgrims into six groups: the nobility; the upper ecclesiastics; the knights; the lower ecclesiastics; the gentry, merchants, artisans; the unskilled, the peasantry, the poor, and the unspecified. These six classes will be used in discussing social composition at individual shrines and when considering the overall characteristics of the pilgrims. This is not the only, nor perhaps even the best way to classify pilgrims involved in miracles. There are, admittedly, difficulties in assigning some of the pilgrims to their 'proper' social classes. The easiest to identify are the nobility and upper ecclesiastics, since as mentioned the scribes were eager to advertise the high social tone of their shrines, just as eighteenth-century proprietors of English spas published names of the rich and powerful who came to take the waters. Things become less well-defined lower down the social ladder; in medieval England the social boundary between noble and non-noble was not as clearly drawn as it was in France or Germany. Even in the process of settling the kingdom after the Conquest the knights were moving away from continental feudalism, and by the thirteenth century the process of subinfeudation on the one hand and a shift from birth to wealth as a basis of knighthood on the other softened the boundaries at both ends of the class. In any event, when a man is called a 'knight' by the registrars, we will assume that in fact he was a knight. As for the *literati*, the educated men who administered noble and royal affairs, most were clerics who doubled as secretaries. This classification problem is avoided but not solved by considering them as ecclesiastics, not secular functionaries. Simple country folk usually present no difficulties since in few things was the demarcation so distinct as between peasant and prince and prelate. It was the difference between the colourless world of poverty and the fine gowns and brilliant jewels, the processions and banquets of cathedral and great hall.

Unfortunately this system is too crude, too simple, to allow compensation for the unalterable fact that most medieval women lacked social status *sui generis*. In the late fifteenth century when the Parisian printer Marchant wished to bring out a new *danse macabre* featuring women instead of men he found that he had a major problem: it was not possible to find forty social roles for women (to match the forty for men), so his artist ended up representing the fair sex in its few poor professions, supplemented by the varying conditions of the female as such—virgin, bride, mother and so on.[11] In the miracle records, most women were either given no social designation or were viewed as social reflections of their fathers or husbands. When counting up the social classes we have to use the ascribed social status of the male, so that if a miracle happens to involve the wife of a knight her social class will be that of the knights. With infants or children the status of the parent(s) will be applied. The anthropologist's concept of the extended family is also useful for laymen whose lives were inseparable from the ecclesiastical world, such as a monastic servant who spent his working life within conventual walls with the 'father' (*abbas*) and 'brothers' (*fratres*) of the establishment. He is placed among the lower ranks of the church, along with the concubines and children of the clergy. It is less important to discover whether someone was tonsured or knighted than to know the general social milieu in which he spent most of his time. In animal cures the social position of the owner is taken into account: pigs and cattle were usually associated with the lower classes but horses and falcons were 'upper-class' creatures. Sexual distinctions present few problems, since the sex of the pilgrim is clearly indicated in the records. In animal cures the owner's sex is counted; with infants, the sex of the active parent—the one responsible for recourse to the saint—or if both parents, then the father. Children past infancy are classified by their own sex.

Using only rough averages, therefore, and by means of these categories, we can work out a *general* impression of the people undergoing and reporting miracles at any given shrine. False readings result if the system is applied too rigorously because of the censorship exercised by the medieval registrars and because of the inherent defects of the evidence. Now, like those pilgrims who journeyed from one holy place to another, let us visit each of the major shrines—that is, those which have left accounts of at least a hundred posthumous miracles—to examine their origins and discover who their miracle-blessed pilgrims were.

William of Norwich

When Bernard Malamud settled down to write *The Fixer*—the story of a twentieth-century Russian Jew accused of 'ritual murder' of a Christian child—whether or not he knew it, he was re-telling an old English tale. William was born in a Norfolk village and became an apprentice leather-worker in Norwich some eight miles away; in 1144 his corpse was discovered in a wood on the edge of the city. According to the *Anglo-Saxon Chronicle*, the

> Jews of Norwich bought a Christian child before Easter and tortured him with all the torture that our Lord was tortured with; and on Good Friday hanged him on a cross on account of our Lord, and then buried him.[12]

At first few people seemed interested: the body was reburied on the spot, but when the boy's relatives learned about the discovery and accused the Jews to the Norwich cathedral monks the corpse was dug up and reburied in the cathedral cemetery. Within a decade this practically unknown child was an uncanonized Norfolk 'saint', the first purported victim of a Jewish 'ritual murder'.

First his family, then the Church, then the citizens of Norwich made him notorious. William's family disliked Jews. His aunt had a nightmare about them, his mother ran wildly through the city clapping her hands and screaming that the Jews had killed her son. His uncle, the priest Godwin, who was a key figure in the cult, had warned the boy to stay away from Jews; Godwin had 'interpreted' his concubine's dream to show that 'they' were to blame for the death of the child. Godwin also accused the Jews of the boy's murder in a Church synod at Norwich in 1144, and he was still reputed about 1150 to to be a special patron of the 'saint'. William's second cousin and his brother (who became a Norwich monk) also played a part in the cult.[13] Family prejudice was echoed in the attitudes of certain ecclesiastics, three of whom helped to send William on his way to popular canonization after 1150. Norwich was a cathedral priory, in which the bishop of the diocese was *ex officio* 'abbot', while the monastery was actually under the guidance of a prior. A bishop who strongly supported the anti-Jewish accusation was consecrated in 1146. Perhaps he was aware of the financial value of pilgrim offerings, especially desirable since his recently-refounded cathedral had no important relics of its own; perhaps he merely hated Jews. The monastic prior, who disbelieved the charge, died in 1150—his successor was a partisan of William's cult. The third member of the ecclesiastical trio, Thomas of Monmouth, became a Norwich monk about 1150 and for some unknown reason made himself William's champion and chief propagandist. Thomas completed his *Life and Miracles of St. William* (dedicated not surprisingly to the bishop) about 1173, having tended the shrine and recorded miracles for over twenty years; he even kept relics of the child as his own personal property.

After 1150, then, the trio of bishop, prior and Thomas of Monmouth stirred up interest in William which was on the wane when Thomas arrived in Norwich, as he himself admitted: 'yea in the hearts of almost all it had almost entirely died out'.[14] Even the most enthusiastic clerical support, however, was sterile without the concurrence of the laity. In William's case the question is why his *cultus* was so strongly supported by the people of Norwich above and beyond the fact that any purported saint would attract at least passing notice. Twelfth-century East Anglian society was prosperous. This heavily-populated region was rich in sheep, swine, fisheries, and salt works. In the twelfth century Norwich was the chief commercial centre of East Anglia and the third wealthiest city in England, but the business of getting and spending there was complicated by the division of the city into English and Norman quarters. As early as 1086 in addition to 655 English there were 160 French burgesses within the city. The 'King's Jews' lived under the shadow of the Norman castle and the protection of a Norman sheriff. Their financial power and association with the French must have given many Norwich debtors even more reason to dislike the Jews, and it is probably no coincidence that the very house where William was supposed to have been killed belonged to one of the principal Jewish money-lenders of the city.

When Thomas of Monmouth joined the Norwich monks William's body was rotting in holy ground next to the cathedral. After three vision/dreams in 1150 Thomas convinced the prior and brethren that a translation was in order. On the appointed night they opened the tomb and then Thomas and another monk took up their candles and peered into the sarcophagus. The skeleton of the boy was fondled, Thomas slipped two loose teeth into his sleeve, the rest of the bones were wrapped in linen and finally conveyed to a new grave in the monks' chapter house, after which many miracles were attributed to William and recorded by Thomas. In 1151, because pilgrims disturbed chapter-house deliberations, or so Thomas alleged, the body was moved into the church itself. Once again Thomas was involved, helping to carry the remains to their new resting place south of the high altar. Little William was again translated—in 1154—from the south to the north side of the altar and there, for the rest of the Middle Ages, he seems to have remained.

The mid-twelfth century was the high point in William's thaumaturgic career, but the cult continued to attract notice until the very end of the Middle Ages. A forest-chapel at the original burial place was consecrated in 1168, an altar was dedicated in the cathedral in 1278, and his feast was still being celebrated by the monks on March 24th in the late thirteenth century. Offerings were recorded in the fourteenth century and in the fifteenth century repairs were carried out on the shrine, though by this time oblations were declining. Even so, most of the surviving representations of the little saint come from the fifteenth century, and offerings were still made at the chapel in the wood as late as the sixteenth century.[15] Though most of the pilgrims were local people and the span of miracle-working was short, the cult had repercussions for centuries: the ritual murder idea migrated many thousands of miles, constantly renewed and consolidated by clerical literacy and common prejudice. William, in the end, was famous not for his merits—he hardly 'existed' until he had died—but because 'the Jews' were said to have murdered him. Insignificant though his life was, after his death something happened in Norwich, a motif was established which constantly re-appeared whenever and wherever anti-Semitism was acute.

It was during the 1150s, as a result of the publicity generated by the translations, that most of the miracles were reported, which presumably coincided with a peak in visits of all pilgrims. Thomas of Monmouth seems to have acted conscientiously, seeking out witnesses, writing down their stories 'as they themselves afterwards told me'. The solicitous monk was also instrumental in some cures, offering tomb-dust in water to one suppliant, for example, and in another case placing an insane woman next to the tomb. Thomas seldom questioned the events themselves, provided he had witnesses (and sometimes even if he had none).[16] He was a faithful registrar for over twenty years and though the miracles declined in numbers he seems to have been as enthusiastic in 1170 as he had been in 1150.

We shall take the number of recorded miracles to be 115; in this as in all the major miracle collections, one might quibble over whether there were a few more or a few less. The essential point about these figures— and this applies to every major cult—is that they only represent pilgrims who had become involved in miracles. The *total* number of pilgrims to William's, or to any other medieval, shrine is unknown. Slightly more than half the 115 were men. As to social class, men and women together, the pilgrims were notable from two points of view. In the first place a great many members of the merchant and artisan class were recorded by Thomas. Few other cults drew so many pilgrims from a single city, and this high proportion of urban occupations is hardly surprising. A second feature is the high level of participation by the lower clergy, many of them Norwich monks who were taking advantage of their wonderful treasure. In the midst of economic and social tensions in Norwich, William's cult provided an opportunity to express anti-Semitism and at the same time gave the monks the 'saint' that their cathedral needed. The cult was born and bred in the cathedral and nurtured and developed by the city. The implications of these findings about class participation will be examined after all of the cults have been considered.

Thomas Becket
There is only a single extant manuscript of the *Life* of William of Norwich, which puts a limit to what one can say about him. Quite the opposite is true of the next saint, as famous as William was obscure. Among the 250 august volumes of the *Rolls Series* there are seven fat tomes called *Materials for the History of Thomas Becket*, two of an Icelandic *Life* of Becket, and scattered references through many of the other volumes. Within fifty years of his death at least twenty biographies were circulating, and each succeeding century has produced a new batch of *Lives*; the twentieth is no exception.[17] In addition, there are a great many unpublished manuscripts in cathedral and secular libraries in this country and abroad (especially in France). Becket's career and death were rehearsed in contemporary chronicles, collections of letters, liturgical observances; they were a topic of conversation at all social levels in the later twelfth century. News of the *immanissimum scelus*, most monstrous crime, as the pope called it, flew to the ends of Europe. The murder of 1170 threw suspicion on King Henry II and resulted in at least a temporary reaction in favour of Church liberties over royal prerogatives. The cult of Becket became the most famous in the land and remained so until about 1400 when it was joined in notoriety by that of the Virgin of Walsingham.

Becket was murdered in his cathedral on the grey Tuesday evening of 29 December 1170. After the lethal blow crashed down upon his head and sliced off a piece of skull one of the assassins thrust his sword-point in and 'stirred the brains' of the prelate. The terrified monks slowly crept back after the murderers had gone, removed the body to the high altar and prepared it, as best they could in the unsettled circumstances, for burial. The very next day word came that unless the corpse were buried at once the knights who had assassinated the prelate would cast it into a refuse pit or suspend it from the city gibbet. The body was put into a sarcophagus in the crypt; then the monks came up, shut and locked the door behind them, and left the future saint alone in silence and darkness.

But Becket was not forgotten, at least not by local people, for at the place of his murder bystanders pressed their fingers into his blood and made the sign of the cross on their foreheads and eyes while invoking his name. Another contemporary noted that the very first miracle occurred on the night of the murder, when a Canterbury man cured his paralysed wife with some of Becket's blood he had wiped up on a cloth. As other remnants of the archbishop were being furtively carried away by local people that night the monks, realizing that they were allowing a precious commodity to escape, collected what they could of the blood and brains, retrieved the bit of skull. The space where Becket fell—today marked only by an elegantly simple statement of his death—was closed to public access. For a year cathedral services were curtailed, the statues and crosses veiled, the altars *denudata* because of the pollution of blood and the magnitude of the atrocity.[18]

As news spread, miracles followed. There were cures in Sussex on 31 December, in Gloucestershire and Berkshire in early January. A London priest, healed after a night spent at the tomb, went home praising Becket, but secretly (*occulte propter metum*), because he was afraid. Becket's enemies were having a limited success in intimidating those who lauded the dead prelate. They kept watch at Canterbury hostels, ready to silence any unsuspecting visitors who praised Becket and to hustle them off to an impromptu 'trial'. Many dared not speak openly; nevertheless there was *murmur multum in populo*. Some secretly planned but deferred their pilgrimages until 'less dangerous times'. Miracles happened in private homes—regardless of Becket's enemies—in the usual ways, with water, measured-candles, vows; a few desperate pilgrims even went into the crypt secretly and there received their miraculous healing.[19] By Easter of 1171 (28 March) at least twenty miracles had occurred. The insistent demand for access to the thaumaturgic tomb eventually had results and on 2 April 1171 the monks publicly opened the crypt. More and more miracles were reported, many occurring at or near the tomb itself. Becket's enemies, goaded on by the growth of the cult, grew more hostile. The monks, hearing about plans to snatch the body, removed it to a secret place (hiding it behind an altar in the crypt) and after the threat blew over they not only returned it to its sarcophagus but built a protective outer casing around the tomb, with two holes on each side through which kneeling pilgrims could kiss or touch the coffin inside. In June 1171 the archbishop's enemies fired their Parthian shot, accusing the monks of effecting cures through magic, but admitted 'There is nothing we can do. Look: all England is going to him.' By now Canterbury pilgrims were wearing the ampoules of curative water around their necks where they could be seen and not, as they used to do, secretly under their clothing.[20]

The cathedral was 'reconciled' on 21 December 1171. It is probable that unusually large crowds celebrated the Christmas feast which ran into the first anniversary of the murder (29 December). The numbers of pilgrims must have been tremendous in mid-April 1172, the first Easter celebration in the cathedral in more than a year. The Church absolved King Henry II of complicity in the murder in May, by which time the influx of pilgrims reporting or experiencing miracles at Becket's tomb required the services of two registrars. The period between late 1171 and mid-1172 would have been what a contemporary had in mind when he wrote that at first there were few miracles, but soon they became numerous and then very frequent, occurring first 'about his tomb, then through the whole crypt, then the whole church, then all of Canterbury, then England, then France, Normandy, Germany' then over the 'whole world'. The famous cult attracted the interest of all ranks of society from Canterbury street urchins who sang songs about the martyr, to the pope himself.[21]

Pope Alexander III, whose legates were examining Becket's death and miracles within four months of the murder, canonized him in February 1173, a little more than three years after the archbishop's death; Osmund of Salisbury had to wait 357 years for his title. Three years, however, might seem unnecessarily long, considering the circumstances of the assassination, and certainly John of Salisbury, Becket's old friend and colleague, thought and said so in letters to the pope and other prelates. Although the pope was somewhat reserved in his formal bulls of canonization, in earlier private communications he strongly condemned the murder, declaring that Becket was killed *atrociter et crudeliter*; as early as 1171 he had informed the French king that Becket was a martyr. Certainly Alexander III could have canonized Becket sooner; it had taken him less than a year to canonize Edward the Confessor.[22]

The cult quickly became popular in England and abroad. In 1172 William, Archbishop of Sens, wrote to John of Salisbury that the

French miracles were so frequent that they could scarcely all be counted, in 1176 Abbot Peter de Celle claimed that crowds of French pilgrims were going to Canterbury and in 1178 the Archbishop of Rheims came to the tomb. The greatest of all French suppliants was King Louis VII, who arrived in August 1179, the first French monarch to set foot in England. He offered a jewelled ring and an annual shipment of wine which French monarchs sent to the Canterbury monks (with occasional interruptions, for example, during part of the Hundred Years' war) to the end of the Middle Ages.[23] This first, and from Canterbury's point of view, very successful decade was rounded off in 1180-1 when the crypt was rebuilt after a fire of 1174—Becket's tomb was housed under a temporary wooden shelter during the construction.[24]

Before the end of the twelfth century his relics, especially the Canterbury water in its metal ampoules, were spread throughout England and much of Europe: fragments of his clothing, cups or knives he had used, beds in which he had slept, Mass vestments he had worn were revered in homes and churches from Scotland to Sicily. Through them, Thomas cured people of all degrees, *riche e povre e haut e bas*, as a St. Albans monk put it in the 1180s.[25] Versions of Becket's miracles, different redactions of the biographies, hymns and other liturgical commemorations circulated widely, especially among religious houses here and in France, where he had fretted out so many years in exile.

Ecclesiastical recognition of his cult was crowned in 1220 with a translation of his bones to a resplendent new shrine at the east end of the cathedral. This had been long planned but delayed for various reasons. Archbishop Langton was finally able to launch his publicity campaign in 1218 and by July 1220, fifty years after the murder, an enormous crowd gathered in Canterbury at the appointed date. The young King Henry III was present, though he was too young to assist when the holy relics were solemnly carried from the crypt up to the elaborate shrine (not many representations of this shrine exist). The east end of the cathedral had been rebuilt and redecorated to provide a suitable setting: many of the miracles of the crypt were commemorated in coloured glass and the vault above the shrine was newly painted. Poems were commissioned, banquets arranged for the occasion, and until the shrine was destroyed in the sixteenth century a great July Jubilee was held or at any rate planned every fifty years.[26] Becket thus came to have two feasts, the anniversary of his death on 29 December and of his translation on 7 July.

Although the cult had probably reached the fringes of Christendom within a few decades of the murder, the translation of 1220 carried the martyr's fame to a new generation and stimulated or renewed interest in the saint. Relics continued to multiply and pass to and fro, many of them ultimately coming to rest as the foundation of yet another chapel or church. Fifty-nine 'points de culte' have been identified in the French ecclesiastical Province of Rouen alone and in just one French pilgrimage-centre (in Artois) over seventy miracles were attributed to a relic of the martyr.[27] Besides relics Europe received iconographic and liturgical notices of the saint, such as wall paintings, mosaics, statues, medals and badges, which reminded everyone of the atrocity. One of the windows at Sens cathedral, for example, shows his original tomb with the two apertures in the side, exactly as represented in Canterbury glass. The tracing of such vestiges of *cultus* through Europe and beyond has already taxed the skills and patience of more than one scholar and, as recent publications suggest, new items continue to be discovered.[28]

There is plenty of evidence for the popularity of Becket's shrine as a pilgrimage centre, but by far the most detailed, and that which brings us closest to the pilgrims themselves, are the 703 miracles recorded during the very first decade, when Benedict and William sat at the tomb in the crypt and assembled the 'greatest collection of miracle stories connected with any single shrine ... in the whole Middle Ages'.[29] Benedict, Prior of Canterbury in 1175 and Abbot of Peterborough in 1177, had been prompted in early 1171 by visions (and the suggestion of his brethren) to collect Becket's miracles. He noted that they gradually increased even though the cathedral was closed, and then became abundant after Easter Week 1171 when the church and crypt were opened to the faithful. He recorded miracles in chronological order until about Whitsun, or mid-May, 1171. After that, however, the church and crypt being open and the tomb secure within its protective shell, the pilgrim crowds must have been too great and the miracles too frequent, to maintain this orderly scheme. This is evident when his sequence of miracles is examined. After May 1171 Benedict began to record couplets of miracles of the same type, or multiples of more than two and at one point he recorded six consecutive cures of blindness. This suggests that he was no longer recording events *seriatim* but had re-arranged his notes in some different scheme. The miracles of the first half of his collection of six books have been dated to the year following Becket's death, that is, to about the end of 1171. The rest belong to the decade of the 1170s with a few later additions by others;[30] there were in all 265 miracles in Benedict's collection.

William, another Canterbury monk, started collecting miracle re-ports about May 1172. Except for a few later additions his list—of 438 miracles—ends about 1179.[31] Unlike Benedict, William was from the start quite unconcerned with chronology and grouped his wonder-tales by type of cure or by social class of pilgrim. There are some duplications in the work of the two registrars, which we have tried to reconcile. The two were not working side by side nor, apparently, did they attempt to co-ordinate their two collections. The duplications are valuable, however, sometimes providing quite different versions of the same incident. William's style is more florid than Benedict's and his editors have noticed an interest in medicine, in the circumstances a welcome trait.

William began to record miracles about a year after Benedict, and he approached his task with greater prejudice against the 'lower orders' of society. Benedict had begun writing before the cult was fully 're-spectable', and as a result the poor and insignificant local folk consti-tuted the bulk of his earlier suppliants. William, whose work com-menced about the time that King Henry II was formally forgiven by the Church (in mid-1172), could pick and choose from an ever-increasing flood of pilgrims who no longer stayed home because of 'fear of the king's wrath'. Comparing the two lists it is clear that William recorded relatively more men than Benedict, relatively more participants from the upper ranks of the laity, and more from both the upper and the lower echelons of the Church; in other words, William recorded fewer poor, simple pilgrims than Benedict. William's list also reflects a more cosmopolitan following: he noted proportionately four times as many 'foreign' pilgrims as Benedict. This was due not only to William's penchant for selecting more impressive pilgrims but also, no doubt, to a real expansion of the cult into Europe between 1171 and 1172. Generally, then, from the earlier to the later list there was a shift to more male, upper-class and 'foreign' pilgrims. That this was not wholly due to the prejudices of the later compiler is suggested by the fact that the same trend occurred, though less obviously, at two or three other English shrines. Becket's shrine may have begun by attracting the lower classes and women (as both Benedict and William admitted) but it quickly moved into higher social circles.

Godric of Finchale
There can be no more striking contrast to Becket's masculine, upper-class and clerical pilgrims than the ill suppliants who trekked to the shrine of Godric of Finchale, who died in the same year as the Canterbury martyr, 1170. Godric, a Norfolk man, spent his early years as a sea-faring merchant, visiting the great shrines of Christendom in the course of his voyages. About 1112 he gave up his wandering life and became a hermit at Finchale, under the authority of the bishop of Durham. Credited with clairvoyance and healing miracles, Godric acquired a thaumaturgic reputation; he was known even to Becket and Pope Alexander III. Reginald, a Durham monk, composed a *Life* of the venerated hermit, to which posthumous miracles were added during the 1170s.

Godric died in May 1170 and was buried at Finchale about three miles north-east of Durham. The spectacular growth of Becket's cult may have prompted certain Durham monks to speculate among themselves why Godric's relics, too, were not working miracles. Their anxieties came to an end when his corpse began to do so in June 1172.[32] Though never canonized, Godric established himself with the locals as a 'saint'. In the thirteenth century his hermitage was rebuilt and expanded into an imposing priory by the Wear river and gifts to Godric and his shrine continued to be made throughout the fourteenth and fifteenth centuries.[33]

The list of some 244 miracles provides an intimate glimpse of local popular religion in northern England. The most striking thing about his cult was the fact that over two-thirds of the registered pilgrims were women, higher than at any other shrine. In addition, no saint counted among his devotees so many people of the lowest classes, but since most women belonged to these social levels, this is to be expected with so many females involved in the miracles. There was practically no participation by the upper classes or upper clergy, though a few priests and monks put in an appearance. The majority of his pilgrims were local, female, and lower-class; we shall return to this peculiar configuration after all the cults have been examined.

Frideswide of Oxford
Particular saints were chosen for this study because they were 'real' post-Conquest people, whose deaths can be dated, and who were credited with at least one hundred posthumous miracles which have come down to us. The one exception to these criteria is the patron saint of Oxford, Frideswide. Very little is known of her beyond the legendary tales recorded long after her death, but she is nevertheless included—although she herself was certainly pre-Conquest—because her posthumous miracles were attributed to her and recorded in the twelfth century.[34] In addition, since she is the only female saint we are considering, it may be worthwhile to see how her pilgrims differed from the crowds who resorted to the other, male, wonder-workers.

It is not easy to imagine what life was like for a Saxon girl whose father—according to tradition—was 'ruler' of Oxford about the year 700. Even the place itself would not be mentioned in historical documents for another two centuries. If Frideswide was indeed alive in A.D. 700, the society around her was far different from what it became in the twelfth century. In her day the kingdom of Mercia had not so many years earlier lost its great and ruthless leader, Penda, while Ine the lawgiver still reigned as king of Wessex; control over the Oxford area was sometimes disputed by these two kingdoms during this troubled era. The Northmen or Vikings had not yet discovered how easy it was to plunder England, but there was no lack of internal conflict as the petty and the major kingdoms—collections of Germanic tribes we conveniently abbreviate as 'Anglo-Saxons'—tried to carve out spheres of influence for themselves. Though Frideswide may have lived in a violent age it was paradoxically a period of great respect for the cloistered religious life, at least in some parts of England; after all, one of her contemporaries would have been the monk-historian Bede. Frideswide decided to give herself up to prayer and seclusion, so her father built a convent for her in Oxford where she settled down to the contemplative life with a band of like-minded maidens under her care.

All went well, so runs the legend, until her father died, but then a local 'king' seized the opportunity to try to force her into marriage, which she resisted. After a number of unusual rebuffs—on one occasion the king's men were miraculously struck blind—her suitor attacked her convent and Frideswide ran off to a nearby boat and escaped into the watery maze of streams and rivers which still meander through the university city. She spent her remaining years in self-imposed exile, during which she established a reputation as a healer and woman of great piety. One of her refuges was a place now known as Binsey, on the verge of the city of Oxford. The village—a short row of houses and a pub—becomes very muddy and dismal at certain times of the year, but if the traveller perseveres he will find a tiny church a few hundred yards beyond the village, and a healing well reputedly dating from the years of Frideswide's exile. This well retained its reputed curative powers even in the early years of the twentieth century, but now it is more often used for wishing than for curing.

Frideswide was buried in her Oxford nunnery in the early eighth century and on this site in the early twelfth century a church was built (the Danes had razed an earlier structure in 1002) which came under the control of the Augustinian Canons. As we have seen, from 1170 the cult of Becket was expanding through England. Robert de Circklade, a prior of the Oxford canons of St. Frideswide's was cured by, and wrote a life of, Thomas Becket in the 1170s. This may have encouraged the next prior, Philip, to emphasize the glory of his own saint by translating Frideswide's remains to a new shrine in 1180. There had already been premonitions of her greatness; visions and dreams as early as 1172 (just when Becket's cult was enjoying tremendous acclaim and Godric's was coming into being) suggested that the precious relics should be moved to a more honourable place. The translation drew crowds of pilgrims and the usual reports of miracles followed.

Pilgrims, including that inveterate shrine-goer Henry III, visited her tomb during the thirteenth century, though there is no extant record of further miracles. Medieval charters continued to name the Saxon maiden as beneficiary of sundry gifts, and ongoing interest brought on another translation in 1289 to a more elaborate shrine, parts of which can still be seen in what is now Oxford cathedral. A few references to indulgences come from the fourteenth century and by the end of the fifteenth Frideswide had secured the honour of liturgical commemorations at least in the Province of Canterbury, though she was never officially canonized.[35]

About two-thirds of Frideswide's 108 posthumous miracles involved women. This distribution, with that for Godric, is unusual, since at all but these two shrines most of the pilgrims were men. Unlike Godric's pilgrims, however, Frideswide's were not overwhelmingly from the poorest social sectors. Some represented the craftsmen/artisans/gentry of the city and surrounding countryside, and there were relatively more upper-class pilgrims than in Godric's following. In general, Frideswide's was an unspectacular, local cult drawing mainly upon the women of the area who may have felt some affinity with the long-dead Saxon princess.

Of these four twelfth-century English saints' cults obviously Becket's stirred greatest interest and had the most significant effect upon later English hagiography. In both Godric's and Frideswide's cult there is mention of pilgrims who had also visited the shrine of the Canterbury martyr, and one of the last miracles attributed to William of Norwich also involved a visionary appearance of Becket. For the rest of the Middle Ages, comparisons would be made between Becket and other reputed or canonized saints such as Simon de Montfort, Thomas Cantilupe, and Edmund Rich, all of whom died in the thirteenth century.

Chapter 8

Saints, Sickness and Snobbery: Shrines and their Clientele

Miracles are marvellous works; but that which is marvellous to one may not be so to another.

Thomas Hobbes

More saints have been canonized by the papacy in the twentieth century than during any previous century, including the Middle Ages. Before the Reformation, however, the great age of saint-making was the thirteenth century. In this chapter we are concerned with men who died in the thirteenth century, but the question of their subsequent canonization is really of secondary importance. We have chosen them, just as we chose the saints examined in the last chapter, because their cults, involving at least a hundred posthumous miracles, flourished before the eyes of literate clerics who recorded what they saw and what reports they heard. The posthumous miracles of these thirteenth-century figures, together with those reported in the twelfth-century cults, should provide a sufficiently-broad basis for some general conlusions about the cures and other miracles reputedly experienced by twelfth- and thirteenth-century pilgrims, and what relationship those miracles had to particular categories of medieval people. As it happens, the first cult to be examined developed around one of the saints who was officially canonized by the pope in the thirteenth century.

Wulfstan of Worcester

Frideswide's pilgrims were neither numerous nor exceptional and the same may be said of the 103 people involved in posthumous miracles attributed to Wulfstan, Bishop of Worcester, who died in 1095. Having earned a reputation for statecraft as well as sanctity, Wulfstan died as the last representative of the Anglo-Saxon episcopate; the first suggestions of canonization were made about the the middle of the twelfth century, but the papacy failed to respond. Toward the end of the century, however, it seems that the dead bishop requested (through visions) that he should be translated, a task undertaken in 1198 by John of Coutances, Bishop of Worcester. One September night after all the laity had been sent from the cathedral, the Worcester monks approached the tomb where Wulfstan had lain undisturbed for more than a century—since the day his tearful companions had washed his body, dressed it in sacerdotal vestments, and sealed the lid in place.[1] The monks bent to their task; as soon as the lid was raised a sweet odour seemed to fill the church. They found the ancient corpse not reduced to powder, but dressed in tattered remnants of clerical garments, the body still covered with skin, with hairs still attached to the scalp. Wulfstan's skin and bones were put into one portable shrine or feretory, what remained of his garments into another and both caskets were placed upon the high altar.

A new bishop, Mauger, was consecrated in 1200. In early 1201 while he and his monks were celebrating Wulfstan's obit a woman was cured after coming to pray for the dead bishop's assistance. Other miracles followed and Mauger asked the pope for a canonization inquiry. Since the new bishop thought that the 1198 translation, carried out neither publicly nor with papal approval, might prejudice his case he had the good sense to return the remains to their original resting place. His petition was a success: after the pope's *ad hoc* committee of English prelates sent their report on Wulfstan's life and miracles to Rome in 1202, Pope Innocent III canonized him in 1203. The corpse was re-translated to a new shrine in 1218 and on this occasion several bits and pieces were set aside for distribution as precious relics. At least one contemporary chronicler looked back on this *morcellement* as sacrilege, clinched by the death of the bishop responsible (Sylvester) five weeks later.[2]

Just over half of Wulfstan's 103 registered pilgrims were men and the great bulk of pilgrims of both sexes came from the lowest classes. Neither the upper nor lower levels of the clergy were particularly well-represented in the pilgrim crowds, which is somewhat surprising considering the saint's venerable position in the hierarchy.

Simon de Montfort

Miracles occurred at the tomb of Simon de Montfort, although he had been excommunicated—twice—by the time of his death. Theological formalities were swept away by popular interest and pilgrims crowded to venerate the relics of the man who ravaged the south of France in the 'crusade' against Albigensian heretics during the early thirteenth century. In England, forty-seven years later, his son—another Simon—also died excommunicated but became a popular 'saint' nevertheless. Simon the younger was the Earl of Leicester, who led the baronial movement of the thirteenth century against Henry III and was killed by royalists in 1265. His mutilated corpse was taken to the Benedictine abbey in Evesham and buried before the high altar, soon miracles were attributed to him, and a popular cult developed.[3]

There is little doubt that by the end of his life Simon had acquired followers from all ranks in English society, among the clergy and laity alike. In the former group he was supported by the bishops of Ely, Winchester and London, to name only three of at least eight sympathetic prelates; the abbots and priors of Bury St. Edmunds, Notley, Abingdon, St. Albans and several other houses also rallied to his cause. Clerical support was particularly strong in Worcestershire, the county in which he was to meet his death. It was an area dominated by ecclesiastical landholders, of whom one of the most powerful was Simon's close friend Walter Cantilupe, Bishop of Worcester, whose nephew Thomas—the future St. Thomas Cantilupe—was for a short time Chancellor of England under Simon's regime. This ecclesiastical support was not universally applauded. In 1264 Pope Urban IV ordered his legate to reprimand prelates, clergy, barons and others who were keeping the civil war alive, and this legate, as Pope Clement IV, repeated the order. Measures were to be taken

> in regard to those bishops and religious and secular clerks who in their preaching have spoken of Simon de Montfort and his accomplices as men zealous in a good cause, and have praised their actions.

This prohibition was aimed against the friars as well, for Simon had long been associated with the Franciscans and was no enemy to the Dominicans. Scholars and leaders of Oxford University, like Grosseteste, were also powerful allies.[4]

Montfortians were found at all ecclesiastical levels and the same was true of lay society. To be a baron or knight was *ipso facto* to be a friend or enemy of the earl. Royalist confiscations of land and manors after the battle of Evesham, with scant regard for the definition of 'rebel', led to confusion in the shires and also served to keep Simon's memory fresh in his partisans' minds—especially those whose lands were taken from them. About a hundred lesser landowners of the west Midlands, for instance, had their property confiscated after (if they had not been killed during) the battle of 1265. As for the peasantry, there are only indirect signs of involvement by the 'common people' before the earl's death, though proclamations and promises of better govenment for all, read out in the shire courts from 1258, may have boosted support for Simon's political programme at the grassroots. As a modern historian puts it, 'public opinion had been stirred in England, public propaganda and popular preachers had excited it, and now an incentive was given . . . to rally round a new leader. This new leader was Earl Simon.'[5]

The civil war culminated in August 1265 at Evesham where, in the midst of picturesque surroundings, Simon's army was trapped between Prince Edward's forces and a loop in the river Avon; his followers were defeated and he himself was slain. Simon's head and testicles were sent to the wife of one of his enemies, one foot is supposed to have ended up in a miracle-working silver reliquary in (pro-Montfortian) Alnwick, while the other came into the possession of Llywelyn ap Gruffydd, Prince of Wales, who eventually married one of Simon's daughters. One of his hands, originally destined for an enemy, was reputedly returned to Evesham.[6] Simon's weapons and armour were also distributed to the victors, and we have already seen how he worked a miracle for a man who kept some of this booty at his bedside. Simon's friends carried the mutilated remains from the field on a dilapidated ladder and gave what was left of the corpse to the Evesham monks, who buried it by their high altar. Their church has long since disappeared, but a modern plaque is set into the ground at the presumed site of Simon's burial. Not long after the battle a curative spring arose miraculously at the place where he fell; it is now a weedy pond known as Battlewell. As late as 1910 its water was used therapeutically, for weak eyes.[7]

The kingdom was in turmoil for two or three years after Evesham. Certain regions, such as Worcestershire itself, came under royal control only after great 'persuasion', and in such areas the memory of Simon's fate may have strengthened resistance and encouraged his apotheosis. Simon's popular canonization took place, therefore, against a background of anti-royal resentment and disappointment in the failure of the champion of 'liberty and justice'. Some of his biographers or hagiographers discovered analogies between Simon's death and Christ's: the sun was darkened, the heavens thundered over Evesham when he fell; his garments and armour were distributed by lot amongst the victors standing round the corpse; like Christ, Simon had come to save the world from oppression. One modern writer's observation, that 'in many a house of friars and nuns and throughout the countryside he was a popular saint', was vividly illustrated by the Aconbury nun who was so stricken by the news of his death that, after blaspheming the God who had allowed such a thing, she imagined that she held, and kissed, Simon's severed head.[8]

Article Eight of the *Dictum de Kenilworth*, a document drawn up by some of the victors in 1266, called for the condemnation of anyone who claimed that Simon was a saint or a just man, since he had been excommunicated at death; furthermore, no one was to spread tales about the miracles attributed to him. Clearly Simon's cult, like that of Becket but unlike, for example, the cults of William of Norwich or Godric, arose almost at once and evoked equally favourable and hostile responses. Opposition to his popular veneration came from high places. Pope Clement IV said that Simon had been a 'wicked' man, and for good measure the papal legate Ottobuono again excommunicated the month-old corpse.[9]

Regardless of the *Dictum* or the pope, many people thought of Simon as a martyr, a hero who died for peace in the realm and for the sake of the Church. His miracles proved, according to his followers, that Jesus was well pleased with him. A song written within twenty years of his death compared him to both Christ and Becket—Simon died for his country, as they had died for the Church. Another song also linked him with Becket: *Come ly martyr de Caunterbyr, finist sa vie.* One of the people who benefited from a miraculous cure called him a 'martyr for the sake of justice' and in a prayer composed in his memory he was likened to Becket and styled 'Blessed Simon the Martyr' who had died for the renewal of Britain.[10]

Since popular veneration, prohibited by the *Dictum*, could be dangerous, no one dared openly to discuss the cures at his tomb or at the spring 'because of fear of the king and his people'; the miracles—as in Becket's case—were not 'set out publicly'.[11] It is little wonder that people hesitated to report miracles at Evesham and that the first half-dozen or so miracles happened not in public in the abbey church but at the curative spring over a mile away.

His cult does not seem to have survived, at least as far as miracle-working at Evesham goes, much beyond 1300, though vestiges of sympathy for the fallen earl persisted even in the most unlikely places. For instance, while King Edward II rested at a Yorkshire castle in 1323 he heard two women singing songs about Simon de Montfort. The changed political conditions which followed the accession of Edward I in 1272 may have deprived Simon's cult of most of its *raison d'être*. This change in fashion is evident in a certain manuscript which describes the events of 1265: a passage mentioning the miracles of Simon's corpse was scratched out during the Middle Ages.[12] It is even possible that the Evesham monks may have disinterred and secretly reburied the corpse. There was some confusion at the burial itself, in 1265: though one contemporary writer claimed that Simon was buried with royal permission, another declared that things were done hastily and unceremoniously. Perhaps the victorious royalists had further plans for Simon's remains. A third source noted that sometime after burial some of the Evesham monks began to murmur that Simon, an excommunicate, was unworthy of Christian burial *and* that he was tainted with treason. This attitude grew in the abbey until finally 'he was exhumed and cast into a remote place' *usque hodie est occultus et incognitus*, 'unknown and hidden to this day'. The question is unresolved. In 1267 one of Simon's sons complained to the pope that his father 'did not have church burial', but on the other hand in 1290, in some circles at any rate, it was believed that de Montfort was still buried at Evesham, though there is no mention of Simon or his shrine in the customal of Evesham Abbey drawn up at the end of the thirteenth century.[13]

Whether or not his bones were eventually removed from the abbey, pilgrims came to his tomb and to the curative spring for at least a decade, and experienced or reported their miracles, which were recorded by two or more anonymous registrars. Some 190 miracles were listed, covering the period from August 1265 to Whitweek 1279. In many ways Simon's pilgrims resembled those who reported miracles at Becket's shrine. It was a masculine cult, attracting relatively nearly as many men as found in Becket's cult; in fact, Simon's was second highest of all the cults in proportion of male to female pilgrims. Simon's pilgrims included more members of the noble class than any cult including Becket's and was second only to Becket in relative numbers of upper ecclesiastics. The lower ranks of the Church were also well-represented. These findings are not surprising since his life had deeply involved the politically important people of the realm as well as many clerics and prelates in the Church; those who attributed miracles to him after his death tended to come from these same classes. Ordinary local people also sought out his relics for the healing of their ills, once the rumours of miracle-working began to spread.

Thomas Cantilupe

Thomas Cantilupe was closely associated with Simon de Montfort, both in this life and (at least in visions) in the next. Thomas had the good luck to be born into a comfortably-off family. His Norman grandfather William, who established the English fortunes of the Cantilupes, was one of King John's 'evil counsellors' and sheriff of Herefordshire, with his principal seat in Warwickshire. Thomas's father, for a short time in 1238 keeper of the Great Seal of the realm, was steward of Henry III's household. He inherited the family estates in 1239. Thomas himself, a second son, did not succeed to his father's lands, which fell to his elder brother William in 1251. The family was large. Besides William, Thomas had three brothers and three sisters.[14] The tradition of eldest son for the family estates, second for the church, was faithfully kept in this Cantilupe generation, though when Thomas was a child and his uncle asked him what he wanted to be when he grew up, he said a knight.[15] That uncle was Walter Cantilupe, later Bishop of Worcester, who was especially interested in educating Thomas for the clergy. Walter's plans for his nephew succeeded far beyond what he could have imagined when Thomas became not only a bishop but a saint, shedding his spiritual patronage over the west country where the Cantilupe name was so well known.

Thomas was born in Buckinghamshire about 1218 in Hambleden, now a prosperous-looking, well-kept little village in the pleasant hilly country near Henley-on-Thames. He studied at Paris, Orleans and

Oxford, collecting several church livings and two canonries (London and Hereford). He was Chancellor of Oxford University about 1261 but resigned to enter fully into political affairs. Thomas and his uncle Walter were ardent Montfortians and for a time—in 1264 during Simon's brief 'reign'—Thomas was Chancellor of England. After Simon's death at Evesham Thomas prudently removed himself to Paris 'to study theology'. Having received royal permission to do so, he returned and continued his interrupted career, which culminated in 1275 when he became Bishop of Hereford. At the same time, he was an adviser to King Edward I. This successful career in the Church was marred by a quarrel which broke out between Thomas and his superior, Archbishop Pecham, over a conflict of ecclesiastical jurisdiction. In the end Pecham excommunicated Thomas, who set off to appeal to the pope in Italy, where he died in 1282.

His bones were brought back and buried in Hereford Cathedral and in 1287 transferred to a new tomb, where miracles began to occur. A papal commission examined the evidence for canonization in 1307, Pope John XXII canonized Thomas in 1320, and a final translation of the relics took place in 1349. His death and the growth and decline of his cult are treated at length in a separate chapter; he is singled out for special examination because the circumstantial evidence presented in his posthumous miracles is far more detailed and extensive than in any other English cult, with the possible exception of Becket's.

Although his friends praised him after his death, Cantilupe seems to have been an authoritarian, somewhat aloof man of the sort of dour piety one could expect in a conscientious, educated, but basically aristocratic prelate. He was something of a prude; as a young man he tried to avoid even the sight of attractive girls, and once, after he became a bishop, he refused the innocent kiss of his own sister. He was as stern in his prejudices, a notorious hater of Jews. There was no winning sympathy, no warmth such as one associates with St. Anselm of Canterbury or St. Hugh of Lincoln. Who, then, came to the shrine of such an apparently unlovable man in search of miraculous assistance? About two-thirds of the 470 recorded pilgrims involved in his miracles were men, and the great majority of all his pilgrims came from the lower classes. Relatively few upper-class people were involved in the miracles, nor did many upper-level ecclesiastics attract the registrars' attention. Most surprising, however, is the very small proportion of pilgrims from the lower clergy. Of all the cults we have chosen to study, Cantilupe's included relatively fewest miracle-touched priests, monks or friars. Proportionately more than twice as many lower clergy were noted in Frideswide's and even Godric's cult, six times as many were found among Becket's pilgrims. One reason for this extraordinarily low clerical participation may be the excommunication of Cantilupe by the

Archbishop of Canterbury, which was still, as far as most English clerics knew, in effect at his death (although he had been released on his death-bed in Italy by a papal penitentiary). It was not until a separate hearing cleared him of the sentence in 1307 that the papal commissioners could proceed to the canonization inquiry. Few churchmen, meanwhile, seem to have risked a pilgrimage to an 'excommunicate'. The Franciscans were far from enthusiastic about Cantilupe, perhaps because of his controversy with the Franciscan Archbishop Pecham. In any case it is clear that the mere fact that a man had once been in Holy Orders and high in the ranks of the Church did not assure interest on the part of the clergy, at least in his posthumous fame and miracles. This was also evident in the cult of Wulfstan, another prelate whose miracles do not seem to have involved very many churchmen; on the contrary, as the pilgrims of William of Norwich and Simon de Montfort suggest, in some cases relatively more clerics were drawn into the miracles attributed to the bones of laymen.

Edmund Rich
Cantilupe is the last of the thirteenth-century English saints for whom at least a hundred posthumous miracles have survived. In order to determine whether the social class distributions at English shrines presented an 'insular' pattern or whether the results could be matched on the continent, we conclude with two French saints. The first of these was actually an English prelate who died in France and whose cult was essentially French. Edmund Rich was born at Abingdon, about 1180, into a very pious family. His father is said to have retired to the monastery of Eynsham, leaving Edmund's upbringing to his wife Mabel, a more than usually holy woman who was in the habit of wearing a hairshirt and metal bodice. She 'checked the growth of sensuality' in her children as one biographer puts it, and we can well believe it. When she died bits of the bodice were distributed to her sons Robert and Edmund and it was said that miracles were worked at her tomb in Abingdon. Edmund's two sisters, who had vowed perpetual chastity, went off to the convent at Catesby where one of them became prioress, and she, too, was credited with posthumous miracles. Just to complete the portrait of this wonder-working family, brother Robert was also said to have worked miracles after his death.[16]

Edmund left his pious surroundings for Oxford and Paris and by about 1214 he incepted in theology at Oxford and may have been among the first to draw upon the 'new' Aristotle in his lectures. He became treasurer of Salisbury Cathedral and was elected Archbishop of Canterbury in 1233. He interested himself in affairs both of Church and kingdom, playing the role of peace-maker when noble tempers overheated, but running into difficulties with his own cathedral monks.

Their quarrel—arising from conflicting claims to certain churches and other matters—resulted in his appeal and journey to Rome in 1238, but things were still in turmoil after his return to Canterbury. By 1239 there was extreme hostility between Edmund and his own monks; he went so far as to suspend them from entering the cathedral church, though he relented enough to allow four of them to receive pilgrims to Becket's tomb and to watch over the relics. Once again he set off to see the pope, leaving England in 1240. He never came back.[17]

Edmund died at Soisy (about sixty miles south-east of Paris) in November 1240 and his viscera were buried at nearby Provins. The quick-witted abbot of Pontigny claimed the corpse for his monastery, where Edmund had enjoyed the Cistercians' hospitality during his journey. Hysterical crowds who only days earlier had lined the roads to see the famous 'exiled' archbishop now greeted the funeral procession all along the way back to Pontigny. Everyone tried to touch the body, and more than once the abbot nearly lost his great treasure to these eager mobs; at one point he whispered into the corpse's ear to work no miracles until they had arrived at the abbey. On the way there was some discussion as to whether England had a better right to the body (*nocte illa, cum de corporis possessione iustiori contenderemus*)[18] but the abbot of Pontigny satisfied himself that he had the greater claim, asserting that Becket, while *he* was in exile at Pontigny, prophesied just such a boon and that Edmund, a confrater or associate member of the monastery of Pontigny, had expressed a wish to be buried there. In any case Edmund had excommunicated his own Canterbury monks before he left England, so it was unlikely that they would trouble themselves very much about collecting the remains. The body was interred at Pontigny and underwent an informal elevation some three months later, but even before this the first overtures to the pope had been made.

In 1241 the full weight of the Cistercian order was added to the canonization appeal and during 1242 letters asking for his canonization went to the Holy Father from France and England. Miracles, meanwhile, were going on at the tomb, and by 1244 two commissions (one for France, the other for England) were collecting evidence. Apparently the miracles which came to light were insufficiently attested, since Pope Innocent IV ordered a second inquiry in 1245. Even this seemed destined to fail. One of the cardinals who was involved in the matter confessed that he found the miracles difficult to believe, gratuitously adding that he only believed the wonders of St. Martin of Tours because the Church declared them to be true.[19] Another stalemate was averted when an English cardinal recruited witnesses to the miracles and invited them to see the pope, expenses paid. Even then some of the English witnesses refused to leave their farms, but a handful finally arrived at Lyons, where they were interrogated by the cardinals dealing with Edmund's canonization. Finally, six years after his death, the archbishop was enrolled among the saints in December 1246 and the bull announcing this was issued in January 1247.

The corpse was translated in June 1247 when, in the words of Richard Wych (himself to become a canonized saint) 'with our own hands we have touched his holy body; his head, with its hair lying thick and uninjured, with a comb we have carefully and reverently, and even joyfully, combed and arranged'.[20] There was another translation in 1249, to a very costly and ornate shrine, and it was probably then that one of the arms was separated and enclosed in a second, portable reliquary; since women were prohibited from entering the precincts of a Cistercian house, part of St. Edmund could now be taken out to them by means of this arm-shaped reliquary. The cult was of continuing interest in England through the thirteenth century and many distinguished people including King Henry III visited the shrine, and penitents, too, were sent there by English ecclesiastics. Local centres of veneration grew up in England, at Catesby, for example, where relics of St. Edmund worked miracles, and at Oxford, where the Bishop of Lincoln had to prohibit pilgrimage to St. Edmund's Well (in modern St. Clement's) in 1290 because of superstitious excesses. The outbreak of the Hundred Years' War between England and France in the fourteenth century, however, curtailed pilgrimage from England—hence an English archbishop became a French saint.[21]

Most of the 209 recipients of Edmund's miracles recorded in the mid-thirteenth century were men, about half of whom were of the lower classes. Approximately a third of the pilgrims were women, virtually all from the lowest social levels. Generally, these were simple, local people; only a relatively small proportion were from the upper classes or the clergy. As in the case of Thomas Cantilupe in England, the fact that the deceased was once a prelate did not automatically mean that many clerics would arrive at the shrine with tales of wonderful cures and other miracles. The same was true of the last thirteenth-century saint to be considered, Louis of Toulouse.

Louis of Toulouse
Life in the streets of medieval Palermo must have been, to say the least, colourful: splendid gowns and beggars' rags, exotic scents and the stench of gutter rubbish, melodic sounds of Arabic, Greek, Sicilian and French, the eternal drone of Church Latin. In 1282 a sordid incident on one of these tumultuous streets led to events which would profoundly change the life of Louis, then about eight years old.[22] A French soldier insulted a Sicilian woman, her husband became enraged, blood was spilled, and before the sun had set a full-scale revolt against the French

ruling house of Anjou was under way. As a result of the 'Sicilian Vespers', as the revolt is called, the island fell into the waiting arms of the Spanish kings of Aragon. In the aftermath Louis, as the son of Charles II an heir to the Angevin kingdom of Naples and county of Provence, was sent as a political hostage to Spain. From about his fifteenth to twenty-first years, at the age when most princes begin to enjoy their powers, Louis of Anjou was carefully guarded and, more than that, he was visited by Franciscans of the fundamentalist camp known as 'Spirituals'. He took their teachings very much to heart.

Returned to his own people by the Aragonese, Louis publicly took minor orders in 1295 (he had done so secretly the year before), which did not please his father King Charles. After his eldest son died leaving Louis next in line, King Charles had even less reason to rejoice in Louis's pious proclivities, but there was a greater shock in store for him. Early in 1296 Louis took the step which excited a great deal of public interest when he firmly renounced all of his rich inheritance; he was ordained a priest in May and by December he was offered the bishopric of Toulouse by Pope Boniface VIII, which he accepted on condition that he be allowed to join the Franciscans. The pope agreed: on Christmas Eve 1296 Louis joined the order and within a week he had also become the Bishop of Toulouse.

The new bishop left Italy and followed the old Roman route toward his episcopal see. At Nîmes, however, with Toulouse 150 miles to the west, he changed his direction and paid a visit to Paris, 350 miles north. At last he retraced his steps and in early May 1297 entered Toulouse. A month later he was in Aragon, the land of his honourable captivity, visiting his sister in Barcelona; he remained there until July. While on this visit he decided to renounce his bishopric. He set out for Rome, following the usual route, via Aix and St. Maximin, but at Brignoles (which was probably his birthplace) he fell ill and died on 19 August 1297, at the age of twenty-three.

A papal canonization commission investigated the case in 1307-8 and in 1317 Louis was ascribed to the calendar of saints. There were several reasons for the success of his canonization. Giving up a rich patrimony was a striking act, one of those uncommon instances of an ideal (Franciscan poverty and simplicity) turned into a reality. Like St. Francis himself, Louis had to suffer his father's wrath, but after his son was dead Charles II lost no time and spared no effort to elevate him to sainthood—it was good policy to have a saint in the family. (In the very year of Louis's death his great-uncle and namesake, a king of France, was canonized, and the name 'St. Louis' usually brings Louis IX, and not the Bishop of Toulouse, to mind.) In addition to family interest another reason behind the successful canonization of 1317 was an old friendship between Louis and James Duèze, who had been a member of

Louis's household in Toulouse. Duèze became Pope John XXII in 1316, and it was he who issued the bulls for the cannonization of 1317. Friendship aside, as John, one of the shrewdest of medieval popes, sat with his French cardinals in his French city of Avignon in the midst of the Angevin lands of Provence, he must have seen the advantages of agreeing to canonize an Angevin saint.

Another reason to consider Louis 'saintly', at least in some quarters, would have been his attempted renunciation of the bishopric, an office hardly inferior to many secular princedoms in material rewards. He may have decided that the spiritual life of Franciscan poverty could not be reconciled with the realities of powerful office which would be forced upon him whether he remained prince or prelate. Perhaps a sense of inadequacy also prompted his decisions to give up the kingdom and diocese. Provence and southern Italy were hardly the most pacific lands to govern, and the large see of Toulouse—which Louis accepted reluctantly, entered unwillingly (by way of Paris) and abandoned speedily after a single month—can scarcely have been a sinecure. Though Louis might be accused of shirking his responsibilities, contemporaries chose to look upon him in a kindlier light.

The body was translated in 1319 to a new and elaborate shrine in the Franciscan church at Marseilles and separate reliquaries received smaller relics of the saint. A *chef*-reliquary is mentioned in 1399, with three keys kept by three different individuals. In 1385 the city fathers discussed a proposal to commission a statue of the saint for one of the main gates of Marseilles. Apparently the value of some of the offerings were not insignificant: King John 'The Good' (d. 1364) had to restrain the Franciscans from selling the jewels dedicated in honour of St. Louis and many sumptuous oblations are recorded, including a golden rose studded with gems given by Louis I of Aragon. So much for Franciscan poverty. The body remained enshrined at Marseilles until 1423 when the Aragonese, who had stormed the walls, were said to have agreed to spare the city in exchange for Louis's remains. Although the corpse—except for an arm—was taken to Valencia, gifts continued to be presented in Marseilles: in 1442 Marie of Anjou vowed 253 *livres* to the saint on behalf of her nine-year-old son (who would one day be known as 'The Spider King', Louis XI of France).[23] Even after 400 years the Franciscans still cherished the memory of the young bishop, for when they founded a mission in the wilds of California in 1772 they called it San Luis Obispo de Tolosa. It is now a pleasant city dominated by what is still known as Bishop's Peak.

The canonization process of 1307-8 has been printed with other pertinent documents including a list numbering 211 but containing in fact 221 posthumous miracles. They are undated but probably occurred in the late thirteenth or early fourteenth century. Louis was well-honoured by the people of Marseilles in whose midst the holy corpse lay. Over half the pilgrims were men and, apart from the usual lower-class majority, the best represented social level was the artisan/ craftsman/merchant, typical of urban shrines. Only William of Norwich claimed a higher proportion of city-dwellers as devotees. There were very few ecclesiastical pilgrims involved in his miracles, in spite of Louis' association with the Church, and there were few upper-class secular pilgrims, whose numbers were unexpectedly low considering the social background of the dead bishop. Evidently prelates and wealthy nobles and titled dames could find other ways to express their interest than by becoming involved in miracles. Although as we have seen they were not illiberal when it came to bestowing gifts, very few joined the simple folk who came to the shrine to give thanks, or to pray, for a miracle.

The records of the posthumous miracles of seven English and two French saints, which we have been examining in this and the last chapter, provide us with information concerning more than 2,300 pilgrims. It is clear that the social and sexual characteristics of the crowds involved in the miracles could differ a great deal from one shrine to the next. For example, there were more women (69%) and more lower-class pilgrims (87%) involved in the miracles of Godric of Finchale than in the miracles of any other saint, and most of these pilgrims were local people. During his life as a hermit Godric limited his attentions to the local inhabitants and apparently the tradition continued after his death. Besides this, Cuthbert, the famous saint of nearby Durham, was as we mentioned not sought out by women, so Godric probably seemed to them to be an acceptable alternative. Of all the saints, Frideswide and Wulfstan were the most 'remote' from their pilgrims. The first died some 400, the second more than one hundred, years before their bones began to work miracles; their personalities had dwindled from memory long before their relics were curing suppliants. In a sense each of their shrines was a *tabula rasa* with no particular social, political or economic associations to affect the interests of pilgrims. Most of the suppliants involved in their miracles were lower-class people, and two-thirds of Frideswide's and just under half of Wulfstan's visitors were women. The upper classes of Church and lay society showed scant interest and the lower clergy and what would some day be known as the 'middle class' were only moderately represented. The same general pattern was observed among the pilgrims at Cantilupe's shrine, but of all the English saints the defunct Bishop of Hereford had fewest ordinary monks and priests among his miracletouched followers.

Becket, Simon de Montfort, and William of Norwich, each of whom died violently, are in a different category. Political, social, and economic interests played a part—beyond the 'religious' and therapeutic— and these 'special interests' are reflected in the people who became involved in their cults. They worked more miracles for the upper classes and clergy than the other saints did, and Becket's pilgrims were very conspicuous in this regard. In the two French cults, however, the miracle-reporting pilgrims at Edmund Rich's shrine at Pontigny conformed very closely to Wulfstan's cult, while Louis of Toulouse resembled Frideswide's in social class distribution, though with relatively fewer female pilgrims.

Given the limitations of the evidence, these shrine-by-shrine comparisons and generalizations may be too ambitious and unenlightening in themselves. Alternatively we may combine all the pilgrims and observe overall patterns as well as the differences between the French and the English suppliants as a whole. In general, nearly two-thirds of the 1,933 English pilgrims (61%) were men. About a third of all English pilgrims were men from the lower classes, another third were lower-class women, and most of the rest of the males of other social groups, the lower clergy being most numerous. To express these differences in another way, most female pilgrims (86%) were of the lowest class, but only slightly more than half of the men (56%) came from this social level. A comparison with the 430 pilgrims from the two selected French cults turns up some interesting figures. In both England and France exactly the same proportion of the sexes was found among the pilgrims (61% men, 39% women); in both England and France exactly the same proportion of all female pilgrims (86%) belonged to the lowest social classes. The miracle-reporting pilgrims of the two countries differed mainly in the fact that French men were more 'lower-class' than English male pilgrims. The similarities firstly as to overall sexual distribution, and secondly in class distribution among the women, suggest that for these two elements at any rate there was a remarkable uniformity of composition among the people who were drawn to curative shrines in France and England. These similarities, it must be emphasized, refer only to the *mass* of miracle-touched pilgrims; as we have seen, the sexual and social make-up of such pilgrims might vary markedly between particular shrines.

It is desirable to know how the social levels observed among the pilgrims were related to the overall structure of medieval society, the make-up of which continues to engage historians in research and controversy. There seems little disagreement about the main features:[24] English society was dominated socially by the nobility and upper clergy, and numerically the lower classes were overwhelmingly superior; in between were the knighthood and lower clergy, with an embryonic 'middle class'. When we set the pilgrims next to this hypo-

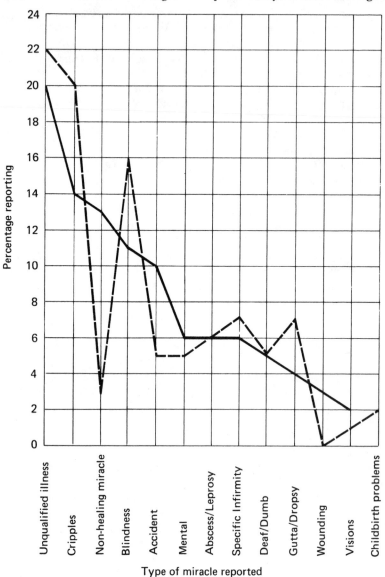

1   Miracles reported by lower-class English men and women in the twelfth and
thirteenth centuries (women = broken line; 645 men, 649 women)

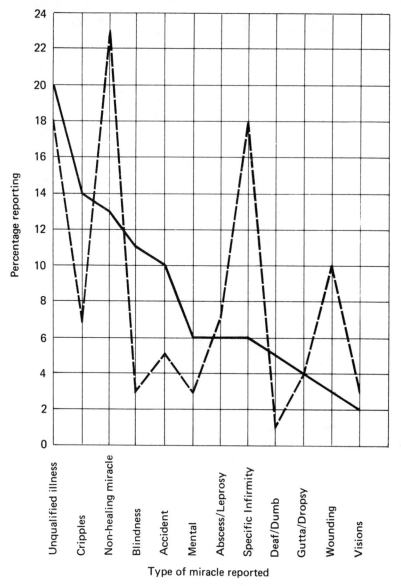

2   Miracles reported by upper- and lower-class English men in the twelfth and thirteenth centuries (upper-class men = broken line; 645 lower-class, 194 upper-class men)

thetical model, it would appear that the English shrines attracted relatively fewer lower-class people than were found in the population generally or, to turn it around, attracted more from the upper social ranks. Participation by priests and monks and other lesser clergy was higher than their numbers in society would warrant and even bishops and abbots, as well as the nobility and knights, were well represented. In France the pilgrim population departed less from the general population than in England, that is, social participation at the two French shrines seems to have followed the general social structure more closely than in England.

'Pilgrims', then, or at least those affected by miracles, can be stereotyped but only in very general terms. Not all saints attracted the same crowds: much depended on the entombed individual, on his influence upon society while still living, on how 'spontaneous' or contrived was the veneration he enjoyed. Saints whose posthumous fame was based solely on a reputation for holiness seem to have drawn a generally lower-class pilgrim crowd in which the sexes were not markedly unequal, but even with saints who exerted special social attraction the lower-class pilgrims constituted at least half of all the recorded suppliants at their shrines; this foundation was present at all the shrines. The recorded pilgrims sometimes turned out to be quite different from what might be expected. From the mere fact that the enshrined individual had held office as bishop, for instance, it did not follow that the clergy participated in his miracles as a matter of course. In addition, the level of clerical participation had very little to do with any official canonization. The officially canonized Bishop Thomas Cantilupe's pilgrims included fewer clergy than any other English saint; William of Norwich, the unfortunate boy found dead in the woods, stirred up much ecclesiastical interest, although he was never canonized. As for 'international' comparisons, though English upper-class men seem to have taken slightly more interest in their saints than their French counterparts, the majority of the suppliants at the French shrines were not significantly different in sexual and social 'profile' from those at similar curative centres in England.

Moving now from social and sexual traits to the events reported at the shrines, let us re-arrange the mass of recorded miracles into the separate categories of our classification system. The first and most obvious point is that the pilgrims seem to have reported, or from their point of view the saints seem to have preferred working, certain types of miracles. The wonders most often reported by the nearly 2,000 pilgrims at the seven major English shrines, disregarding the French saints for now, were cures of unqualified illness, then crippling ailments, then non-healing miracles, and then blindness. The miracles of over half the pilgrims belonged to one of these four categories. If the

English pilgrims are divided by sex (1,176 men, 757 women) and then the type of miracle is considered, we find that the sex of the pilgrim had an effect upon what type of miracle was reported. To ascertain precisely the effect of the pilgrims' sex upon their miracles we should consider only men and women of the same social level. Since most women came from the lower classes, this will be our test group (consisting of men and women from the peasantry, the poor, and the unspecified, to use the terminology of our classification system). When the miracles most often reported by these two numerically equal populations of the same social level are examined (see graph one), it is clear that the incidence of certain miracles—especially those involving the blind, lame, and non-healing events—varied according to the sex of the pilgrim. These findings are limited to lower-class men and women. In order to discover whether there were differences between the social classes similar to those we have found for the sexes, we should compare the miracles of lower-class English men with those reported by upper-class men (that is, members of the nobility, upper clergy, and knights). When this is done (see graph two), it is evident that miracles tended to vary with the social class of the person reporting them, as well as with the sex. From these analyses it would appear that relief from crippling diseases and blindness were associated with the lower-classes, more commonly with women than men, but relatively rarely with upper-class men. On the other hand non-healing miracles and specific infirmities were seldom reported by lower-class women, more frequently by lower-class men, and most often by upper-class men, who also recounted most cases of deliberate violence. Pilgrims of different social classes and sexes reported, and presumably thought they had experienced, distinctive types of miracles.

Why did comparatively more pilgrims from the lower classes suffer crippling and blinding infirmities? Dietary differences probably had their effects since, as we have seen, the food of the peasantry was inferior to that of the well-off in quality and in sheer bulk. As Langland remarked, poor men went hungry while 'the Friars feast on roast venison'.[25] The rich probably ate too much meat and not enough vegetables but the pernicious effects of vitamin deprivation and dietary imbalance were probably more serious among the lower classes. The link between these deficiencies and eye trouble, for instance, was pointed out above, as was the debilitating effect of a winter diet. The quantity of food was also important, and no doubt the poor suffered much more than the rich in times of famine. The poor were also badly sheltered and although the manor-houses and halls of the rich may have been draughty and uncomfortable, they were far superior to flimsy peasant hovels of mud and sticks, some light enough to pick up and carry away. The cold, damp English climate must have affected the health of the families who endured life in these shabby huts, perhaps rendering them especially susceptible to certain complaints such as crippling arthritic attacks. We have also noted that some communicable diseases, such as trachoma, an eye disease, thrive where living-space is insufficient. The differences, then, between the upper and lower classes, as to susceptibility to certain illnesses, can be related to the vastly different standards of living of the two groups. But in addition we noticed further distinctions among the people reporting miraculous cures.

Lower-class women tended to become blind and crippled more frequently than lower-class men. It is not unlikely that some cured pilgrims had been suffering from conversion hysteria, and if modern findings about this illness are applicable to the Middle Ages—but only if so—then women would have suffered hysterical debilities more frequently than men; common symptoms would have been paralysis (in the limbs, for example) and blindness. Even though this would only have affected a limited section of the population of female pilgrims it would help to account for at least some of the observed differences between the sexes. Besides the psychogenic possibilities, perhaps the fact that rheumatic arthritis affects the limbs (but not the spine) more often in women than in men may also account for these findings. Of course men would not have been affected by the trauma of childbirth. Parturition may also have lamed and crippled relatively more lower- than upper-class women; we have cited cases in which women were crippled after giving birth, and well-off ladies would no doubt have received better care. Finally, where food is in short supply, it has been observed that women generally suffer malnutrition more acutely than men, since active males and children are usually given available food with left-overs going to the females.[26] If this was also true in medieval England, then the consequences of malnutrition (which, as we know, may lead to eye diseases among other things) would have been even more common among lower-class women, especially when food was scarce at certain points in the agricultural cycle. In the fourteenth century Langland expressed sympathy for poor women in their hovels who consumed their minute incomes

> on milk and oatmeal to make gruel and fill the bellies of their children who clamour for food. And they themselves are often famished with hunger, and wretched with the miseries of winter.

He ends his lament by suggesting that his readers 'comfort these cottagers along with the blind and the lame'.[27]

We also noted that men reported non-healing miracles more often than women. This was probably a result of the circumstances of such miracles, which often involved rescue at sea, escapes from captivity and similar adventures closely allied to male roles in medieval society. For the same reason men reported more miraculous cures of deliberately-inflicted wounds; about nine out of every ten cases of violence involved men, just as three of every four accidents afflicted the 'stronger' sex. Upper-class men, though small in numbers, were the most common victims of deliberate woundings, perhaps because the bearing and use of arms in war and tourney was not only a noble and knightly prerogative but also, as it were, an occupational hazard. Another peculiarity of the miracles of upper-class males was the highest occurrence of specific diseases. We noted in an earlier chapter that among those who consulted *medici* the upper classes, who could afford the fees, were disproportionately well-represented. Perhaps they reported so many specific diseases at shrines because, even though the doctors may have failed to cure them, they provided their patients with a carefully-formulated diagnosis which the sufferers would have passed on to the registrars at the shrines. In addition, upper-class pilgrims would presumably have been more articulate than most simple peasants; as one registrar commented, he was unable to record the details of some illnesses because of the faulty descriptions provided by illiterate pilgrims.[28]

Non-healing miracles, as noted, were associated with male roles, but this does not explain why the top (male) level of medieval society reported such events more often than any other single category (graph number two). One reason may be the already-discussed greater opportunity which upper-class people had for resorting to alternative sources of healing, especially *medici*. Many were thereby 'filtered out' of the mainstream of therapeutic pilgrimage and when they *did* arrive at the tombs of the holy dead they came not so much for healing but to recount some wonderful tale which had nothing to do with physical debility. Another reason may have been a desire to dissociate themselves from their social inferiors by refusing to acknowledge that they too suffered the same obvious bodily failings and deformities as common peasants. It must have been as evident to the medieval pilgrims who were there at the shrines as it is to anyone who will consult the registrars' reports, that blindness and lameness and contorted limbs were most often associated with low social station.

There may have been another reason for the upper classes to 'prefer' reporting non-healing miracles to cures. In many twentieth-century peasant societies illness is thought to bring shame upon the affected individual, to belittle all his family.[29] In the Middle Ages, *virtus*—manliness—was to the nobleman what *machismo* is to a modern Mexican village headman. To be ill was to admit weakness, shameful imperfection. Sensitivity to shame, if not to sin, was one of the burdens of the *noblesse*. In the twelfth century the Bishop of Clermont arose before a council at Bourges and described how a knight had been miraculously cured of leprosy after spending six months at Canterbury. When the knight was asked to come to the council and confirm the miracle, he refused; he was ashamed to admit that he had once suffered from the disease.[30] This knight's attitude toward leprosy may have similarly encouraged a tendency in other individuals to deny or hide their illnesses, to consult *medici* privately, or to report invisible, specific diseases. They refused to admit the common, manifest ailments, the lameness or open sores or swellings or blindness which lesser beings paraded in the publicity of wonder-working shrines. Of course there were noblemen and knights who suffered from ghastly ulcers and blindness and leprosy, but relatively few of them show up in the records of posthumous miracles. In one of his childish outbursts Aucassin, the thirteenth-century lover of Nicolete, illustrated these social and psychological prejudices. He refused to associate, he ranted, with

> halt old men and maimed, who all day and night cower continually before the altars, and in the crypts; and such folk as wear old mantles and old tattered frocks, and naked folk and shoeless, and covered with sores, perishing of hunger and thirst, and of cold, and of little ease.

He would rather live and even die and roast in Hell with 'the goodly clerks, and goodly knights that fall in tourneys and great wars, and stout men-at-arms, and all men noble'.[31] Here is the flagrant snobbery which made the lower classes so repulsive to the upper, as well as the explicit association of lower-class people with shabby sore-covered folk who crouched at altars and in crypts. Here, too, is the implicit denial that goodly knights and proud nobles were tainted by the common sufferings of mankind, though they might fall wounded in tourneys.

The foregoing comparisons between upper- and lower-class men have excluded the lower clergy, who cannot very easily be ascribed to either social level. In general the lower clergy conformed to the patterns observed for the upper classes: there were relatively few cases of lame or blind priests or monks in the miracle records. The same proportion suffered specific infirmities as found in the upper classes and even more men of the cloth reported unqualified illness than knightly and noble pilgrims. The turbulence of medieval society seldom—in the central Middle Ages in England, anyway—rolled through chancel and cloister; very few priests and monks were victims of physical violence. Another mark of their vocation was evident in the fact that they reported more visions than any other single social class.

Finally, drawing upon the cults of the saints of Pontigny and Marseilles for comparative material, we find that the 430 French pilgrims reported specific infirmity more often than the English simply because of the many cures of fever at the shrine of Louis of Toulouse. Tertian and quartan fever was common in that part of the world. Other than this, the patterns of illness observed among visitors to English shrines are also characteristic of French pilgrims. More women were involved in cures of blindness—and by just the same proportion as in England—and, as in England, more men in non-healing miracles. In general, the observed correlations between social class, sex and miracle type are the same in both countries—at least for the thirteenth century.

The events recorded by registrars at shrines tended to be related to the sex and social classes of the pilgrims. There were many exceptions, but on the whole men and women from different social backgrounds seem to have become involved in miracles in predictably different ways. To recapitulate, after examining some 2,300 alleged miracles we have found that cures involving blindness and crippling ailments were most common among lower-class women, less so among lower-class men and least of all among upper-class men. Non-healing miracles, however, were rare among lower-class women, more evident for lower-class men but most characteristic of all the miracles reported by upper-class men. In addition, lower-class men reported accidents more than other classes, and upper-class men experienced deliberate woundings and specific infirmities more often than lower-class men or women. It is not unlikely that these correlations were generally true for all medieval curative shrines at least during the same medieval centuries. We have suggested a few reasons, environmental, social and psychological, for these differences. That is the overall picture but, as we have seen, particular shrines attracted particular pilgrims, and these suppliants experienced characteristic miracles. In addition there was a distinguishable geographical 'field of participation' around each shrine. Having established who our pilgrims were and what miracles they believed they experienced, we shall now find out where they came from.

Chapter 9

Maps and Miracles:
The Geography of Pilgrimage

The divinity of our Lord and Saviour Jesus Christ,
being famed abroad among all men, in consequence of
his wonder-working powers, attracted immense
numbers.

Eusebius

Eleanor of Alnwick was tormented by illness for months until she
learned that two of her neighbours, one deaf and the other partially
paralysed, had been cured by the holy corpse of Gilbert of
Sempringham. She made her candle and her vow, went to the tomb,
and she too was cured. As Thomas of Monmouth put it, 'The frequent
success of those who had gone before, invited others to favourable
expectations.'[1] It is clear that the spread of news about miracles was
essential to the development of popular cults. But how and by whom
was such lore broadcast? who were the potential or passive and who the
active, carriers or agents? what were their motives?

At its simplest, someone unexpectedly stumbled across a fledgling
curative cult and then carried the news to others, often their relatives,
at home. One man, for example, had heard about Becket's miracles
while travelling about on business, and Lady Mabel de Bek learned of
William's wonders when passing through Norwich on her way home. In
several cases the miraculous healing of one family member was
followed by that of others, like the two children cured of blindness
after their aunt returned from Hereford with exciting stories of
Cantilupe's wonderful powers. Tales of miracles passed round the
family circle and made each member a potential enthusiast, but when a
saint was also related by blood, marriage or friendship, family interest
knew no bounds.[2] 'Family' in the wider sense included retainers, and
the master-servant relationship was another channel for news of curative shrines. The seneschal of Battle Abbey, miraculously healed by
William of Norwich, came home, found his miller ill and recommended
a pilgrimage to the Norfolk city. Sometimes news about miracles went
from lower to higher social levels within the 'extended family': a

Pembroke knight followed his reeve's example in seeking saintly aid and a Lincoln matron acted upon similar advice from her own serving-girl.[3]

The news of miraculous relics often, but by no means always, came into villages in this way, brought by individuals to their families, and then there was a chain-reaction from one family to the next. In the close-knit society of the English village, where gossip was—and is—the stuff of social life, anything unusual in an individual or family could not be kept secret for long. News of a miraculous cure flew from hovel to cottage to manor-house and the claims of the latest 'saint' were soon acknowledged by many of the village folk and became common knowledge. When a woman returned to her village in the thirteenth century after being cured at a shrine everyone rushed out to look at her as if she had returned from the dead; after a drowned boy's revival, his parents lost no time in passing the news along to their neighbours, *immediate miraculum convicinis eorum puplicantes*. Serious illness and other life crises, though personal, were not particularly private. The sickbed or accident scene buzzed with friends and neighbours, some of whom would later testify at a shrine or before a papal commission about the miracle they saw when they called down the saint to ease the pains, or restore the life, of a fellow villager. One man struck down by illness was advised 'by his friends' to put his trust in Becket; elsewhere friends crept into a sick-chamber to suggest that candles be sent to William of Norwich.[4]

A whole village sometimes supplied witnesses to miracles, or so the registrars claimed. The 'whole island of Thanet', for instance, reportedly came to Evesham to verify a cure of Simon de Montfort; of course in most cases such expressions are not to be taken literally. In England generations of villagers were used to sending three or four of their number—usually of the more substantial sort—to various courts and meetings to represent 'the whole village'. A parish priest, for example, arriving to give evidence of a miracle, was accompanied by the more respectable villagers, *majoribus et melioribus villae*, a phrase which would not have been out of place in a writ for a local inquest before the sheriff. More than one village could easily become involved in a single miracle. After a young girl 'drowned' one Sunday in a tavern garden but later revived thanks to Cantilupe her overjoyed father swept her up and rode toward Hereford, accompanied by several villagers. Others joined them as they passed through one village after another; even the Hereford people came out (for the news had preceded the party) to greet the girl 'brought back from death'. Few villagers along that route could have been ignorant of Cantilupe's powers after that. After a French boy had been reputedly snatched from the arms of death by saintly intervention, the bells of his village church rang so energetically that the clangour disturbed three nearby villages; in another case the bells of Hereford Cathedral and of all the surrounding village churches and chapels rang out as news of a wonderful cure spread into the countryside.[5]

As a saint's fame grew, so would his successes within particular villages, even to the point of stimulating two or more villagers to experience a miracle. In William's cult, for example, eight villages outside Norwich boasted more than one miracle-touched resident, and about sixty-three villages and towns outside Canterbury and London and twenty-eight places in France witnessed at least two (sometimes several) instances of Becket's miraculous virtues. In some cults the closer the village was to the shrine the stronger was the saint's influence: three-fourths of all the places containing at least two cured villagers were less than twenty miles from Godric's tomb at Finchale.

Villagers may also have had special ties with saints. Becket once carried out a confirmation service at Newington about eighteen miles west of Canterbury. After his death the place became a secondary curative centre where at least fifteen miracles were supposed to have occurred. The village-saint relationship was expressed in various ways. A cripple from a village belonging to the Worcester monks remained at Wulfstan's shrine several days without a cure. Addressing the saint he complained, 'Was I not born and raised on the land of your church? You cure foreigners and strangers daily' but not, he continued, 'your special servant.'[6]

Such villages were sources of propaganda for a saint. Strangers to the village market-place or ale-house might overhear—or perhaps be told—the story of local people who had been blessed with a miracle, or perhaps someone would be pointed out whose miracle was *notorium in parochia*, as one Cantilupe witness put it. Places, too, became magically endowed with miraculous associations: strangers in a certain French village were shown 'the well where Ernulphus was drowned' and had been revived by saintly assistance.[7]

Those who learned such things in the villages through which they passed would themselves become potential agents for the wider dissemination of a holy cult. Some travellers were more involved than others in this labour of love and hope. They were the active, as opposed to the passive, carriers, of whom perhaps the most effective—because they were the most enthusiastic—were those people who had personally experienced a miracle. A certain Henry who had a relative among the monks of Rievaulx spent all day telling them about his wonderful cure at Godric's tomb. That regrettable weakness, a compulsion to tell others about one's medical experiences, was utilized by medieval monks who encouraged such eager folk to remain a few days at the shrine as living proof of the saint's powers. Afterwards they set off to tell anyone who would listen about their happy encounter with the other world. Some already-cured pilgrims played even more active roles, like the stranger passing through a particular village who was drawn by the sounds of lamentation to the side of a 'dying' child. He recommended that she be given water from Canterbury; after all, it had cured *him*—of insanity.[8] Many miracles were suggested by such 'strangers' who happened by, and in so doing stimulated yet another village to rely upon the new saint. These strangers need not all have been personally cured, and many an outsider, *ignotus quidam*, simply offered the recommendation he had heard from others on his travels.[9] On the other hand a few pilgrims who discovered that their 'cures' were merely temporary could be found bewailing their misfortune up and down the public roads.[10]

The records sometimes illustrate the peaceful chance encounters among wayfarers, striking up conversation as they walked or rode along.[11] In the usual search for apt topics for discussion, the latest saint would be a natural selection. A knight and cleric would exchange greetings as well as news of Becket's miracles; a party of Welshmen going home told an abbot about the cures of Canterbury; a crippled cleric met some prelates while travelling in France and as a result of their conversation he eventually found himself giving thanks at Pontigny for his miraculous cure.[12]

The people who spread the word about saintly deeds were of all sorts and conditions, the merchant on his business rounds, the homeward-bound miller cured at a shrine who launched into praise of the new saint whenever he had the chance, the peasant who passed some strangers as he plodded toward the village market and overheard wondrous rumours of the dead resuscitated and the crippled unbent. The higher the social status of the teller of the tale the more weight his words carried whether he repeated his story on the road for the benefit of strangers or at the side of the holy dead, at the shrine itself. Becket's scribe, William of Canterbury, as we know, expected beggars to be liars and the nobility to tell the truth. In fact, whether he spoke wild lies or uttered truths upon a Bible, to a registrar the miracle of a single nobleman was worth a dozen dead and revived peasant children. In the matter of propaganda, it meant a great deal if a nobleman or a knight was on one's 'side'. In addition, the greater wealth of the upper classes provided them with the mobility which was very important in developing a new cult. For example, a knight who was healed by Godric (he was one of the few knights involved in the cult) told his story to other knights at a royal residence (*palatio regis*) after which they all devoted themselves to the dead hermit of Finchale. Matthew, Count of Boulogne, was at the Canterbury shrine with his entourage when he overheard a Berkshire knight report a miracle.

News of the wonderful event went back to France with them.[13]

In a few of the Cantilupe miracles these movements in the upper echelons can actually be traced. A knight took his falcon to the Hereford shrine and told the story of its miraculous cure, in the hearing of the Earl of Cornwall and other noblemen preparing to go into Wales, and in their presence a cleric with crippled hands was healed. The nobles and their men then went off to attack Dryslwyn Castle. During the course of the siege one of the knights was hit under one eye with an arrow and part of a wall fell and crushed several others, burying one unfortunate warrior under the rubble so that only his feet were visible. These calamities were alleviated, however, by prayers to Thomas Cantilupe.[14] It is unlikely that the wounded and upended knights—or their friends—would have thought of Cantilupe had they not seen and remembered the miracles of the clergyman and the knight's falcon, nor is it likely that they would soon forget them.

These examples suggest that unqualified statements about the 'growth of the cult' of a saint may be misleading, suggesting that such 'growth' was an abstract, even automatic, process unrelated to the society in which it occurred. The awareness of curative cults was not silently and mysteriously communicated to peasants in their huts or to knights in their halls, but was physically carried to them by living individuals. Who these individuals were, and how far they travelled, to a great degree determined the effective limits of a curative cult.

Prelates, clerics and monks were more important than the laity in spreading news of miracles because of their influence over the spiritual welfare of laymen, their literacy, and their more efficient channels of communication. Naturally news of miracles was thickest in the air at the centre of a cult, near the entombed saint. The clergy who manned these centres were usually quite willing to have the bells rung and a *Te Deum* sung after a miracle. Solemn announcements of miracles could be heard now and then above the murmuring crowds of ill and healthy travellers in the nave or round the holy shrine. After letters confirming a miracle were received at Lincoln, for instance, a procession was formed and the cured woman was led to the tomb while the cathedral bells rang out and the faithful offered up their joyous prayers. A public announcement about the miracle followed. Pilgrims who did not witness miracles or join in the liturgical jubilation which followed them could, if literate, turn to the written accounts of saintly wonders which were hanging up near many shrines.[15]

Just as the members of a family were all involved in the miraculous experience of any one of them, so all the members of spiritual 'families' such as monasteries were equally involved. At an early stage in William's cult seven persons associated with the Norwich priory were affected by miracles or visions, one after another; two monks even experienced a second miracle. Just as demons might infect entire religious communities, saints could cure several inmates at once. Of fifty-five recorded miracles attributed to Gilbert of Sempringham's bones, sixteen involved Gilbertine nuns, monks or dependents. We can identify two or three members of St. Frideswide's priory at Oxford, and four from the great monastery of Reading, reporting miraculous interventions of Thomas Becket. These self-stimulative tendencies in monasteries and cathedrals were sometimes jogged by the recital of miracles in chapter. After a knight was cured he told his story in the Lincoln cathedral chapter-house, *in publica audientia*, and another miracle was made known *multitudine cleri et populi in capitulo Lincolniensi*; after which a canon from another house, present in chapter, added his own report of a miracle. The chapter-house was, among other things, a place where the beliefs and expectations of tonsured and lay auditors were confirmed and guided, as the nave was for *hoi poloi*. This applied to other tales as well: the abbot of Bury was so impressed by a vision described to him by a passer-by that he 'told the story in full Chapter with some sharp comments'.[16] Monastic and cathedral institutions were important, then, because knowledge of miracles was instantly carried to all members who in turn communicated such information to lay and ecclesiastical visitors (unless perhaps a new saint might rival their 'own').

Some individual clergymen were very active indeed in spreading the good news, not necessarily about saints of their own diocese or house. Secular priests, who usually got out and about more than regulars (monks), sometimes appeared at shrines with two, three or four different miracles to report. Henry of Houghton, a priest, knew of two and Ralph of Froyle four miracles credited to Becket; a rector reported two cures involving himself, one of his cow and another of a pet bird belonging to a local noblewoman. When such individuals reported multiple miracles it is possible that they themselves had suggested the ghostly remedy in the first place. Paulinus, a priest of Leeds, witnessed a blind girl's cure at York in June, 1171; a few days later a blind man who had lodged with Paulinus was also cured at St. William's tomb at York. Shortly afterward a man with internal afflictions was healed there and the affair was witnessed by—Paulinus the priest of Leeds.[17]

The clergy popularized cults in other ways, for instance by making saints' relics available to their parishioners. Just as families treasured relics and passed then down as heirlooms, parish churches (and of course cathedrals and monasteries) stored up relics too. Sometimes, it is true, parish priests were rather over-protective and tight-fisted with their thaumaturgic possessions.[18] Customarily ampoules of Canterbury water were suspended in churches as relics, *in ecclesiis pro reliquiis sanctis suspendunt*, to be taken down and rushed to the dying or ill as needed.[19] One twelfth-century rural pastor had a church or oratory about eight miles from Canterbury, in which he used to hang the *ampullae* brought back by his parishioners from Becket's shrine (at that distance the availability of such relics may have lowered their value if not their curative powers, hence his 'collection'). Some of them he thought less full than they ought to have been, no doubt because of evaporation, so he poured out what was left of all of them into a basin, added 'ordinary' holy water from the church supply, refilled them, and then hung them up out of reach. No one would know the difference, anyway.[20] Such supplies of Canterbury water were kept in monasteries as well, for example at Reading, where a monk was cured through its virtues, at the Premonstratensian house of St. John of Croxton and at a great many other religious houses both English and foreign. Besides collecting their relics, the clergy also encouraged saint-veneration by dedicating altars to them, as the Archbishop of Rouen did for Becket at Barfleur.[21] More directly, they advertised the cult and miracles by means of the spoken word, through preaching.

The sermon, more and more common in later medieval England, was often very close to the realities of village life. We have seen that mothers were warned about crushing their infants, and so on. The priest might also inject an element of levity or entertainment into his spiritual instruction, perhaps assisted by one of the many collections of amusing but moralistic sermon-tales or *exempla*. It was standard form to embellish miracle stories if this would keep the flock from dozing. The recitation of miracles in sermons was hardly a novelty in the thirteenth century, since St. Augustine of Hippo and Ambrose of Milan were doing it about nine hundred years ealier. Some of the English miracles suggest that a sermon was going on in the background, as it were. A Berkshire knight lay at home ill in bed with a swollen arm on 3 January 1171, a Sunday, when

> the lady of the house, having come home from church, broke out in gentle weeping. The knight, supposing that she was weeping out of sympathy for him, chided her in soothing language, declaring that the scourge of the Lord was good for him; he would be able to escape it when it pleased the Divine Pity. But the woman replied in these words: 'It is not, most beloved lord, it is not as you think. I am disturbed not only on your account, but I mourn for our father and the father of the whole realm, that is the Lord Canterbury, who was slain in his church with the swords of the most villainous conspiritors.'

And she then explained everything she had heard. No doubt many congregations, as in this village some 115 miles from Canterbury, heard the news of the martyrdom from the local priest on this first Sunday after the murder. Becket remained to the end of the Middle Ages the 'national hero among the saints of the English pulpit'.[22]

We may contrast the foregoing example of a simple village priest passing along news of Becket's death, with the following impressive exposition of one of St. Wulfstan's posthumous miracles. The resuscitation of a dead child at Wulfstan's tomb at Worcester (in 1220/21) having been investigated and proven to the satisfaction of Bishop William of Blois, a solemn procession was formed from the cloister into the church. Then, as it was Sunday, the mitred bishop himself followed. The procession ended, silence fell, and the bishop preached at length about the miracle. Afterwards he came down into the nave and briefly narrated the miracle to the royal justices who were holding court in the western part of the cathedral church. And then, beginning a *Te Deum* with a sonorous voice, the bishop processed with all the people to Wulfstan's shrine to give thanks to God.[23] When cures occurred, or as in the foregoing case were proven, on Sundays or feastdays, they naturally became known to an augmented congregation. It is clear that in the early history of most cults miracles tended to 'bunch up' on these special days, when more people were present. Although preaching about miracles is documented in many English (and in the French) cults, the sermons were not necessarily based upon recent miracles. Lessons read on major feastdays might include an account of a few famous miracles attributed to the commemorated saint, and these same events were repeated year after year. Preaching, to sum up, reinforced belief at cult centres and introduced the saint and his miracles to more distant congregations. In addition to the spoken word, however, the clergy had at their command an even more powerful tool for influencing opinion.

The advantages of clerical literacy were heightened by a network of communication which spread, in theory, from the pope to the lowliest vicar and then through all ranks of lay society. An abbot in Yorkshire could send a letter to a sister-house in Provence and expect it to be duly received and considered, perhaps in chapter, in 'the usual manner'. Few secular rulers could hope for the same, on such a wide scale. These letters from the clergy flew above and beyond the limited horizons of the peasantry who relied on the spoken vernacular, not the written Latin, word. Within the two spheres the same ends were attained but at different rates and by different means. Letters about saints and miracles aroused interest not merely in nearby regions but across whole territories, between realms. In Becket's cult there was a flurry of letter-writing on both sides of the Channel, French prelates reporting local miracles ascribed to Becket, English churchmen writing to encourage the cult among their French colleagues. One such letter went from Canterbury to the abbot of St. Remi in France and then to the convent at Mt. Dieu where one of the brethren read it and cured himself by applying it to his body. Nor was it merely single letters. Odo, once prior of Canterbury, sent a copy of William's whole collection of Becket's miracles to the Cistercians of Igny in France; this was lost so he sent a second collection (this time the one made by Benedict) which was in turn copied and sent on to other French monasteries.[24]

Looking for a moment at a small selection from the corpus of printed letters for Becket's cult, the prior and convent of Canterbury or sometimes the archbishop and even individual monks, received letters about miracles from, for example, the abbot of Welford (Sulby), the Bishop of Norwich, Reading monks, the abbot of Shrewsbury, a chaplain of Luton, the dean of Gloucester cathedral, the Bishop of Glasgow or his archdeacon, a member of the house at Much Wenlock, clergy of Exeter cathedral, abbots of French houses, Pontius, Bishop of Clermont, Hugh, Bishop of Durham, Richard, Bishop of Coventry, the prior and convent of Taunton, Robert, Prior of St. Frideswide's, the abbot of Derby, the treasurer of Lisieux cathedral, and so on. We must imagine the registrars receiving these letters and adding or copying them, often without comment, into their lists of miracles. In one of the French accounts of a miracle the writers ended by pleading 'that you cause this to be written down among the miracles of the precious martyr'.[25] And so it was. John of Salisbury exchanged several letters about Becket's *cultus* and miracles with French prelates in 1171 and 1172. When he moved to France as Bishop of Chartres he wrote to Canterbury between 1177 and 1179 to report a miracle he himself brought about with one of Becket's relics.[26] People wrote about other miracle-working saints as well, but there is no collection—for an English saint, at any rate—to match the letters which have survived for Becket. The importance of the letter-writing clergy and occasionally the laity (including English kings at times) cannot be overestimated. Their messages not only spread the news of miracles to distant regions and educated audiences, they also moved the saints within the range of a papal canonization.

An awareness of miracles at a particular place was broadcast in these diverse ways, from simple villager to villager, parish priest to town-dweller and up and down the ecclesiastical ladder in England and abroad. The result of this activity was the development of an area around each shrine within which tales of miracles worked by the holy dead became common knowledge. By tracing pilgrims back to their towns and villages and plotting these sites on a map we can obtain a rough picture of the region which included most of the people directly involved in the miracles of a particular cult (as it stood when the list of posthumous wonders was completed). It is not always easy to locate the places the pilgrims lived. What the editor of Becket's miracles said about this is just as true for the other cults examined in the present study:

> The attempt to identify the places which are mentioned in the miracu-
> lous narratives . . . has cost me very considerable labour; but this labour
> has often been vain, and has no doubt often resulted in mistakes, for
> which . . . I have to beg the reader's indulgence.[27]

There is often no mention of an origin, or the origin is sometimes
indicated in general terms, as 'from Suffolk' or 'of France'; sometimes
it is difficult or impossible to locate certain places even when a name is
given because such a place has ceased to exist or more often because
more than one place of the same name exists or once existed, or
because orthographical changes have made indentification questionable. The approximate proportion of pilgrims' origins we have managed
to locate (including cases in which distance but not site is known) will
be noted in each cult. Distances between origin-sites and shrines are
expressed in simple linear terms, without regard for actual travelled
distances. In this attempt to establish a geographical field of participation around each of the major cults we begin with that of William of
Norwich.

Most of William's miracles were reported by local folk. More than
half (57%) of his recorded pilgrims (94% located) lived less than ten
miles from the shrine and most of these came from the city of Norwich
itself. After ten miles or so there was a sharp decline in pilgrims'
villages. This decline continued until, at a distance of about fifty miles,
very few individuals felt sufficient thaumaturgic radiation from the
child's bones to experience a cure or undergo a pilgrimage to seek one.

William's is one of the few cults in which we can trace the changing
geographical pattern in time as well as in space. Thanks to Thomas of
Monmouth's extraordinary affection for the dead boy the body was
translated several times, and each translation can be dated and the
miracles then assigned to periods between successive translations.
When this is done it becomes evident that, as time passed, the average
distance between pilgrim-villages and the shrine increased. People came
from more and more distant places. In 1150-1 the average was twenty-
three miles; in the period 1151 to 1154 it rose to thirty-two miles, and
for the long stretch between 1154 and 1172 the average distance had
increased to forty-five miles, twice the original average. In determining
the above figures only pilgrims extraneous to Norwich were considered. By asking whether more pilgrims came from Norwich or from
outside the city over these same periods, we find that in each successive
stretch between translations fewer and fewer people who lived in the
city of Norwich became involved in the miracles of the saint. At the
peak, in 1150-1 when Thomas of Monmouth's efforts were first rewarded by public interest, two-thirds of those concerned in the
wonders were Norwich denizens. By the last period, however, less than
one-third of the pilgrims actually lived in Norwich, the majority being

'outsiders'. These figures, if plotted on a graph, will show a constantly declining participation-level on the part of Norwich citizens over the years. And as the folk touched by miracles tended to shift from the city there was also a concomitant shift in their social classes, from urban workers to rural peasantry, from shoemakers to shepherds.

These findings may be taken as demonstrating the expanding sphere of attraction around the shrine over the years, drawing more and more distant folk into the cult. This may indeed explain some of the shifts, but it is hardly realistic to suggest that—even in the barbarous state of medieval communications—it took several years for news to travel some thirty or forty miles into the countryside. There is another reason: a decline of interest at the centre of the cult. Perhaps after a few years the new saint, having ceased to be a novelty, no longer excited Norwich citizens in whose midst he resided in his easily-accessible shrine and therefore no longer worked wonders for them. The same circumstances have been observed at a modern shrine where,

> except for the original cures, Lourdes has failed to heal those who live in its vicinity. This suggests that the emotional excitement connected with the preparatory period and journey to the shrine may be essential for healing to occur.

And the immediate neighbourhood provided no 'patients' among the possessed girls said to be cured in a cave in modern Spain.[28]

There is little doubt that the *frequency* of Norwich miracles declined steeply after the outburst of 1150-1 stimulated by Thomas of Monmouth and other cathedral officials. The wonders of William dropped from about one every ten days to one every five months or so, though these are averages and can only give a very general impression. Summing up, then, between about 1150 and the end of the 1170s, diminishing numbers of Norwich people were involved in William's miracles as more outsiders tended to show up in the records. At the same time, fewer and fewer miracles reached the ears of Thomas of Monmouth. In this sense, at least, the cult languished and nearly died out.

To pass to the next saint is to move from small things to great, from a one-city cult to one which attracted notice throughout England and in foreign lands as well. At first glance Becket's widespread fame would seem by its very magnitude to present insuperable problems. If the whole of Christendom acknowledged him, can a geographical pattern be identified for all those masses of pilgrims? Sympathy for Becket, or at least knowledge of his plight, had affected Christians from one end of Europe to the other, so that the emotional reaction to his death has the appearance of being spontaneous, after which miracles occurred everywhere at once. Nearly every British town of any size from Dover to Scotland contributed pilgrims, sometimes several pilgrims, to the two miracle collections. In addition, no other cult involved so many 'foreign' visitors. Nearly a third were external, most of them from northern France. Many French prelates, as we have seen, exchanged news about the miracles and some of their enthusiasm must have rubbed off on their associates as well as on the laymen whose souls were within their jurisdiction. The social status of the laymen who came from other lands was, on the whole, higher than that found among English lay pilgrims, another way of saying that people from distant parts tended to come from higher social ranks (in Becket's cult at any rate). Many places in France such as Clermont, Eu, Liseux, Poitiers, Pontigny, and Rouen sent three or more cured visitors to Becket's tomb. Northern France contributed many pilgrims because of geographical proximity to Dover and because of the associations between the northern regions (Becket's ancestors were Norman) and Becket as Chancellor as well as exiled archbishop. He left behind him scores of relics and after his death any French church possessing such treasures was quick to make use of them.

We have discussed the importance of the dispersal of relics in the fortunes of a cult. In Becket's case this is obvious. English churches and monasteries came almost as a matter of routine to possess—or be expected to possess—the Canterbury ampoules, and they found their way to the continent as well. Each phial, when carried about as a talisman, was in effect a perambulatory shrine. Whether stationary or not, the pious might use Canterbury water as a source of miraculous virtue instead of travelling to Canterbury. Rather than postulating ever-widening circles of influence growing outward from Becket's shrine, a better model includes many intermediate epicycles representing places where several cures were wrought, often by the miraculous water. Other Becket-relics had the same effect, like those carried home by a Cheshire nobleman which were credited with no fewer than twenty-two miracles at Whitchurch, on the Welsh border. This must have happened at many other places in England and abroad. Chapels and crosses erected in Becket's honour were as effective as material relics: a French knight cured at Becket's shrine went home and built an oratory in the martyr's name; that very night a paralysed woman was cured and over 300 local folk came to marvel at the miracle. Cures happened, too, at the small altars or *aediculae* mentioned by pilgrims, wayside shrines on the route to Canterbury, as well as at places associated with events in the archbishop's life such as Newington, mentioned earlier.[29] These circumstances make it difficult to recognize a 'pattern' among the pilgrims since there were so many ways to broadcast Becket's cult and they were all in play at the same time. Another complication arises from Church support. No other saint could number so many bishops, abbots or other highly-placed church-men among his followers, actively exchanging letters, relics and accounts of miracles.[30] The significance of the letter-writing campaign is obvious. An immobile little clique of Norwich monks, for instance, might be able to interest the local city people in William's cult, but their powers were limited. It made a great deal of difference whether a cult was supported by ten monks or ten bishops, and Becket's fell into the latter class. Becket also claimed a high proportion of the upper social levels among the laity, precisely those elements in medieval society with greatest wealth, mobility and influence outside the Church.

Although this cult is complicated, with great interest shown by the *literati*, with French associations, with several secondary shrines and an abundance of relics circulating from one end of Europe to the other, still it is possible, by examining the 700-odd pilgrims listed by Benedict and William, to reach certain conclusions about the geographical patterns of participation built up around the English Delphi, Canterbury.

Subtracting all pilgrims for whom no origin is given (99) and all those whose origins cannot be pinpointed on a map (71) leaves 531 individuals. About a third of them (171) came from places outside the British Isles, leaving 360 recorded British men, women and children who were personally involved in a Becket miracle, and whose places of origin are known. Generally speaking, more than half (56%) came from south-eastern England, hardly surprising since this was the most highly-populated area of the country. But the localization even in this great cult is striking: one-quarter of all of the recorded British pilgrims originated in Kent or Canterbury itself. After Kent the greatest numbers of pilgrims came from London, followed by Berkshire and Oxfordshire, Sussex, Essex and Suffolk. There were relatively fewer pilgrims from more distant counties such as Devon, Somerset, Cornwall, Hereford, Shropshire, Durham and Northumberland, though York contributed rather more than the other northern, midland and western regions.

Within England, then, although many cured pilgrims travelled many days to pray at the tomb, most of them came from areas at no great distance from Canterbury, many from Kent itself. In this respect Becket's cult was not much different from many others. As mentioned, many bystanders dipped cloths and fingers into the archbishop's blood at the cathedral on the night of the murder and later wrought cures with these relics. These Canterbury people, a short walk from their homes in Ruttington Lane or Monastery Street, were the first modest ripples before the tidal wave of the later 1170s. On the other hand, even from the very first there were indications of the long-distance influence of the cult. As early as the fourth day after his death, Becket's power

2 Places containing two or more individuals affected by the miracles of Thomas Becket in the twelfth century (open circles = two individuals, solid circles = three or more)

wrought a cure in Gloucester, about 170 miles away, and next day someone in Berkshire, 115 miles distant, felt the dead archbishop's healing hand.[31]

The pilgrims did not, therefore, come 'from everywhere' to become involved in Becket's thaumaturgy. Nor did the excitement reach all parts of Christendom at once. It is true that relatively few of the miracles were dated either by Benedict or William, but Benedict, who began writing a year earlier than William, tried through the first few months at least to keep his records in chronological order. From an examination of the first 100 entries in Benedict's list (which brings us to about mid-May 1171) it is clear that there was at first a noticeable degree of localization, with twenty-two pilgrims coming from Canterbury and seventeen more from the rest of Kent, a total of thirty-nine 'local' pilgrims out of 100. Only a single person among those with an identifiable origin was 'foreign'. William's later list presents a different picture: at least nineteen of the first hundred pilgrims were 'foreign' and only eleven originated in Kent and Canterbury. We already know a thing or two about William and will not be surprised to see him preferring the foreign to the local visitor. Although he listed not quite twice as many pilgrims as Benedict, in total, William included seven times as many foreigners. In addition to illuminating William's prejudices, however, these differences probably also indicate a real shift away from purely domestic participation—evident in Benedict's earlier compilation—to European interest in the cult.

As noted in an earlier chapter, there was a shift in the social levels among the pilgrims from the lower, during the first few months, to the upper at a later stage in the cult's development. While this was going on the geographical origins of Becket's suppliants were also changing, moving outward from the immediate vicinity of his simple tomb and eventually involving, as the twelfth-century monk wrote, 'the whole world'.

The pilgrims who visited Godric's tomb at Finchale, like those at William's shrine at Norwich, were local people. Nearly all of them (89% of the two hundred-odd pilgrims with known origins) came from villages within forty miles of Finchale, but, unlike William's followers they were more evenly spread over the Durham countryside (graph number three). There was a heavy concentration of William's pilgrims in Norwich and then an abrupt decline as the city was left behind. In Godric's case there was also a decline, but a far smoother, gradual and regular one, which suggests a relatively constant diminution of interest or enthusiasm at increasing distances from the shrine. Both were local cults but Godric's was, if it may be put this way, less local.

A chronological framework is absent from Godric's miracles but by

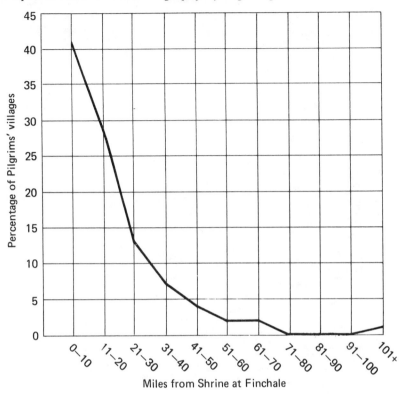

3   Geographical distribution of 204 pilgrims' villages in a 'local' twelfth-century
cult (Godric of Finchale)

assuming that they were recorded more or less in order of occurrence—
the compiler uses no obvious system of categorization—then at least
their sequence may be of some help. Examining the miracles as they are
listed, it would appear, first of all, that there was no significant
difference between the average distances of the earlier, and of the later,
pilgrims. It cannot be shown, in other words, that earlier pilgrims came
from local villages, later pilgrims from distant ones, the sort of thing
noted for William and even Becket. The second point is that there was a
shift in the proportion of male to female pilgrims. When the cult started
out in 1172, the majority of the pilgrims were women (forty-four out
of the first fifty listed) but gradually the ratio changed. More and more
men appeared until, among the last fifty pilgrims, men outnumbered
women (thirty to twenty). It may be that women, having found an
alternative to the unkind misogynist St. Cuthbert of Durham, led the

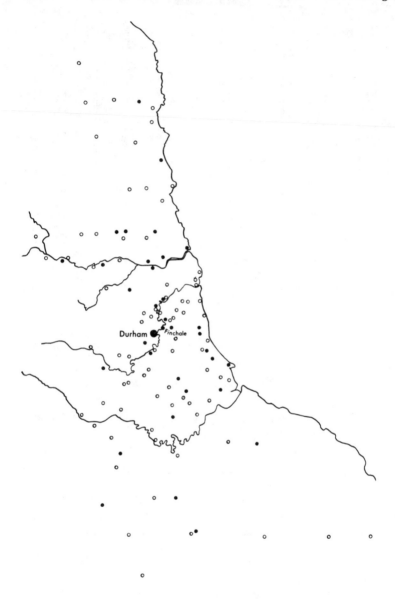

3   A local cult: Godric of Finchale (open circles = town or village with one person affected by Godric's miracles, solid circles = two or more people affected)

way and that men turned to Godric after several cures had demonstrated to them that the cult was no mere flight of female fancy.

Regardless of changing levels of participation, the majority of Godric's pilgrims were women and most of his suppliants were indigenous northerners whose very names recall their mixed Anglo-Scandinavian past: Acke, Addoc, Brictiva, Crin, Eccoc, Goda and Iggus, Sungiva and Thoke, Tunnoc and Ulfkill. Their villages lay between the Pennines and the sea, and not much more than forty miles to the north and south of the Finchale shrine. Godric's miracle-working powers never seem to have reached much beyond this northern region. The cult remained simple, local, unpretentious—like the hermit himself.

There is little to be gained by a detailed study of Frideswide's or Wulfstan's cults. Both were local, drawing upon nearby villages for most of their pilgrims. Half of Frideswide's visitors lived twenty miles or less from her shrine, three-quarters less than forty miles. In Wulfstan's case there is very little evidence to go on since over half his pilgrims had either no stated origins or were described in very vague terms. Of the few who can be traced back to particular villages and towns it seems that—as in Frideswide's cult—three-quarters lived less than forty miles from Worcester. Mere physical or geographical descriptions cannot, of course, tell the whole story about these two or indeed about any of the other cults. Frideswide continued to be mentioned in a variety of documents up to the fifteenth century and Wulfstan became an officially-approved saint, to be remembered by the Church Universal on his feast day. But in their beginnings there was nothing remarkable in their cults or their recorded pilgrims.

When we turn to Simon de Montfort's cult, there are reasons for expecting more unusual geographical patterns since the circumstances of his popular 'canonization' were hardly routine. Political interests, which ran like a minor chord through Becket's posthumous career, have in Simon's come to the fore as a major theme. Much of this political propagandizing has been mentioned in earlier chapters, as well as the deliberate comparisons of Simon with Becket. In addition Simon's was a cult in which more men participated than women, many of these males coming from the upper classes and the ranks of the Church. Against such a background, does the pattern of pilgrim-origins (just over half mapped) show anything of these influences? In the first place, though more pilgrims lived within twenty than within forty miles of the shrine as in 'local' cults generally, the differences were negligible. There was no great concentration around Evesham with a gradual decline over increasing distances. In the second place, *most* of Simon's pilgrims lived *more* than forty miles from his tomb. In every cult so far examined (except Becket's) most pilgrims came from places *less* than forty miles from the shrines. Though he was buried in their midst, many of the anti-royalist knightly and noble families of the immediate area probably chose to honour Simon with prudent reserve. The *Dictum de Kenilworth* called for an end to his cult in no uncertain terms and many people were unwilling to risk royal displeasure or ill-treatment at the hands of roving, victorious king's men. This also occurred during the early stages of Becket's cult, when anyone who praised the dead prelate might be intimidated by self-appointed protectors of the king's interests. Even with all these risks, however, many of Simon's pilgrims did come from this unsettled region, an irregular area bounded by Derby, Oxford, Hereford and Northampton. Other more distant regions which had also supported Simon's cause while he lived and sent their contingents of suppliants to his tomb, were London, whose citizens had been notoriously pro-Montfortian, and, surprisingly, Canterbury. Considering Becket's nearby shrine this emphasizes the political—rather than pious or therapeutic—interest in de Montfort. Perhaps this is what is to be expected of the chief city of the rebellious county of Kent which was only subdued by the king with difficulty after Simon's death. A few pilgrims even came from the little hilltop village of Brill, over forty miles from Evesham. It is probably not just a coincidence that Brill had been condemned as 'contumacious', that is, anti-royal, after Simon's death.[32]

Ecclesiastics were prominent among Simon's pilgrims. Simon had established close ties with many churchmen and he had also attracted the sympathetic attention of the friars, whose habits of perambulation and preaching were eminently suited to spreading the influence of his posthumous cult over wide regions and through many social levels. Because of special interest among people living in widely separated parts of England the geographical pattern for Simon's pilgrims is not a neat, regular falling off in participation at greater distances from his shrine. It is a combination of mild local interest with continuing involvement up to and beyond one hundred miles from Evesham.

The patterns of some of the English cults are also found in the two French examples. In one, the cult of Edmund Rich, there is no need for much comment. His pilgrim-field was quite similar to what was observed in Frideswide's and Wulfstan's cults. Most of his suppliants were local people, many drawn from the villages and towns through which he had passed while alive and dead. Louis of Toulouse, however, like William of Norwich, was a one-city saint as far as miracle-touched suppliants were concerned. Most of the pilgrims with identifiable origins (93%) came from Marseilles itself—about three-quarters of the total. This suggests that the miracles, which are undated in the manuscript, were recorded not long after his entombment of 1297. His life and death had attracted some notoriety and it may be that miracles eventually began to affect people from places far beyond Marseilles, but the evidence does not indicate this. Many of the city folk who were cured by the saint lived along the waterfront and in the eastern district between *Porte de la Frache* and *Porte du Lauret* (to be decorated in future years with a statue of the sainted 'prince'). They were craftsmen, artisans, skilled and unskilled city types, and the lower—unspecified—levels, who lived in streets with homely names like Skinners' Street or Fishmonger Row (*Rue pelliparia, Rue pecherie*). Some came from the less-crowded suburbs, the *Bourg Ste. Claire*, or the *Bourg de Sion* beyond the eastern walls of the busy seaport. It was a crowded, not particularly healthy place where, as we have seen, one-quarter of all the pilgrims complained of (probably malarial) 'fevers'. In spite of the modest following suggested by his miracle-touched suppliants, however, Louis became a canonized saint and eventually attracted the greatest nobles of France to his shrine.

Cults differed as to the origins of their recorded pilgrims. One way to 'rate' this difference is to answer this question: if we were to set an imaginary pilgrim in motion and direct him to walk away from a shrine, at what point would he find that one-half of the pilgrim-villages were behind him? The case of William of Norwich and Louis of Toulouse cannot be considered since they were so closely associated with a single city, and there is not enough information to help with Wulfstan's cult. But for Godric, for example, our hypothetical pilgrim would only have to walk beyond a circle with a radius of about fifteen miles from Finchale to leave behind him half of all the villages containing a miraculously-cured resident. At Oxford he would walk twenty miles to reach the half-way point and for Cantilupe just beyond twenty miles from Hereford. About forty-five miles from Simon's tomb at Evesham would take the pilgrim to the imaginary circumference; the distance cannot easily be calculated for Becket. Turned around, these figures mean that the pilgrim-villages would become noticeable some distance from Becket's shrine, but our traveller would have to draw closer to Evesham to encounter such places, closer still to Hereford or Oxford before many villagers personally knew of the powers of Cantilupe of Frideswide, and closest yet in Godric's case.

Not only were there differences in pilgrim-sites from one cult to the next, there were also changes within each cult. Although the dead saints attracted local people at the start of their careers as wonder-workers, eventually more and more 'outsiders' were noted in the records as enthusiasm declined at the centre. At the same time, at least in some cases, fewer and fewer women were involved; with this change there was a correlated change in the social levels of the pilgrims as well as in the types of miracles they reported. While all this was going on the frequency of miraculous cures declined. These conclusions, reached by piecing together information from separate cults, are tentative since medieval scribes so often failed to identify the pilgrims clearly and were especially careless about dating their reported miracles. There is one medieval English cult, however, with an appreciable number of miracles, most of them clearly dated, which would allow us to put these conclusions on a firmer basis. That cult was made up of the followers of the thirteenth-century prelate, Thomas Cantilupe, Bishop of Hereford.

Chapter 10

The Changing Fortunes of a Curative Shrine: St. Thomas Cantilupe

Even from two hundred leagues away people came on
pilgrimage to the Hereford church and hastened to his
tomb as if to a saint.

Witness at 1307 inquiry

A life of Thomas Cantilupe published in Ghent in 1674 is still the only
substantial study of the saint. Most modern articles about him and his
cult are based upon a fourteenth-century manuscript edited in *Acta
Sanctorum* in the eighteenth century, but unfortunately both the
author of the 1674 book and the *Acta* editor used second-hand
materials provided by others who had transcribed the Vatican manuscript for them. *Acta* is a difficult source to use because only parts of
the original process were transcribed, the sequence of events was
disrupted, and errors are all too common. For instance, the 'Willelmi de
Vrap, de Enthfolk' of the printed version turns out in the manuscript to
be 'Willelmi le Draper de Suthfolk'. The arbitrary rearrangements
which the editor made in his materials have misled nearly every
historian who has used the printed edition of the process for his
information about the cult, and the errors, once committed, have been
perpetuated by successive modern writers. In what follows we have
relied upon the manuscript (in microfilm) for details concerning this
cult, supplemented by additional printed documents.[1] A proper
edition of the entire work would provide historians with what appears
to be the longest complete process of canonization of any medieval
English saint—the only Englishman canonized in the fourteenth
century and one of the last saints of medieval England—and, after
Becket's, the largest collection of English miracles to have survived
until the present day.

Some of the miracles provide wonderfully detailed descriptions of
the events of a single day—even a single hour—in the lives of the

ordinary villagers of Herefordshire, whether we credit their 'miracles' or not. Take the Saturday morning of 28 May, 1300, for instance. The view from the village church of How Caple has probably changed very little during the past seven hundred years. Rough pasture slopes down to the River Wye some four hundred yards to the south, the hamlet of Ingestone lies just visible through the trees on the other side of the river, still as insignificant a place as it was when Edward I was king, and on all sides the hills seem to shut out the rest of the world. This peaceful scene was transformed on that May morning by the shouts of How Caple villagers scrambling down the field to the riverbank, where John Fisher was dragging his son's body from the water. Margaret Francis from Ingestone had seen him slip and fall in, as he searched for something in his father's boat tied to the bank, but she could do nothing since no one heard her screams and there was no bridge to bring her across the river to his aid. The rigid victim, measured to Bishop Thomas Cantilupe, recovered within a few hours. On Tuesday the parents and their neighbours walked eight or nine miles to Hereford cathedral, told the canons the story, and then joined in the general celebration of yet another miracle attributed to the dead bishop.[2] When the Fisher family arrived at the cathedral they would have found the saint's tomb in the north transept surrounded by a mass of candles, wax votives and jewellery and guarded by a *custos* or two. It was not always like this. When Thomas was buried in his episcopal church in 1282 his tomb lay elsewhere. It was devoid of pilgrims' offerings, and his bones worked no miracles.

Thomas had gone to Italy to appeal to the pope against Archbishop Pecham in a conflict over ecclesiastical jurisdiction. Here he died, on 25 August 1282, at 'Castro Florenti' (Ferento), six miles south-east of Montefiascone on Lake Bolsena (seventy miles north of Rome). The body was transported to the monastery of San Severo near Orvieto and the flesh and viscera, separated from the skeleton, were buried in the abbey church. The heart and bones were taken to England, the former to Ashridge—heart-burial was a not uncommon medieval form of commemoration—the latter to Hereford.[3] The bones were buried in the Lady Chapel in the east end of the cathedral under a large flat stone of a type customarily used for prelates and the nobility. Nothing more is heard about the dead man for three years, until 1285 when three bishops allowed indulgences in exchange for prayers for his soul, and next year another bishop offered a further indulgence. These were probably issued at the request of Cantilupe's successor Richard Swinfield, Bishop of Hereford from 1282 to 1317, one of the main promoters of the cult. In 1286 he instructed two Hereford proctors in Italy to find out whether any miracles had occurred at San Severo and to inquire about the pope's attitude toward Cantilupe's canonization.

Meanwhile, he had his own plans for his predecessor: on 3 April 1287 he moved Cantilupe's bones to a new tomb constructed in the north transept of the cathedral. On the same day a handful of people claimed miraculous cures. The popular cult was under way.

During the next fifteen years Swinfield wrote to the pope, sent Hereford proctors to the papal curia, busied himself in lobbying for his 'saint' at English church councils and parliaments, and solicited further letters from his fellow-prelates. It was not until King Edward I became involved, however, that the papal wheels began to turn. Edward I and Thomas Cantilupe had both, at one time or another, supported Simon de Montfort's programme. After Edward became king, Cantilupe was one of his counsellors. The king wrote to the pope in 1305 requesting Thomas's canonization so that his friend on earth could be his patron in heaven. Edward also wrote to seventeen cardinals.[4]

At first glance 1305 was not a propitious year for asking favours of the Supreme Pontiff since the newly-elected French Pope Clement V was wandering about the plains of his beloved homeland, Gascony, reluctant to go to that volatile capital of the Italians, Rome (he was to enter Avignon, not Rome, in 1309). He was attended by a skeleton administrative staff who had with them only the essential collections of official documents, the viatory archives, for routine matters. Although Clement was unable to consult the Cantilupe dossier because he did not have it, papal organization and expertise easily overcame these obstacles. He wrote to three cardinals at Rome and instructed them to look into the matter. They replied that they found in the bishop's file letters from the English king, the Archbishop of York, fifteen bishops, seven abbots, eleven earls and several barons and nobles urging canonization (the fruits of Swinfield's labours). Meanwhile the Hereford chapter, with an eye on the way things were going, set up their own commission to investigate local miracles in September of 1306.[5] They could not yet have known that on 23 August 1306, in Bordeaux, the pope had at last issued his mandate for an inquiry into the life and miracles of Cantilupe, appointing three commissioners to carry out the examination in England, and setting the time limits. A week later, however, someone reminded the pope that Cantilupe might have died excommunicated (by Archbishop Pecham, with whom he had quarrelled). Obviously it would not do to sanctify one who may have been forever barred from heaven. Clement sent a second letter instructing his agents to hold a preliminary hearing and, if they found no evidence for the alleged excommunication, to proceed to the canonization inquiry.[6] The excommunication hearing began in London on 15 April 1307, and Cantilupe was found to have died reconciled to the Church. This cleared the way for the second stage.[7]

The three men who formally opened the canonization hearing in

London on 13 July 1307 constituted, in modern terms, a board of inquiry sitting to collect sworn testimony. It would be up to the papal curia to decide whether this testimony was evidence which warranted canonization. The commissioners were William de Testa, a papal tax collector whose fiscal duties took him away from the inquiry on various occasions; Ralph Baldock, Bishop of London, who—as it happened—became Chancellor of England a week after the excommunication inquiry opened, found himself even more distracted by the death of King Edward I a week before the canonization inquiry opened, and was called away on matters of state several times throughout the hearing. The third member of the panel was William Durand the Younger, Bishop of the French see of Mende, who appears to have been the only member of the trio who sat through the entire process. The hearing itself was conducted in a relatively formal way. On one side sat the commissioners, and by them the three or four notaries who jotted down the testimony *verbatim* in clerical shorthand and later compared notes and prepared a formal transcript. Sometimes the notaries went to the homes of sick witnesses to record their statements and some of them also acted as interpreters, for although clerical and upper-class witnesses gave evidence in Latin or French, most laymen spoke English, and one witness testified in Welsh. It all had to be turned into good ecclesiastical Latin: an English witness who said 'alas, alas' meant, one of the notaries explained, '*heu, heu*'.[8] Facing the bench was the proctor or official representative of the Hereford canons, sometimes assisted by a co-proctor. And in the middle, the witness. He or she was called in, took an oath on a Bible and was then asked a pre-arranged set of questions, or interrogatories, about the life and miracles of Cantilupe. Other witnesses were brought in and asked the same questions: it is little wonder that the hearing took the full four months allowed by the pope.

Both sides, the commissioners and the Hereford proctors, called witnesses, just as both sides—plaintiff and defendant—call their own witnesses in modern trials. Naturally, the proctors' witnesses (Cantilupe's friends or associates and people cured by him) spoke favourably of the dead bishop. The commissioners' witnesses, however, in theory people who could provide an unbiased account, were not always full of praise for Thomas. Most of these witnesses were systematically summoned by the commissioners from the monasteries and friaries of London and Hereford, and many Franciscans called by the commission denied knowing anything about his miracles, or replied in a derogatory manner to questions about them. Perhaps they were still irritated by his old conflict with the Franciscan Archbishop Pecham. Altogether, by the end of the hearing the notaries had listed 223 witnesses (in *Acta Sanctorum* an extra hundred witnesses were added in error), which is somewhat misleading since the witnesses who testified more than once were given a different number each time. In fact, the Hereford proctors called 164 witnesses, the commissioners called thirty-nine *proprio motu*, and two witnesses were called by both sides, a total of 205. Only thirteen men were called by the Hereford proctors to give testimony about the virtuous and saintly *life* of Thomas, without reference to his miracles.[9]

To return to the chronological development of the process, after more than three dozen people in London told what they knew of the life and posthumous miracles, the hearing was adjourned on 12 August for a change of venue to Hereford, where it re-opened on the 28 August. Next day the commissioners carefully inspected and inventoried the offerings at the shrine (a second inventory was taken at the end of the hearing), interviewed the past and present *custodes tumuli*, then settled down to hear more testimony about the bishop's life and miracles.

About September 15 the notaries began to record testimony under a new rubric, 'The Beginning of the Second Part of this Process, on the Proof of the Miracles'.[10] They used this heading even though they had already collected a great deal of information about miracles in London and Hereford. Several of the miracle witnesses were passing through or lived in London when the commission first opened the hearing there in July, and at Hereford some of the witnesses who were called to discuss Thomas's *vita* included a *miraculum* or two as well. This unobtrusive detail about the rubric is interesting—for two reasons. It shows that there was still room for procedural flexibility—even clumsiness—in a canonization inquiry in the early fourteenth century, and secondly it illustrates yet again why the printed version of this process is difficult to use. The *Acta* editor, perhaps misled by his secondhand sources, separated the testimony about Cantilupe's life from that concerning his miracles, disregarding the fact that the two were mingled day by day through half the hearing. He thereby made a muddle of the chronological sequence and form of the inquiry, and the process has remained more or less incomprehensible until the present study.

The last 'official' day of the hearing was 13 November 1307. For four months the commissioners had listened to testimony about Cantilupe's life and twenty-five of his posthumous miracles. Now, on the final day, the Hereford proctors offered as further proof of his spiritual powers a list of 207 miracles arranged by type—raising the dead, cures of the blind, and so on. Nor was this all: they persuaded the board to allow them to present witnesses to twelve more miracles, witnesses selected from the 'great part of the citizens of Hereford congregated in the cathedral to give evidence'.[11] The commissioners, meanwhile, noticed that many of the 207 miracles were undated, so they requested the proctors to remedy this. Apparently it was easier for the Hereford canons to copy and submit their entire chronological list of miracles (out of which they had chosen the 207). When duplicates are eliminated from this mixture of oral and written posthumous wonders, about 470 miracles remain. This bulky file—now containing testimony from 205 witnesses to Cantilupe's life and thirty-seven miracles, two long lists of miracles (one chronological and the other topical), two inventories of the shrine, copies of official letters from the pope and Hereford chapter and postulatory letters from various prelates—was finally sent in December 1307 to the papal curia with a 'covering letter' summarizing the year's work. At the same time the new king, Edward II, urged the pope to expedite the inquiry 'undertaken by the urging' of his father King Edward I; he also sent similar letters to no less than twenty-five cardinals.[12]

King Edward II continued his epistolary prompting of pope and cardinals and in 1312 also wrote to the King of France, who was by then exercising greater control over the Avignonese papacy and who, apparently, had expressed an interest in Cantilupe in the recent Council of Vienne (1311-12).[13] As a result of this the file was taken out and inspected in 1313, the contents were listed, but once again the dossier was put away to gather more archival dust.[14] Edward persisted, sending not only letters but special envoys to hurry up the long-delayed canonization. At last on 19 March 1320 Pope John XXII in consistory in Avignon opened the formal scrutiny of Cantilupe's case. A few well-attested miracles were discussed by the cardinals (only those attested by *viva voce* witnesses; the two long lists were ignored), and by March 22 the pope expressed his satisfaction that Thomas should be enrolled among the saints, but because Easter was near (30 March) these findings were kept secret until after the Paschal celebrations. On April 16 the pope opened the formal ceremony of canonization and brought it to a conclusion next day, on which he established Cantilupe's feastday as 2 October.[15] At long last the Bishop of Hereford was a canonized saint, and although Bishop Swinfield may have been responsible for 'creating' a popular saint out of Cantilupe, it is no less certain that royal interest had made him an official saint as well. Edward I and II between them wrote to various popes seven times or more and sent at least fifty-nine letters to the cardinals on Cantilupe's behalf. In addition, both the Hereford cathedral chapter and the kings kept proctors at the papal curia for years and paid particular cardinals to forward their interests, including this canonization.

After news of the canonization arrived in England, some prelates issued indulgences to stimulate pilgrimage to the new saint, and the Bishop of Hereford, Adam of Orleton, wrote round to his colleagues and to all the parishes of his diocese inviting everyone to Hereford for the first celebration of the saint's feast on 2 October. A parliament called for 6 October may have prevented some bishops from being present in Hereford, but a few managed to break away from parliamentary affairs long enough to send indulgences from London.[16] A translation of the corpse to a more prominent place was usually the next step. King Edward II authorized seven Hereford proctors to circulate through England and Wales to collect donations toward a new shrine and he instructed his own bailiffs to co-operate with the proctors. The collection must have been profitable, for in the single archdeanery of Norfolk (the diocese was divided into four archdeaneries) the collector came away with over £45, by medieval standards a considerable sum of money.[17] Preparations went ahead: materials were purchased, craftsmen were hired, indulgences were issued, but year after year the bones remained where they had been since 1287. Finally, after a crescendo of letters from the king to the pope, the pope to the Bishop of Hereford, the bishop to his episcopal colleagues, and after their replies and excuses for non-attendance, the day of the translation was set for Sunday, 25 October 1349.[18]

In the presence of many clerical and lay notables—Edward III had fallen ill but miraculously recovered on his way to the ceremony—the cathedral clergy and honoured guests assembled in the north transept. The tomb was opened and inside they found a wooden chest—so fragile that it crumbled to powder at the lightest touch. The bones and skull were taken out of this container, passed among the privileged onlookers to be kissed with pious joy, then placed in the new shrine in the Lady Chapel at the east end of the church. Sixty-two years after he began to work miracles, St. Thomas Cantilupe was at last put to rest in the same chapel where he had originally been entombed, but now in a shrine which suited his celestial status. There, a medieval prayer predicted, he would remain until Resurrection Day. The translation was thought to have had far-ranging beneficial effects, for afterwards 'they said' that God stayed his vengeful angel's hand and the Black Death, which had raged for more than a year, abated in England.[19]

This was the last time that Cantilupe's name and sanctity stirred up popular excitement and devotion, at least in medieval England. His feast was celebrated every year in all the English churches and three times yearly at Hereford, when the miracles listed in the papal bull were read to the assembled public; his image was put up in stone and coloured glass in some Herefordshire churches, though all of these marks of official recognition came decades after the great outburst of miracle-working in the late thirteenth century.[20]

The development of Cantilupe's *popular* cult—his career as a dead miracle-worker, distinguished from the steps leading up to his formal canonization and translation—can be reconstructed from the posthumous miracles themselves and from other records. During the 1290s there was a considerable influx of pilgrims. Some of the more famous were Edward I, his two queens, Eleanor of Castile and Margaret of France, his brother Edmund of Lancaster, Gilbert of Gloucester and other noblemen.[21] The income from oblations of both famous and insignificant pilgrims, and wax offerings, was sufficient to excite a controversy among the Hereford canons who eventually, however, agreed on a just division of the spoils. In nearby Worcester it was said that pilgrims *en route* to Hereford left about £10 per year, some giving a farthing, a half- or a whole penny before moving on to Cantilupe's shrine. If these figures can be trusted (which is doubtful), and if most gave a halfpenny, this suggests about 1,200 Hereford-bound pilgrims annually leaving an offering at Worcester alone.[22] Pieces of Cantilupe's clothing were dispersed among friends and family, and even a few of his bones had come into private hands, presumably during the trip from Italy to England. At his birthplace, Hambleden, his image and a knife he used to eat with were working miracles, and votive offerings were hanging there just as at Hereford. In fact the Bishop of Lincoln had to prohibit pilgrimages to Hambleden in 1296—the cult was not officially authorized at that time—though the bishop himself had written to the pope asking for Cantilupe's canonization a few years earlier.[23]

In 1307 when the commissioners were gathering evidence, many witnesses tended to refer to past, rather than to presènt, glories of the saint. By that date, too, there are indications that the offerings left by pilgrims were already in decline. A comparison of the two inventories of the oblations at the shrine (taken seventy-eight days apart) leaves us less impressed than the seventy-year-old witness who claimed that a six-horse wagon would hardly suffice for all the votives.[24] On the one hand, the commissioners noted that during their stay pilgrims brought in one wax and two silver ships, one silver and eighty-five wax images of people, two children's shifts, and candles. But on the other hand, the *total* number of such wax images at the shrine, besides coins and candles (the most common offering) had actually declined—by 127— while the inquiry was being held in Hereford. In addition, one *custos* claimed that only one-tenth of all wax offerings remained, another (the shrine-keeper of 1307, in fact) said one-third, the rest having been consumed with age or put to other uses.[25] During the two-and-a-half months of 1307 there had been no increase in offerings of wax animals or birds, crutches, carts of wax, cloths of gold and silk, chains and anchors and, more surprisingly, rings and other jewels, a common gift from well-off pilgrims. Based upon the commissioners' own inventories, then, there is an impression of a slowing down or stagnation in ordinary offerings at the tomb and, for one very popular oblation—wax images—there was actually an overall decline.

Although pilgrims still went to the tomb all through the rest of the Middle Ages, voluntarily and as penitents,[26] and crowds had been attracted by the 1349 translation, the fortunes of the shrine eventually dwindled. Even before his canonization new would-be saints were beginning to steal Cantilupe's potential pilgrims. About 1316 a local Herefordshire man who fell into the Wye and 'drowned' was measured not to the defunct bishop of his local cathedral but to the Archbishop of Canterbury, Robert Winchelsey, who had died in 1313.[27] In 1336 the pope indirectly acknowledged the decline in offerings and by 1387 the cathedral Fabric Fund took in less than £2 in oblations from the shrine, whereas in 1291 the figure had been over £178.[28] At the end of the Middle Ages a hospital's income was united to the cathedral's revenue because, among other losses, offerings at Cantilupe's shrine had fallen so low that lights could not be purchased for his chapel and other altars. In 1535 in his will the Bishop of Hereford left a gold ring with a sapphire to Cantilupe 'to ornate his shryne'[29] which must have been scantily ornamented by then. The great wealth of silver ships and golden jewellery had gone long before, to meet cathedral expenses. Perhaps the bishop's ring was one of fifteen found by the Dissolution Commissioners when they stripped the shrine of its valuables in 1538. In 1307 there had been over 500 rings of silver and gold, some with precious stones.

The miracles themselves provide much more information about the development of the popular side of the cult. Once miracles begin, others follow. The first thing to note is the lapse of five years between Cantilupe's entombment and his posthumous wonders. Obviously this was not a case of spontaneous thaumaturgy. His corpse lay in the east end of the cathedral without giving the slightest hint of supernatural powers from 1282 until 1287, and then for some reason the wonders began. Someone had to stimulate the popular cult, and Bishop Swinfield seems a likely choice. Before 1287, as noted, he procured indulgences and directed his agents into preliminary negotiations abroad; he also had a new tomb built to a rather unusual design, almost but not quite a shrine.[30] Before he moved the bones into this new tomb in 1287 he took the trouble to invite certain friends along and he scheduled the event for 3 April 1287 knowing full well, no doubt, that since Easter was very near (it fell on 6 April in 1287) the cathedral would be packed when Cantilupe's bones were shifted.[31]

A week before the translation, however, Cantilupe obligingly performed his first posthumous miracle, or so it seemed, for we must admit that the event was very liberally interpreted in the dead bishop's favour. On March 28 Edith, a *furiosa* or mentally-disturbed woman, was praying at the altar of the Holy Rood in the cathedral, her husband having taken her there along with her measured-candle dedicated to the Holy Rood. During her wait at this altar, however, a 'certain cleric' of the cathedral suggested that she might be cured at Bishop Cantilupe's tomb, at that time still a simple affair in Lady Chapel. She was obviously not as disturbed as one might think, being rational enough to follow this advice. She went there but nothing happened.shortly after returning to the Holy Rood, however, the *furiosa* felt sufficiently improved to claim that she was cured. The interesting point is that Edith did not ascribe the cure to the Holy Rood, but to Cantilupe, and so did the clergy; if all the story were known, perhaps it was the other way around. However, the bells were set going, the *Te Deum* sung, and the first posthumous miracle of the good bishop made known to the crowds.[32] It seems more than coincidental that this happened only a week before the shift to the new tomb, but it does not necessarily also point to conscious fraud.

After the move to the new tomb/shrine on 3 April, it was claimed that the shift had taken place according to the last will of the dead man and with the concurrence of his executors. This carefully-prepared statement shielded Swinfield from a possible accusation of carrying out an unauthorized translation of an unofficial saint.[33] The translation, or whatever it may have been called, had predictable results: five people were cured at the new tomb on that Thursday and the miracles continued daily thereafter.[34] Swinfield even had the foresight to prepare for such wonderful events since, the day after the translation, the new tomb was already under the care of not one but two custodians,[35] ready to write down any evidences of Cantilupe's miracle-working powers. The first cured pilgrims had been attracted by news of the transfer of the bishop's bones, or were already in Hereford awaiting the celebration of Easter. In addition, some cured pilgrims said that they had come to the shrine after hearing rumours of Edith's cure and other subsequent miracles. Although some miracles still occurred at the site of original burial (in the east end of the church) until about 20 May, the second tomb was the real focal point of the new devotion. The cult was on its way, though not everyone approved—the day after the cure of mad Edith an official of the Archbishop of Canterbury suspended the canon responsible for publishing the news of her miracle.[36]

After Swinfield had had the satisfaction of seeing miracles performed by the score for some months, he instituted on the Feast of All Souls, 2 November, 1287, an annual obit or commemorative service for Cantilupe, to begin on the next anniversary of his death, 25 August. Obits were sometimes established for the dead as a way to honour their memory, and there was usually no implication of sanctity in the deceased (though Swinfield did mention the possibility of a canonization when he instituted the obit). Again it seems curious that Swinfield waited five years to carry out this rather elementary commemoration of his predecessor.

In the end, it is probably not unreasonable to conclude that at the high point in the Christian year Swinfield performed a pseudo-translation to a mock shrine and later established a quasi-feastday (the obit) for Cantilupe in order to stimulate popular veneration which he hoped would lead to canonization. As we know, it did, thirty-three years later and three years after Swinfield's own death. The tomb he built for Thomas still stands in the transept of Hereford cathedral, scarred by the marks of the sixteenth- and seventeenth-century vandalism common to so many memorials of the Middle Ages; as for that sumptuous shrine in Lady Chapel where the bones were taken in 1349, not a trace remains.

Once the miracles began in 1287, by the usual self-stimulative means further miracles followed. These tell us a great deal about the people whose ills were relieved by Cantilupe (as they believed) and about the rise and decline of popular devotion in general. Although Cantilupe was credited with some 470 miracles (about 500 when all manuscript evidence is considered), we shall limit ourselves to the 450 miracles which were conveniently arranged, by medieval scribes, in chronological order. The first point to consider is the frequency of these events. It is clear that the tremendous burst of miracles of 1287 was followed, with occasional exceptions, by a steady annual decline, for instance from 160 miracles in 1287 to thirty-four in 1288, nine in 1300 and only one 1312. They cease to be recorded after this last date, with the exception of a solitary cure written up in the back of an Oxford college manuscript in 1404 in what appears to be a contemporary hand.[37] This decline began even during the very first year: in April 1287, seventy cures were recorded, in May thirty-eight; the frequency was down to two or three a month by the year's end. Month by month, year by year, fewer people called on Cantilupe in their distress—or, shall we say?—fewer were answered, with a miracle.

These pilgrims, about three-quarters of whom we have been able to locate on the map, were relatively evenly spread out around Hereford. Nearly half lived less than twenty miles from the city, with a decline thereafter. This is the static view, but in the dynamic it is evident that changes were occurring from one year to the next. Most of the miracle recipients of the first year, 1287, were local people, over half living less than ten miles away, within easy walking distance. After this the proportion of 'strangers' increased while at the same time the miracles were becoming less frequent, a trend that is apparent from the start. In April 1287 when seventy miracles were recorded the people reporting them lived on average nine miles from the shrine; next month, the pilgrims' villages lay twenty miles from Hereford; in June, when only

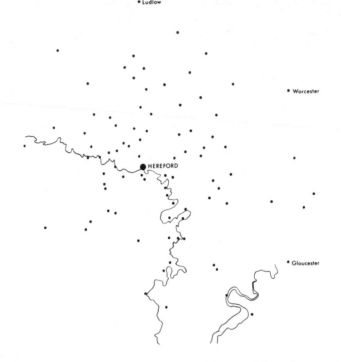

4   Thomas Cantilupe: villages, towns and cities containing at least one individual affected by his miracles

eighteen wonders were registered, the average distance to the pilgrims' villages had increased to twenty-two miles and by July (eleven miracles) it was thirty-four miles. Even though diminishing samples imply less significant averages, there could be no better illustration of the 'shock-wave' of enthusiasm spreading out into the countryside from the point of origin and at the same time losing its power to attract cure-seeking pilgrims to the shrine. As enthusiasm declined at the centre, there was 'infilling' from the outside. These trends continued to the early four-teenth century; ironically, when the papal commissioners were meeting in London in 1307 the active phase of the popular cult—the 'miracu-lous' period—was already practically at an end.

These were not the only changes at the shrine. For example, over the years there was a shift away from female to male registered pilgrims,[38] the same change we observed in Godric's cult. In Cantilupe's case, besides allowing that men may have waited until several woman had 'proven' the miraculous powers of the saint, there may have been another reason for increasing male participation, applicable to other

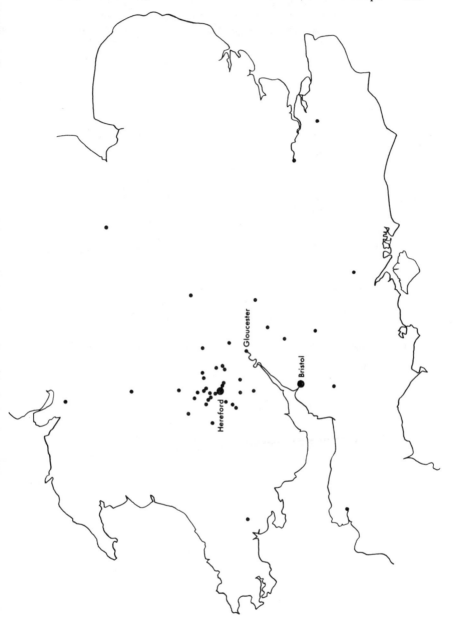

5   Thomas Cantilupe: places containing two or more individuals affected by his miracles (small circles = two or more places, large circles = ten or more)

cults as well. Men were more mobile than hearth-bound women: as mileage to the shrine rose the proportion of women fell and that of men increased. This was especially noticeable after about forty-five or fifty miles, when the participation-level of women dropped very sharply, while that of men continued as before. This is roughly a two-day journey or four or five days altogether from village to shrine and back again; apparently women were able to manage one or two days easily enough but the more the distance increased beyond twenty miles the less able were they to go to the shrine. Until about April 1289, when the average distances rose above forty-five or fifty miles, most cures occurred at the bishop's tomb, but after that at the pilgrims' homes or elsewhere. At such distances most people preferred to wait for their cures in their own homes rather than journey all that way and risk disappointment at the shrine and, in any case, most of the people who *did* make the long journey were men.

These changes had two consequences. Since the population of women fell, and since, as we know, women were predominantly lower-class, the overall level of upper-class pilgrims increased slightly (by 11%). But a second and even more striking change occurred in the type of miracle reported. Contrasting the first with the last hundred pilgrims, cures of the blind and lame dropped from nearly three-quarters in the first group to less than one-quarter in the last (73% to 21%). Conversely only one out of the first hundred pilgrims reported a miracle involving accidents or woundings or non-healing events, but forty-four out of the last hundred had experienced one of these, especially accidents (thirty-one). At least part of the reason for these contrasts must be the correlation we have discovered between certain social classes and sexes, and certain types of miracle. But changed attitudes may also have affected what miracles pilgrims believed they had experienced.

The scenes at Cantilupe's shrine in 1287 were probably quite different from those which would meet us around 1300. At the first date we would see a multitude of miracles and pilgrims, much bell-ringing and *Te Deum* singing, and general commotion in the north transept by the tomb. The participants in the miracles would usually be simple women who lived within walking distance of the church, whose miracles were cures of typically 'physical' ailments, especially blindness and crippling debilities. Most cures occurred at the shrine itself. By about 1300, however, the noise of crowds has given way to quieter cathedral sounds; the flurry of miracles is now only a memory although of course miracles still happened now and then. The average pilgrim of 1300 is a man from some village forty miles away or more. He is often somewhat elevated in social status, his miracle is less 'traditional' in type, and anyway it has probably already occurred in the privacy of his home or some other distant place.

These changes at the shrine were themselves caused by changing attitudes. The first hundred registered pilgrims, having heard that—in effect—there was a new healer in town, eagerly flocked to the tomb animated by that hopeful expectation which is essential to faith-healing. The enthusiasm of such local potential curees was eventually exhausted, and by the time the last recorded hundred pilgrims were arriving in Hereford a decade or so later, local enthusiasm was no longer prompting so many suppliants. On the contrary, many of the late-comers had appealed to Thomas only after some unforeseen and infrequent calamity and not in the midst of their common illnesses. The saint, for the second group of pilgrims, was no longer thought of in the ordinary distresses of life but only in the *extraordinary*, and to that extent Cantilupe was already slipping away from the thoughts of Herefordshire villagers. Most of the 'early' pilgrims came to the tomb at once, ill but in hope, while many of the last group only called in tardily, for other reasons. Put another way, at first Cantilupe was sought out as a remedy for illness, a common or ordinary part of life; but after the passage of ten years or so he was appealed to not in common sickness— the ordinary side of life—but only in uncommon accidents, woundings, non-healing situations, the more extraordinary problems. He had ceased to be a source of immediate therapy; other newer. saints, perhaps, were now turned to for healing. At some point even these 'emergency' cases ceased; the distant, male pilgrims stopped coming to Hereford to report miracles, and Cantilupe's unrecorded visitors were casual callers drawn by curiosity and conventional piety to the once-famous healer of Hereford.

Local enthusiasm, sparked off by a burial or translation or miracle, probably gave way to more distant, occasional interest with concomitant changes in the sex, social class and miracles of wonder-touched pilgrims at other shrines as well, though at different rates and, as in Becket's and de Montfort's case, for example, in different circumstances. Some of these changes have also been noted in a French cult which was recently investigated.[39]

The fact that holy bones eventually ran out of miraculous power—at many of the shrines, within a decade—had little to do with the later history of the 'official' cult. Though Cantilupe's spring of healing was already beginning to fail in 1307 and had run dry by 1320, this did not affect the canonization commission or the papal bull which raised him to sainthood. By then, the whole matter had shifted into another plane, and by 1307 and 1320 it was in the hands of the pope, not the pilgrims. After the translation of 1349 the cult seems to have faded into the quiet respectability of a lawful feast of the established Church and the only miracles the clergy and people of Hereford came to know were the same ones, repeated year after year, mentioned by John XXII when he raised the bishop from the ecclesiastical to the spiritual nobility.

Cantilupe's cult and canonization demonstrate the many complicated operations in the business of saint-making, which incidentally has become no simpler since the Middle Ages. The records of his miracles also establish quite clearly that popular movements which centred on such holy places had a history of their own, an inner development (only glimpsed when dealing with the other major cults). There were changes in the types of people who reported miracles, as well as changes in the miracles themselves. In addition, both the geographical area of attraction and the frequency of the miracles, and presumably overall numbers of pilgrims, changed from one decade to the next. These conclusions are applicable to Cantilupe's cult and are very likely true of many other thaumaturgic shrines of medieval England. But society had its inner developments too, and in the England of the fourteenth and fifteenth centuries criticism of pilgrimages and relics grew even while new shrines were becoming more popular. That conflict would be resolved only in the aftermath of the Reformation.

Part Three

The End of the Middle Ages
and the Reformation

Chapter 11

Shifting Loyalties: New Shrines and Old Saints at the end of the Middle Ages

I bequeath 26s 8d. to a priest to go on pilgrimage for me to Bridlington, Walsingham, Canterbury and Hailes.
Fifteenth-century will

Life in later medieval England was in some ways no better or worse than it had been in the Conqueror's reign. Towns may have grown larger and merchants richer but the peasantry, the vast majority of the population, were still at the bottom of the social ladder, the nobility still a privileged, ruling minority at the top. Medicine was just as impotent to help the sick, housing still as inadequate, sanitation and hygiene as primitive: disease, filth, ignorance and poverty continued to haunt Everyman, and hope-sustaining and health-promising shrines were still attracting suppliants. It could even be argued that the physical environment was less hospitable than during earlier centuries. The fourteenth century opened with widespread famines, then the Black Death arrived to extinguish perhaps one-third of the English people, and in the late fifteenth century the less deadly but mysterious 'sweating sickness' appeared in the records, yet another affliction added to the melancholy list. Society was disturbed by more than plague and famine. During the fourteenth century the agrarian economy began to show signs of depression following the boom years of 'high farming' in the thirteenth century; the Black Death only aggravated matters. Though some people benefited by these economic fluctuations, many peasants were forced from the land (which in many cases was turned over to flocks of sheep) and into the impersonal relationships of town life, a movement which continued to the end of the Middle Ages. Taxation also became more than usually troublesome in the fourteenth and fifteenth centuries since English kings were engaged in the Hundred Years' War, which brought glory at Crecy, Poitiers and Agincourt, but defeat at Orleans, Bordeaux, and Paris. Win or lose, it cost a great deal of money. After the nobles and their hired bands of soldiers came home, the fighting continued in the Wars of the Roses, a dynastic struggle between York and Lancaster which ended with a Tudor victory. Though it was fought mainly among the aristocrats and did not involve the people at large, the battles still had unsettling effects upon English society. 'So violent and motley was life', Huizinga wrote of late-medieval Flanders and France, 'that it bore the mixed smell of blood and of roses', an equally apt description of the aristocratic ambience on this side of the Channel.[1]

Besides all these anxieties, some of which lay behind the peasants' insurrections of 1381 and 1450, there were religious problems too. Papal claims to the right to tax, to appoint 'foreign' bishops to English sees and to interfere with English ecclesiastical affairs generally, resulted in much anti-papal feeling, especially in the fourteenth century. In addition, for most of that century the popes lived at Avignon and were thought to be open to the influence of France, England's enemy. The reputation of the See of Peter fell even lower when the papacy split into two and then into three rival camps in the early fifteenth century. There were also signs of discontent with the Church within England itself: John Wyclif was only the most vociferous fourteenth-century critic of many of the claims made by the Church, and his followers, the Lollards, continued to trouble the hierarchy during the fifteenth century. Worldly bishops were attacked by sober Christians (Langland, for example) and it cannot be denied that some members of the English Church were far better politicians and business executives than guardians of souls. The regular orders, too, seem to have forgotten their earlier ideals. There were only a few new monasteries founded in later medieval England, and some older houses were even dissolved because their inmates had fallen in numbers, or they had gone under in the economic depression. Others held on only by involving themselves even more deeply in the secular world, for instance, by becoming boarding homes for lay people. The friars too lost their thirteenth-century zeal and ended up quarrelling among themselves, with the seculars, and with the laity. Chaucer chose to aim his sharpest arrows at two-faced, avaricious mendicants. By the end of the period many cathedral chapters had become exclusive clubs, wealthy, jealous of their rights, content to carry on the liturgical services through hired underlings.

One could of course always find exceptions to this gloomy picture, and in any case *some* changes in the later medieval centuries were encouraging. The increasing use of the vernacular, for instance, drew more and more laymen into the life of the Church; manuals of instruction and devotion in English proliferated, and preaching seems to have been more frequent and of a higher standard. Lay piety was expressed, too, in the foundation of chantries, arrangements for priests to say Masses (in many cases 'forever') for the repose of the souls of the founders and their families. The number of chantry chapels grew in the fourteenth and fifteenth centuries, and Chaucer criticized the priests who rushed off to sell their services to the highest bidder. *Pace* Chaucer, the chantries do seem to suggest growing concern on the part of laymen for the fate of their immortal souls. This emphasis on 'personal' religious devotion is also suggested by another later-medieval phenomenon, mysticism. Mystics had played a part in Christian history from the earliest centuries but in most European countries and England this inner contemplative drive grew stronger from the thirteenth century. Yet another indication of the growth of later medieval 'lay piety' was the development of the third orders, in which the laity of both sexes associated themselves with established religious orders. There were also other secular confraternities, more or less independent of strict Church control.

How did these changes affect traditional attitudes toward saints' shrines? There is no simple answer. Some holy places seem to have declined in popularity, or at least in oblations offered by pilgrims. In Lincoln, for instance, the income from St. Hugh's shrines had fallen significantly by the early sixteenth century, and at Cuthbert's tomb in Durham it dropped from about £35 yearly in the 1380s to about £16 per year in the 1450s. At the shrine of an obscure local saint in the same cathedral, pilgrims' gifts worth £5 in 1456 had fallen to less than a shilling in the early sixteenth century. The decline in offerings at Cantilupe's shrine has already been noted, and a similar trend is evident at Canterbury, where even the most famous saint of England began to earn less in the later Middle Ages. From the peak years around Becket's translation (in 1220 over £1,000 was offered), income dipped and then rose: the fourteenth century was the most lucrative for Canterbury monks, and the greatest gains of that century came from pilgrims who were grateful for surviving, or worried about escaping, the Black Death. After the Jubilee of 1420 income fell sharply and never revived; in 1535, for instance, pilgrims left only about £36 in Becket's honour.[2] Besides suffering a fall in offerings many saints ceased to work miracles as enthusiasm cooled, even at Canterbury. After the great outburst of over 700 twelfth-century wonders, a few miracles were inspired by the 1220 translation of Becket, and then little is heard about such things until 1394 when King Richard II wrote to the archbishop about a recent cure at Becket's shrine, clearly a novelty. Presumably Chaucer's line about pilgrims going to thank the martyr who had helped them 'when they were sick' referred to earlier, and not contemporary, attitudes. In 1445 the monks issued a public announcement of a miracle and in 1474 there was correspondence about a cure in

Coventry, which seems to be the last recorded notice of Becket's thaumaturgy.[3]

Figures concerning shrine incomes, however, are subject to many different interpretations, and in any event miracle-working was but one—and the most transient—function of the entombed heroes. The mere fact that oblations declined and no more miracles were performed does not necessarily mean that the saint and his shrine had completely disappeared from the public consciousness. Money was spent for the upkeep of William's shrine at Norwich for example, until the Dissolution in the 1530s, and most surviving pictorial representations of William come not from the twelfth century but the fifteenth. Evidently interest had not died when his miracles ceased. Other uncanonized saints such as Godric continued to be granted lands and burning tapers to the end of the Middle Ages, but the most obvious example of the continuing popularity of a saint who no longer worked physical miracles was Becket.

Evidence of ongoing devotion to, or at least recognition of Becket is varied and plentiful, quite apart from continued offerings from pilgrims. To take random examples, in the fourteenth century a tapestry depicting his martyrdom was mentioned in a will, the Bishop of Exeter composed yet another biography of the saint, Canterbury monks continued to peruse the various *Lives and Miracles* in their monastic library,[4] and Chaucer's pilgrims were on their literary way. In the fifteenth century certain people living in Iceland, claiming to be related to Becket's family, were granted letters of fraternity by the Canterbury monks, the king of France asked for a Becket badge to wear in his hat with all his other holy medals, and many people left sums of money in their wills for vicarious pilgrimages to his shrine, as in the example quoted at the very beginning of this chapter.[5] Even in the sixteenth century, the age of the Reformation when the medieval shrines were destroyed and once-holy bones scattered, the first two or three decades were seemingly no different from all those which had gone before. People still provided for Canterbury pilgrimages in their wills, the Pageant of Becket—a travelling platform on which his martyrdom was re-enacted on his feastdays—continued to trundle through Canterbury streets and money was still spent on the children who acted the parts of Becket and the knights, on leather bags of fake 'blood' and 'in goldefoyle' to decorate the wheeled stage. Henry VIII continued to make offerings at Becket's shrine which his own commissioners would one day knock to pieces, foreign ambassadors and fine ladies still visited and grew wide-eyed at the shrine on their way up to London. Erasmus himself found its pilgrims, its wealth, and its owners in need of a satirical blast from his restless pen.[6]

Many of the older shrines then, and certainly Becket's, continued to attract pilgrims, though less, perhaps, for physical healing than for spiritual comfort and the less 'religious' reasons. This does not mean that society could do without curative centres or that they ceased to spring up in the fourteenth and fifteenth centuries. On the contrary, in the later Middle Ages new shrines came into being and seemed to follow the traditional pattern, in which the death of a well-known or reputedly holy figure was followed by reports of miracles at his tomb, and then by formal application for papal canonization. For example, miracle-cults grew up around the tombs of Robert Winchelsey, Thomas of Lancaster, Archbishop Scrope, John Dalderby and Robert Grosseteste (both bishops of Lincoln), Bishop William de Marchia of Wells, Richard Rolle, and others—even Edward II. The quotation at the head of this chapter mentions one of these later medieval saints of England who was in fact canonized in the early fifteenth century, John 'of Bridlington'. These traditional thaumaturgic cults continued to appear, and then lapse into obscurity, until the sixteenth century. King Henry VI (d. 1471) must have been the last Englishman whose canonization was sought at the papal court before the break with Rome. Following the lead of Henry VII, Henry VIII himself was mildly interested in the project, but gave it up about 1528 as relations with the pope deteriorated. During the last few decades of the fifteenth century over three hundred miracles of Henry VI, buried at Windsor, were recorded in English. A Latin abridgment has survived, including about 174 wonders, presumably destined for a papal board of inquiry.[7] This is the last extensive collection of 'traditional' posthumous miracles at an English saint's shrine. Henry's cult, though 'political' and though half the miracles can be classified as accidents and non-healing wonders, hence not 'typical',[8] indicates that the wonder-working saint in his shrine was still an important part of popular religion. But were these 'traditional' saints as important as they had been in the twelfth and thirteenth centuries?

In the later Middle Ages devotion to Christ and his mother became a more distinguishable feature in 'official' as well as 'popular' religion in Europe and England. There were many signs of this shift in emphasis, for instance in liturgical innovations such as the late-medieval feasts of Corpus Christi, the Crown of Thorns, the Compassion of the Virgin, the 'Ikon of the Saviour', the Presentation of the Virgin, the Name of Jesus, the Transfiguration, the cult of the Five Wounds of Jesus.[9] Mystical writings of this period often dwelt upon the suffering of Christ or of Mary; a still widely-read product of late-medieval piety is not concerned with saints but with the very centre of things, the *Imitation of Christ*. Collections of miracles of the Virgin, which became more popular, were—unlike lists of posthumous miracles—'literary' compositions usually unattached to physical shrines and stressing the spiritual rather than merely physical succour to be had from the influential Lady. The Angelic Salutation and saying of the Rosary were popular forms of devotion. Her cult was fostered in many other ways: churches were graced with special chapels built in her memory, the 'Lady Chapels' so familiar to students of English ecclesiastical architecture; in the later thirteenth century the Bishop of Exeter ordered her image to be placed in all the churches of his diocese, and by the fourteenth century the Feast of her Conception was observed throughout the province of Canterbury. Mariolatry, as it is sometimes called, was a movement guided by the Church from above but welcomed, too, by the ranks of the laity for whom religion was becoming a more directly personal matter.

The best indication of a change on the popular front, even of a rivalry between the 'old' wonder-working saints and the 'new', is an increase in centres of pilgrimage associated with Christ and, to an even greater degree, with Mary. In England she was venerated at Walsingham, Ipswich, Doncaster, Caversham, Knaresborough, Worcester, Penrice, Westminster and Willesden, and these are only the more well-known shrines. Some of these began to attract pilgrims in the thirteenth century or even earlier, but they were most popular from the fourteenth century to the Reformation. To return for the last time to our opening quotation, pilgrimage was to be undertaken not only to the old and well-established shrine of Becket and to a new cult-centre at Bridlington, but also to the most famous Marian shrine in England, Walsingham, and to one dedicated to the blood of Christ, at Hailes: the old-style devotion to thaumaturgic saints here complements the 'newer' worship of Christ and his mother. These changes were in part due to the promptings of the official Church in its attempt to implement a more refined piety (a programme which had taken centuries to have effect), unhindered by superstitions associated with magical bones and free of the sometimes unedifying phenomena associated with traditional curative saints and their shrines. The new shrines were evidence of a shift away from the spiritual middle-men and toward the heart of Christianity; the new feasts, new devotions and new holy places lifted the believer, in theory, to a more sublime plane.

There are, however, indications that the official Church succeeded only to a limited extent in refining the spiritual senses of its members by encouraging Marian and Christocentric devotions, and that the Church itself was influenced by the popular traditions and practical realities of the day. As a result, the traditional outlook and the activities associated with the thaumaturgic dead were carried over into late medieval popular devotion to Mary and Christ. The old tension between spiritual and material considerations which troubled even the Primitive Church was present here as well. To begin with, there were practical advantages to the late-medieval Church in the new devotions, quite apart from any elevation of the spiritual life of the masses. Old-style saints' cults continued to attract popular interest in the fourteenth and fifteenth centuries, as noted above. On closer examination, however, it is evident that very few of these saints ever became officially canonized. In place of the half-dozen English saints so honoured in the thirteenth century only one was similarly elevated in the fourteenth and just two (one of whom had been dead more than 300 years) in the fifteenth century. This was certainly not due to lack of perseverance since English kings, prelates and nobility pressed unsuccessfully for at least eleven canonizations at the papal curia in the later Middle Ages. Some of these unrewarded attempts were even more impressively sponsored than the cause of Thomas Cantilupe. On John Dalderby's behalf in the fourteenth century the papacy received individual and joint letters from King Edward III, the archbishops of Canterbury and York, ten bishops, the dean and chapter, and mayor and citizens, of Lincoln, thirty-four religious houses and sixteen earls. These were followed up by letters to cardinals, the sending of a special envoy to Avignon and at least twenty-six more letters from about sixty-six prelates, monasteries, nobles and even Oxford University. The pope remained unimpressed, Dalderby uncanonized.[10] Besides the political uneasiness which often disrupted Anglo-papal relations in this period, attempted canonizations had grown more and more expensive, the process had become more complicated, definitions and proofs of miracles more technical. In short, it was very costly and very difficult to canonize an English saint in the later Middle Ages.

Fortunately neither Christ nor his mother required papal canonization. Their universally-acknowledged holiness was freely available to all. Rather than bother with expensive canonizations, elaborate shrines and properly authenticated bones, churches could attract pilgrims—in the new religious environment—with a simple statue of the Virgin or a Holy Rood (crucifix) made of the most inexpensive materials. It would be unreasonable to suggest that the new devotions arose *because* of the ease with which cult-centres of Christ and the Virgin could be established, without reference to the pope and without all the cumbersome business involved in traditional saint-making, but this freedom probably helped to encourage veneration of Mary and her son.

Another characteristic of later medieval piety that is perhaps not always sufficiently stressed is the way that popular traditions themselves influenced the form of the new devotions, for example, in reverence shown to the Eucharist or consecrated bread which in medieval theology was the body of Christ. It has been suggested that the ostentatious elevations of the Eucharist or Host by priests, customary from the thirteenth century, arose out of the desire of simple congregations to *see* that God was 'made' in the course of the Mass. From this came the idea that the longer one gazed at the Host the more virtue one earned, a popular misconception which the Church condemned. On the other hand, the Church seems to have accommodated itself to this very belief by instituting—especially from the fourteenth century—the 'exposition' of the Blessed Sacrament.[11] The Host was placed in a monstrance, an elaborate container with a window modelled on earlier reliquaries for saints' bones, and was left on the altar for the gaze of the faithful or carried in procession. It is difficult to avoid the conclusion that the older attitudes toward relics, which were kept in reliquaries, carried in processions and occasionally exhibited to the public in a kind of formal 'viewing', have re-emerged in the midst of later medieval eucharistic devotion. The same may be said of the eucharistic miracle-stories, which treat the Host like any 'traditional' saint's relic; these stories were especially popular from the thirteenth century.

The influence of habit—a thousand-year-old habit—and official accommodation is even more apparent in Marian devotion. The 'saint' may be different, but the customs are very familiar indeed. For many ordinary Christians the 'new piety' seems to have made little difference to the way they actually behaved; it was less a matter of spiritual development than a mere alteration in direction when they stepped out on the high road bound for shrines. For many people, the idea of a physical journey on earth was still stronger than the ideal, contemplative ascent to the eternal Christian truths.

First of all, beginning with the obvious, there *were* pilgrimages, with vows and offerings, sometimes stimulated by indulgences,[12] to Marian shrines, as to any other saint's cult-centre. In addition the relics of Mary, such as her 'milk' at Walsingham and Ipswich, or bits of her clothing at Durham (and remnants of Christ like the blood of Hailes, pieces of the Cross at Bromholm, or of the crown of thorns at St. Albans) further 'materialized' and trapped the new devotion in the visible world. Suppliants brought their votives, candles, wax images and golden crowns—for Mary's statues—to the new shrines just as to the old. The Countess of Warwick, for instance, made offerings in 1439 to Our Lady of Caversham, Our Lady of Walsingham, and Our Lady of Worcester. Pilgrims carried away ampoules of water from Marian shrines, they committed the same excesses at these shrines, were subject to the same cautions as earlier generations of pilgrims to Becket's or Godric's shrine had been. In 1313 the Archbishop of York prohibited unauthorized pilgrimage to a parish church where an image of the Virgin had recently been placed and in 1386 the Bishop of Lincoln was disturbed by reports of unverified miracles at a newly-erected wooden cross.[13] Pilgrims found, as the last example emphasizes, that statues of Mary and Holy Roods performed 'traditional' miracles, including those of physical healing. Although lists of these cures have not survived as they have for 'ordinary' shrines, there is other evidence. In the fifteenth-century Pynson Ballad extolling Our Lady of Walsingham, it was claimed that at her shrine the dead were revived, the crippled and blind restored, the possessed, leprous and 'defe, wounded and lunatyke' healed.[14] One might object that this was mere literary ornamentation, but there are also other references such as wax votives and cures of disease at Our Lady of Penrice, Thomas More's reference to a girl cured at Our Lady of Ipswich, a miraculous resuscitation of the drowned wife of Robert Leche through the virtues of the statue of Our Lady of Doncaster in 1525,[15] and a wax image which Margaret Paston sent to Walsingham for her ailing husband in the fifteenth century.

The same customs are evident in European mariolatry. In the diocese of Strasbourg, about thirty-four new pilgrimage-centres grew up after 1350. Eighteen of them were Marian shrines. Many of the newer European shrines were also miracle-centres, with thaumaturgic statues, like the image of the Virgin that protected Ypres against the English siege of Henry Despenser, Bishop of Norwich, in 1383. A Marian shrine in Flanders was started in 1455 when someone suspended her image from the boughs of a cherry tree; though it burnt down only four years later, no fewer than 300 miracles had already been recorded.[16]

Returning to England, the same 'old-fashioned' thaumaturgy was going on at many of the newer shrines of Christ. At the Holy Rood of Bromholm there were *tanta signa atque miracula* from the thirteenth century. The Rood was as popular as Becket's shrine had been, or so the medieval chronicler claimed.[17] As for the shrine of Christ at Hailes Abbey, dating from the thirteenth century, Hugh Latimer had this to say about 1533: 'I dwell within half a mile of the Fossway, and you would wonder to see how they come by flocks out of the west country to many images, but chiefly to the blood of Hales.' Latimer was scandalized, for he saw nothing but superstition in these pilgrimages to saints' images which 'can neither help me nor mine ox, neither my head nor my tooth; nor work any miracle for me.'[18]

Centuries of religious controversy lay behind these indignant words. Before the end of Henry VIII's reign that controversy had swollen and burst into violence, destruction and death, but the conflicts were noticeable long before the English Reformation. Criticism of pilgrimages, relics and saint-veneration came from both sides, from conscientious churchmen who objected to the excesses, and from unorthodox or heretical critics who objected to the principles. In the fourteenth century Wyclif disputed the pope's authority to declare anyone a saint, and his Lollard followers reiterated his arguments, and also denied that miracles were proof of sanctity; as a certain Walter Brut despairingly complained, 'If only those who trusted in miracles would heed the word of Christ.'[19] Though it is often claimed that the Lollards had no clearly-formulated religious 'programme', their criticisms of pilgrimage, saint- and relic-veneration was one of their characteristic tenets. In a document posted on the doors of Parliament in 1395 they condemned offerings to 'blind roods and deaf images of wood and stone' as idolatry.[20] In the early fifteenth century one of them, William Thorpe, claimed that nobody should make vows to images of saints, 'nor seek them, nor kneel to them, nor kiss them, nor incense them', and he condemned the   opular hunger for miracles and the extravagance of foolish pilgrims who travelled accompanied by 'the noise of their singing, and with the sound of their piping, and the jangling of their Canterbury bells, and with the barking out of dogs after them'.[21] Walsingham was one of the principal Lollard targets. In 1382 it was said that the Lollards disparaged the Blessed Virgin, calling her 'the witch of Walsingham' and in the fifteenth century some of them referred sardonically to the place as 'falsingham'.[22] These Lollard critics of image-worship and pilgrimages and false relics saw little difference between the excesses committed in the name of the more traditional, and the more recent Marian and Christocentric, devotion. For them the abuses were repugnant whether at a local saint's shrine or at some Holy Rood. Speaking of Bromholm in 1424 a cleric of Lollard tendencies claimed that 'the image of the cross and other images are not to be worshipped'.[23]

Critics from the orthodox side such as Richard Fitz Ralph, fourteenth-century Archbishop of Armagh, were usually not so strident as their opposite numbers, though one does find a more severe approach in some of the vernacular literature of the day. Chaucer blasted the pardoner who went about with his smooth face duping peasants with false relics—'And in a glas he hadde pigges bones'; on one occasion the host replied to the pardoner's invitation to come and kiss the relics with a suggestion that parts of the pardoner's anatomy should be cut off and 'shryned in an hogges tord'. Men at dice swore by the 'blode of Crist, that it is in Hayles' and the miller's wife, who had enjoyed 'so mery a fit' in the night with John the clerk, woke up screaming 'Help, holy croys of Bromeholm'. Langland's criticisms were just as astringent. He condemned foolish wandering pilgrims who came home to tell tales of their travels for the rest of their days, and he has Avarice say, 'I'll make a pilgrimage to Walsingham, with my wife as well, and pray to the Rood of Bromholm to get me out of debt', hardly flattering references to shrines of Mary and Christ.[24]

Lollards preached (and some were executed for their opinions), prelates warned against excessive zeal and occasionally closed local shrines, popular writers drew attention to the ludicrous aspects of the whole business—yet pilgrimages, shrine-offerings, and vows to saints not only continued but were in many ways encouraged. In 1408 Archbishop Arundel enjoined the veneration of crosses and saints' images with 'processions, bendings of the knees, bowings of the body, incensings, kissings, offerings, lightings of candles, and pilgrimages'.[25] In combatting the Lollards, English prelates were called upon to defend the belief in saints' miracles as a matter of course, but not all of them went as far as Archbishop Arundel. Some fifteenth-century vernacular sermons also encouraged the old ways, recommending pilgrimages and recalling the tales of saints and their wonders such as the miracles of Becket which happened 'noght al onely where he lyeth, but also in alle parties of the erthe'.[26] Vernacular saints' lives were popular too in later medieval England, among a people growing increasingly literate. The printing press was playing an important role by the end of the fifteenth century, and among the works produced by Caxton was an English version of the Golden Legend, a collection of saints' lives. A wish to seem fashionable also kept the shrines in operation. Since a great many important men and ladies continued to go on pilgrimage or to send offerings to various shrines down to the eve of the Reformation, lesser folk followed their lead. At Canterbury, for instance, the Bohemian ambassador was dazzled by the costly tomb of Becket in 1446, as was a Venetian diplomat about 1500.[27] In his will King Henry VII (d. 1509) left instructions for a silver gilt statue of himself to be placed by Becket's shrine, not many years later Erasmus visited the place, and in 1520 Henry VIII and Emperor Charles V went to Canterbury. The last recorded pilgrim seems to have been a certain Madame de Montreuil, who looked upon Becket's shrine in August of 1538. Within a matter of weeks it was destroyed down to its foundations.[28]

Marian shrines too continued to attract pilgrims in the sixteenth century, especially at Walsingham. Today Walsingham is a small town of narrow streets and lanes, a neglected, crumbling collection of tea-shops, guest houses and souvenir stalls. A television aerial marks out a modern habitation built within the ruins of the Franciscan convent on the edge of town. Of the great church which housed the Virgin's shrine only some of the east wall and a few conventual rooms are left, but the well which supplied so much curative water for pilgrims' ampoules is still there. These pitiful remains do scant justice to a shrine which ranked with Becket's in the later Middle Ages, and which was still thriving even in the sixteenth century. In 1519 the Duke of Buckingham sent an offering to Our Lady of Walsingham, Wolsey went there on pilgrimage the following year, in 1523 the bishop of Ely paid a visit, and another illustrious pilgrim was Erasmus. In her will of 1536, Catherine of Aragon, that unfortunate lady who had been the first of many wives of Henry VIII, provided for a pilgrimage to the shrine. The last time Henry paid for a candle to burn there was March, 1538, a few months before the famous statue of the Virgin of Walsingham was taken up to London to be destroyed.[29] Other 'newer' shrines of Mary as well as of Christ were similarly honoured down to the Reformation: in 1483 Lord Rivers bequeathed his body to Our Lady of Pontefract, his heart to Our Lady of Pewe (Westminster) and his hairshirt to Our Lady of Doncaster.[30] The Duke of Buckingham provided an oblation at Our Lady of Pewe in 1508 and the king's candle was still burning before Our Lady of Doncaster in 1537.[31] Henry VII's queen visited the Virgin of Ipswich in 1502, Henry VIII's queen, Catherine of Aragon, prayed before the Virgin of Caversham in 1532.[32] Two months before his execution in 1521, Buckingham made his offering at the Holy Blood of Hailes, and in 1530 the prior of Worcester cathedral spent 2s 4d. for 'expenses ryding to hayles from cropthorn in pilgrymage'.[33] A few years later, when Hugh Latimer cast his eye over the people who came 'by flocks out of the west country' to images and especially to Hailes, there must have been many in those pilgrim crowds who were as influential and orthodox as the prior of Worcester.

Pilgrimage, then, especially to the 'new' shrines, was still important to many leading laymen and ecclesiastics in the later Middle Ages and sixteenth century, in spite of the growing criticisms by reformers. Within and outside the Church, to many others the practices associated with pilgrimages were no more than gross superstitions. Perhaps some were also frustrated when they saw that even the purer devotion to Mary and Christ was being debased. The conflict might have continued unresolved for centuries had it not been for certain difficulties in which Henry VIII found himself, for European reforming influences reaching England, and for the advice of ambitious men the king allowed into his confidence, not the least significant of whom—as far as the shrines were concerned—was Thomas Cromwell.

Chapter 12

The Destruction of the Shrines

Sinne is wher our Ladie sate, heaven turned is to hell,
Sathan sittes wher our Lord did swaye,
                    Walsingam oh Farewell.
                        Anon (sixteenth century)

The history both of Henry VIII's difficulties with the papacy and of the English Reformation is a vast and complex subject. This chapter is concerned only with its effects upon the shrines and worship of the saints. Religious changes—or any other changes in human society—are not inevitable. In England the new attitudes were resisted, the government had to use propaganda, even force, and the old religion was a long time in dying. Secondly, it is sometimes misleading to speak of a 'government policy' in the destruction of the old ways of belief; it is convenient, but not always accurate. There were cross-purposes, blunders, differences of opinion among those who managed the business, and between them and their sovereign. The man directing the dissolution of the monasteries and ruination of the shrines was Thomas Cromwell, and it is clear that his support of the more radical reforms—even if it derived from what he conceived to be reasons of state—was irksome to Henry. Ultimately the difference between the king and his vicar-general, a disastrous marriage alliance and political reverses, led to Cromwell's fall and execution in 1540. He was attainted of high treason and of 'being a detestable heretic' who had misled the king's subjects into a 'refusal of the true and sincere faith and belief'.[1] At least that was the 'official' reason. Thirdly, in this chapter a distinction is drawn between the dissolution of the monasteries and the destruction of the shrines. It may seem 'natural' that both of these aspects of medieval Christianity should fall together but in many cases several months elapsed between the pulling down of a shrine and the later dissolution of the monastery which had housed it and, of course, shrines in places other than monasteries were destroyed as well. The motives for ending the monastic life were mixed, but financial gain was probably Henry's primary interest. On the other hand, compared to the wealth of vast monastic estates there was little to be gained from the gold, silver and jewels of the shrines, many of which—such as Cantilupe's—had already been stripped of their most valuable offerings before their destruction in the sixteenth century. The pulling down of shrines and scattering of holy relics in England, as in Luther's Germany, was a matter of religion and policy rather than economics.

Henry, who was awarded the title 'Defender of the Faith' by the pope in 1521 for his anti-Lutheran stand, by 1527 was appealing to Rome concerning his marriage. Cardinal Wolsey fell from grace in 1529 after prolonged and fruitless negotiations with the pope. By 1531 or 1532 a 'new man', Thomas Cromwell, was helping Henry to assert his independence of Rome, and from 1532 to 1534 the Reformation Parliament passed several Acts by which the king became in fact and in law Supreme Head of the Church in England. During 1535 English ecclesiastical property was assessed, in 1536 the lesser monasteries began to fall, and by 1540 all of them, lesser and greater, had been dissolved. The destruction of relics began in a desultory way in 1535, with Cromwell's commissioners removing from the monastic houses they visited items they considered superstitious, such as a 'bag of relics' containing God's coat and Our Lady's girdle (which women used in childbirth), or—on another occasion—the boots of Thomas Becket and Saint Edmund's nail-pairings and 'other reliques in divers places which they [the clergy] use for covetousness in deceaphing the people'.[2] There were further confiscations in 1536 and 1537, but the destruction of the shrines reached its peak in 1538, the year of the Second Royal Injunctions to the clergy to 'forthwith take down, and without delay' the images 'abused' by superstitious rites. The clergy were also instructed to preach against pilgrimages to such objects and to prohibit offerings to images and relics or 'kissing or licking of the same'. In the same year Bishop Shaxton issued an impassioned mandate to his Salisbury clergy condemning relics which were no more than 'stinking boots, mucky combs, ragged rochets, rotten girdles' and such rubbish. As a chronicler put it, all

> images that were used for comon pilgrimages both in England and Wales were taken downe . . . that the people should use noe more idolatrye to them . . . all shrynes of sainctes taken downe throughout England.[3]

Down they came: the canonized saints, Cantilupe, Richard of Chichester, Hugh of Lincoln, Becket for example; the unofficial demi-gods and heroes such as Darvell Gadarn of Wales and John Schorn who conjured the Devil into a boot; down came the alabaster and Purbeck marble shrines at Bury St. Edmunds, Winchester and Reading; statues of the Virgin succumbed at Cardigan, Caversham—with all her wax images, crutches, candles and brooches—Southwark, Worcester,

Ipswich, Coventry, Penrice, Doncaster, Willesden, even Walsingham; Christ's Rood could no longer be seen at Boston, Boxley, Bromholm or Bermondsey, nor his Blood at Hailes; and all the other English saints in all the other holy places were smashed on the spot or taken on a final journey up to London along with whatever offerings had garnished their shrines. In July 1538, for example, the statue of Our Lady of Ipswich was stored in Cromwell's 'wardrobe of beds' and in September she was joined by the statues of Mary of Caversham, St. Anne of Buxton and Modwenna of Burton on Trent—accompanied by her 'red cow and her staff'. Cromwell's 'wardrobe of beds' in London must have resembled the basement of a modern museum. After his death only silver plate, chalices, mitres and other Church spoils were found. Presumably the statuary had been burned in 1538 when most of the public 'executions' of the saints occurred. As Latimer wrote to him in June of that year, the Marian statues of Worcester, Walsingham, Ipswich, Doncaster and Penrice 'would make a jolly muster in Smithfield. They would not be all day in burning'.[4]

The preceding very brief survey of the destruction may give the impression that all went smoothly at Cromwell's behest, that the country had been long prepared—by the Lollards, for instance—to acquiesce in a sweeping away of a thousand years of tradition, that interest in the saints had decayed into indifference and only a slight push toppled the whole structure. But if so, why were the old customs still being followed even in the fateful year itself, 1538? Rather than gradual acceptance and gracious decline, the final destruction seems in many cases to have burst suddenly upon an unsuspecting people in the midst of their traditional devotions. This was true even of the king himself: in March 1538 Henry VIII was burning a candle at the statue of Our Lady of Walsingham; just four months later he permitted the burning of the statue. As we noted in the last chapter, pilgrimage continued in the sixteenth century—in fact it continued down to the eve of the destruction. In 1535 the offerings at Walsingham came to over £260, a larger sum than at any other English shrine including Becket's. Next year Cromwell's men noted that 133s 4d. were offered by pilgrims in a nine-day period, in other words about £270 per year, very near the 1535 figure. This does not suggest a diminution in pilgrim-offerings and, by extension, in pilgrimage at least to Walsingham. In 1536 or 1537 Hugh Latimer was very concerned that the old ways were yet followed: pilgrimage continued, and *'even still the miserable people are suffered to take the false miracles for the true'*. In 1538 a royal commissioner reported that Mary's image at Cardigan was the object of a 'greate pilgrimage *to this present day*' and still in Wales, it was reported that between 500 and 600 pilgrims venerated the image of Darvell Gadarn on 5 April 1538, offering cattle and money.

The Cromwellian agent who plucked down Mary's image at Caversham (near Reading) in 1538 somewhat indignantly complained, *'even at my being* [there] , there came in not so few as a dozen with images of wax' to offer to the Virgin's statue.[5]

It cannot be doubted that many, especially among the less conservative prelates, wished to put an end to the shrines. Archbishop Cranmer—as we might expect—requested Cromwell to examine some blood which was supposed to have been Becket's but which Cranmer suspected was a 'fained thing and made of some redd Oker', and in the rich English prose of the bishop of St. David's some of the laity of his diocese were castigated as 'clatteringe conventycles of barbarous rurall persons' deluded by relics and saints.[6] There would have been little point in episcopal condemnations or the scattering of the relics and images, however, unless these common parishioners and other 'rurall persons' were still under the spell of magical bones. Apparently the supernatural powers of relics were not yet banished from the minds of many of Henry's subjects.

In August 1538, for instance, a Dominican prior in Cambridge wished to remove a statue of Mary from his convent since so many pilgrims visited it especially during Sturbridge Fair, which was drawing near.[7] The inertia of habit no doubt accounts for the continued visits of some pilgrims to holy places or favourite statues which they had known since childhood. But others were actively hostile to the iconoclasm of 1538. Some were lay folk, like the two women 'examined' by an agent of Cromwell after they objected to the general desecration and end of pilgrimage, or the squire who claimed that Cromwell's pulling down of images was all in vain. Many of the clergy added their voices to those of the dissentient laity in 1538: a Shrewsbury vicar re-gilded the statue of the Virgin in his church, the vicar of Newark on Trent urged the kissing of images and foretold the destruction of the destroyers, and others publicly condemned the Cromwellian programme in this year, like a certain monk of Thame, a hermit from Chesterfield, and a priest of Rye. A Windsor priest advised pilgrimage to the tomb of Henry VI, while a vicar in Chichester diocese preached in favour of images and miracles and claimed that the old ways would return in a few years. On Candlemas Day he had the temerity to give voice to a 'ballad of Our Lady' in the chancel of his church and then announce to his parishioners:

> Law, law, Masters, I said we should have the old fashion again; ye may see it comes a little and a little.[8]

These sentiments explain why the image of St. David was removed 'quietly', why Cromwell instructed his men to take away the statue of Our Lady of Penrice 'as secretly as might be'. They also explain why the government devised an elaborate propaganda programme to overcome popular resistance to the destruction of the shrines and prohibition of pilgrimages. This was nothing new. Before dissolving the lesser monasteries in 1536 Cromwell's men travelled about collecting gossip which could be useful in discrediting the monks. The tenor of their 'findings' is suggested in two contemporary tracts, *Of the Sodometry of the Monke of the Monastrey of Lanthony in Gloustershire* and *A Declaration that the Prior of the Croched Friers in London was found in Bed with a Whore.*[9] There was, in some cases, justification for such attacks, but it is generally conceded that most of these scurrilous reports lacked a factual basis and were merely part of a 'smear campaign' to make the closing of the monasteries more palatable.

When attacking the 'traditional' saints the commissioners scattered their bones and demolished the fabric of the shrines, presenting the locals with a *fait accompli*. Sometimes remnants of the saint were carried away secretly by the faithful, but usually the bones were reburied in some unmarked place or—in Frideswide's case, for example—mixed up with another corpse. With the 'newer' devotion, however, the government adopted a different approach. In order to show the people at large that statues of the Virgin and Roods of Christ were human devices unworthy of veneration, these were taken to a public place and, following a sermon suited to the occasion, reduced to smouldering heaps of ashes. They were proven to be mere wood, and quite unsupernatural. These performances often occurred in London and were heralded with a great deal of publicity.

This propaganda programme concerned *inter alia* two items related to the new devotion, the Blood of Christ at Hailes Abbey, and the Rood of Boxley in Kent. Hailes Abbey, a Cistercian house founded near Winchcombe in the mid-thirteenth century, received its precious gift from Edmund, son of King Henry III, in 1270, and the Blood of Hailes soon attracted so many pilgrims that the new Worcestershire shrine was thought by some to rival the Marian shrine at Walsingham in Norfolk. As we have seen, devotion to Christ and his mother increased in the later Middle Ages, and there was probably as much reality as rhetoric in Hugh Latimer's complaint about crowds of pilgrims who were passing by his home on their way to worship their Saviour's blood at Hailes. Today only the base of the shrine remains—a bump in the ground—and near it other bumps and exposed stonework are all that is left of the ambulatory in which those pilgrim crowds gathered to absorb the virtues of the famous relic.

In February 1538 a sermon was preached at Paul's Cross by the Cromwellian Bishop Hilsey during which he asserted among other things that twenty years earlier an abbot of Hailes claimed that the blood of Christ was a duck's blood. The current abbot, who like Hilsey owed his position to Thomas Cromwell, immediately wrote to the latter to deny any knowledge of this fraudulent relic, and to call for an inquiry. By March the offending item had been removed from public veneration though pilgrims still came to venerate the empty shrine, even in September. In October Latimer, who so disliked those pilgrim crowds, was commissioned to go to Hailes to examine the 'blood'. He found it to be a yellowish gum tightly closed up in a round beryl which made it seem red. The relic was placed in a sealed box and left with the abbot, but seems shortly afterwards to have been sent to London. In November Bishop Hilsey once again stood at Paul's Cross, this time to retract his earlier statement about duck's blood and to admit that it was a gummy stuff, perhaps honey coloured with saffron.[10] The ultimate fate of the relic is unknown.

Even though Hilsey, who annoyed some conservatives by his sermons, and was even called 'knave bishop and heretic' by some of them,[11] retracted his blatant claims for a more straightforward account of the Hailes relic, the suggestion had been planted in the minds of many radical Reformers. The more extreme claims reappeared in later propaganda, such as the semi-official 1539 'Declaration of the Faith', and a justification of the religious changes written about 1550 called *The Pilgrim*. This piece of propaganda not only repeated the tale about duck's blood but averred that it was secretly renewed every Saturday by two monks who had 'confessed' to their fraud. In addition, a second legend made an appearance in *The Pilgrim*. It was said that the glass of the container was constructed so that the monks could make the blood seem to appear or disappear; disappointed pilgrims were usually rewarded by the sight of the blood after making further offerings.[12] Latimer had simply described the container as a 'round beryl garnished with silver', but because the outlandish tales were more useful to the reformers (especially those of Edward VI's reign), the yellow gum of Hailes was remembered as duck's blood secretly and periodically renewed, kept in a conjurer's magical glass.

The next object is an even better example of a relic or statue, the fraudulent possibilities of which were embellished in order to make its fate less objectionable and to underline the 'monkish abuses'. On 7 February 1538 Cromwell was told of a discovery within the Priory of Boxley (about twenty-four miles west of Canterbury). In the routine course of statue-demolition the Rood of Grace, a crucifix, was removed from the wall or pillar to which it was affixed. Inside it were found 'certain engines and *old* wire, with *old rotten* sticks in the back of the same, which caused the eyes to move and stir in the head . . . and also the nether lip in likewise to move as though it should speak'. A contemporary chronicler noted that there were strings of hair to move the eyes and lips. The Boxley monks disclaimed any knowledge of these hidden devices and when the Rood was displayed on next market day in Maidstone, three miles away, the locals expressed great surprise and indignation at such a thing.[13] Pilgrimage to the Rood, which may or may not have been common once upon a time, was no longer significant in 1538, for when the priory was assessed in 1535, the commissioners said nothing about offerings to any Rood of Grace. When they visited monasteries they usually reported pilgrims' oblations when these were still coming in, such as the £10 pilgrims offered in 1535 at the Blood of Hailes. The writer of the letter to Cromwell emphasized this absence of pilgrimage himself when he noted that Kentish folk 'had *in time past* a great devotion to the image'. By 1538 the wonderful Rood, possibly designed for processions or pageants, had fallen into disuse, its old, rotten mechanism crumbling into decay.

The Rood was taken to London in February 1538, and on the 23rd a contemporary wrote that the 'abusion' was to be divulged next day, a Sunday, at Paul's cross. Bishop Hilsey, whom we have met, preached a sermon condemning the Rood and then threw it to the crowd, who dismembered it. In April the Swiss reformer Bullinger, who had close ties with the English Reformation, received a report that when the Rood was exhibited at Paul's Cross it 'turned its head, rolled its eyes, foamed at the mouth, and shed tears'. This remarkable augmentation of powers was carried even further by other propagandists, such as Hoker, the minister of Maidstone. About May he wrote to Bullinger that before Hilsey's sermon was delivered, the Rood—'a wooden God of the Kentish folk'—had been viewed by the royal court and had put on a memorable performance for Henry: it 'scowls with his eyes—turns his face away—distorts his nostrils—casts down his head—sets up a hump-back—assents—and dissents!'.[14]

The nimble device became notorious. As one of his diplomatic agents in Brussels wrote to Henry VIII, one Saturday evening in November 1538 after-dinner conversation turned to topics of the day and someone mentioned the common rumour that religion was extinct in England. The diplomat replied by explaining Henry's objectives and declared that only the abuses of religion were taken away, such as Becket's shrine and the Rood of Boxley.[15] In this casual conversation the Rood was brought in as justification of the English Reformation; it was too apt an example not to mention. The Rood, like the Blood of Hailes, had a propaganda value which was exploited for decades. In a work first published in 1576, Lambarde's *Perambulation of Kent*—a pioneering study in local history and topography—the Rood was still undergoing metamorphosis since it was reputedly able to

> bowe downe and lift up it selfe, to shake and stirre the handes and feete, to nod the heade, to rolle the eyes, to wagge the chappes, to bende the

browes, and finally to represent to the eye, bothe the proper motion of eche member of the bodye, and also a lively, expresse, and significant shewe of a well contented or displeased mynde: byting the lippe, and gathering a frowning, frowarde, and disdainefull face, when it would pretende offence; and shewing a most mylde, amyable, and smyling cheare and countenaunce, when it woulde seeme to be well pleased.

Lambarde, we are told, went about his writing with 'stout Protestant scepticism';[16] and, evidently, with inventiveness. Unfortunately he does not describe the sermon and destruction of the Rood, though he had ample opportunity. Lambarde claimed that in his day there were still many people living who had seen and heard Hilsey's sermon, and that there were many books about the Rood in circulation.[17] Such accounts may have been designed to ridicule through satire or, on the other hand, the powers of the mechanical cross may have been so grossly exaggerated in order to emphasize the 'diabolical' skills and craftiness of the monks capable of such tricks.

It was fortunate for the reformers that the Rood was taken to pieces by the London mob, for then the wild stories of its powers—its ability to 'gather a disdainefull face' for example—could flourish unimpeded by the limitations of the object itself. The reformers must have known, as more than one historian has pointed out, that other similar mechanical toys were in existence, even in St. Paul's itself. There are vague references in both the 1539 'Declaration of the Faith', and *The Pilgrim*, to other roods with moving parts.[18] Boxley took pride of place, however, and the legends which grew up around it continue to be accepted, or at least repeated, to this very day.[19]

The final example of how government policy was implemented by exaggeration and falsification is taken, appropriately enough, from England's best-known saint. Although Thomas Becket was widely honoured, even in the twelfth century there were those who were not entirely convinced that he had earned a place among the canonized. 'Some said he was a lost soul as a betrayer of his country', wrote a thirteenth-century monk, 'others that he was a martyr as a defender of the Church'. The heaviest attacks began in the fourteenth century, especially after Wyclif claimed that Becket had been a great 'possessioner', interested in accumulating temporal power who had died while trying to protect this worldly dominion. Wyclif's followers repeated these allegations. In 1395, for example, one of the Lollards' Twelve Propositions denied that Becket had died a martyr's death, and for the rest of the Middle Ages criticism of Becket and of pilgrimage to Canterbury was a standard Lollard exercise. According to them, Becket's death was of no value (1428); he was a false traitor (c. 1429); Wyclif was holier than Becket (1429); Canterbury pilgrims gave their souls to the Devil (1464); Becket was a thief whose offerings were misused (1523); he was not a saint (1531). In 1532 a man was executed as a heretic who had claimed among other things that Becket had been a traitor, murderer and thief.[20] These Lollard reiterations probably made the demolition of his shrine and cult much easier for Cromwell. 'Officially', though, Becket's honour was still being upheld, even in the early 1530s. In 1531, for instance, a book against the martyr was condemned by the bishop of London and in 1533 a certain William Barlow confessed in a letter to the king 'errors' which included his composing a dialogue 'inveynge specyally agaynst Saynt Thomas of Canterberye'.[21]

King Henry was moving farther away from papal authority in these very years, and by the end of 1534 the royal *volte-face* was complete. The business of dissolving the monasteries and pulling down shrines set in motion in 1535 was well underway in the following year, and the first intimations of the end of Becket's cult and shrine were also heard in 1536. In that year the government abolished certain feasts, including the important 7 July commemoration of Becket's Translation; in 1537 the Archbishop of Canterbury, for the first time in more than three centuries, did not fast on the eve of the July celebration, and in the same year the image of the martyrdom of Thomas was removed from the city seal of Canterbury.[22] By 1538 the devastation of the shrine was clearly imminent. In April a correspondent of Bullinger expected St. Thomas of Canterbury 'soon' to go the way of the Rood of Boxley,[23] and in August, 1538, the Archbishop asked that Becket's 'blood' be examined. Early in September the commissioners were in the cathedral and within two weeks the shrine had been dismantled, the bones dispersed or burnt (the question of their fate is still unresolved),[24] the treasures carted off to the royal coffers. In the same month the Second Royal Injunctions definitively abolished all liturgical celebrations in Becket's honour. On 16 November, in a proclamation jointly issued by King Henry and Cromwell, the latter promulgated a 'history' of Becket which was supposed to prove that he had been a rebel and traitor and no canonized saint; in addition Cromwell ordered Becket's images taken down, his name erased from all service books, and (once again) all his feasts abolished. The results of these measures can be seen in surviving medieval calendars (chronological lists of saints' feastdays) where, more often than not, Becket's name is only barely legible since most of it was scratched away centuries ago; in the service books whole pages were cut out or mutilated in compliance with these mandates. Cromwell followed up his injunctions in a circular letter to the bishops in December, repeating his account of 'traitor' Becket's death and calling for an absolute end to his veneration.

Someone in government—one naturally thinks of Cromwell—went to even greater extremes to discredit Becket, by inventing a 'trial' in which his treason was proven and judgment given for the annihilation of his shrine and reputation. Becket was said to have been cited to appear in April 1538 and when no attorney stepped up within thirty days, judgment was passed against him. This 'judgment' was carried out, so it was claimed, in August and completed by the 19th of that month, and it called for the destruction of his shrine and other memorials.[25] The account of the fictitious trial was probably produced not long after the official injunctions of 16 November which, incidentally, make no mention of this earlier citation and 'judgment'.[26] The trial of Becket was probably invented to provide a basis for Cromwell's accusation of treason and to justify the desecration of his shrine. Perhaps foreign reaction to the destruction of one of Christendom's most famous shrines had something to do with the spurious trial. Certainly there was interest abroad. On 5 October 1538, for example, a correspondent in Valencia informed Cromwell that 'every man who seeks news from England inquires what has become of the saint of Canterbury'; in November Cromwell was informed from Padua that the Venetians and others were 'mad against the abolition of the idols in England', which would presumably have included Becket's shrine. Naturally the pope was disturbed by the news, but not everyone on the continent looked upon it as a calamity: Luther's close ally Melanchthon wrote to a colleague that things were going well in England, that Walsingham's Lady had fallen and that 'the monument of Thomas of Canterbury there has been destroyed'.[27]

Although Cromwell's curious 'history' of Becket may have soothed consciences within England, and the imaginary trial perhaps had similar effects here and abroad, it is equally true that English devotion to the Canterbury martyr continued after 1538 even though his shrine was gone, his bones dispersed or destroyed, and his cult outlawed. In 1539 an Ipswich parson was accused of saying the services of Becket against the Injunctions, an image of his martyrdom was still to be seen in the church at Henley, and in another parish the villagers tried to disguise his statue by exchanging his episcopal cross for a woolcomb.[28] Such incidents were probably due as much to misunderstanding the drift of the latest royal policies—which did sometimes contradict themselves— as to overt defiance. The fact that it was no easy thing to abolish ancient traditions and beliefs is evident in the need to repeat and to elaborate injunctions against image-worship to the end of the sixteenth century. In 1541 the king wrote to his bishops that, in spite of his earlier orders, 'shrynes, covering of shrynes, and monuments of those thinges doe yet remayne in sondraye places of our realme' and they were to be taken away.[29]

Henry VIII died in 1547 and during the reign of Edward VI (1547-1553) the reformers pushed their radical programmes much harder. In

1547 the royal guardians of the king (a minor), in particular Somerset, ordered the clergy to seek out and destroy images, pilgrimages, offerings, candles and trindles and any other evidences of image-worship and the reformers repeated earlier injunctions that the word *papa* and Becket's name were to be removed from service books. These instructions were to be followed in the homes of the parishioners as well as in all the churches. In 1548 Archbishop Cranmer, writing to his bishops, repeated these orders and quoted from the royal mandate that

> muche stryfe and contentyon hath rysen and dayly ryseth, and more and more encreaseth . . . and in some places also the images whiche by the saide injunctions were taken downe, be now *restored and set up againe*, and almoste in every place ys contentyon for images.

He then instructed his clergy to take down all vestiges of image worship—whether used with superstitious 'abuse' or not—and end all pilgrimages whatsoever.[30]

In 1549 Latimer was still referring to that old government scapegoat, the Blood of Hailes, as a 'great abomination' in his sermons before the young monarch (who once tried to impress Somerset by collecting biblical passages which condemned idolatry and putting them into his best French). During the next few years Edward, now under Northumberland's control, established an Act against Books and Images and introduced the Second English Prayer Book, which omitted all commemoration of saints. He also assented to the Forty-two Articles, in which it was declared that the worshipping and adoration 'of images, as of reliques, and also invocation of sainctes, is a fonde thing vainlie feigned, and grounded upon no warraunt of scripture'.[31] The result of these injunctions and publications was the smashing of medieval artefacts which had somehow survived the iconoclasm of Henry's reign.

After 1553 when Edward VI died and 'Bloody' Mary began to rule a troubled land, the religious beliefs of her subjects were once again thrown into confusion. The queen installed Catholic clergy, killed some who had offended, or refused to submit to, her regime, and attempted to restore the old ways. In 1555, for example, the liturgy of Becket was once again heard in the precincts of Canterbury cathedral, but although Becket's 'pageant' was dragged from storage and refurbished, no attempt was made to restore his shrine.[32] When Mary came to the throne no one in England under the age of sixteen had ever seen Becket's famous memorial or for that matter any of the other great shrines their parents might still mention now and then. It seems that Mary was content to have the surviving statues put back in their niches, altars returned to the east end of the churches, roods restored to their beams.

All of Mary's work was reversed with the accession of Elizabeth in 1558. Again the churches were stripped of statues, roods, votives, in yet another purge. The variable fortunes of the church at Yatton in Somerset may stand for what probably happened in thousands of other parishes up and down the country, as the religious climate changed with changing sovereigns. During the reign of Edward the church-wardens at Yatton had to pay out over four shillings for the cost of removing the images, including the Virgin Mary in the chancel, and for a carpenter's labour and materials in building a wooden altar-table. After Mary came to the throne the churchwardens spent over twelve shillings in restoring church goods and as wages for the carpenter who rebuilt the old altar. Finally, with Elizabeth, they spent over two shillings in plucking down the images, removing the rood, and taking away the very altar which they had built in the previous reign.[33] The necessary changes were made in other areas as well: that old 'pageant' of Becket was finally sold as junk in 1564 (for 2s 8d.), the 'blessyd archebisshop' Becket mentioned in a popular history published in 1516 became, in the 1559 edition, 'trayterous byshoppe', Elizabeth's Arch-bishop Parker issued the usual injunctions against image-worship, and in the Thirty-nine Articles (1563, officially sanctioned in 1571) the adoration of images and saints was given its final, Anglican condemna-tion as a 'fond thing, vainly invented'.[34]

With the 'Elizabethan Settlement' the theological pendulum came to rest—at least until the seventeenth century—but there were still minor problems now and then, such as the parishioners of Seaton who gathered one July evening in 1564 to celebrate the vigil of Becket's translation.[35] Even though these outward violations of the ecclesiasti-cal norms established by Elizabeth were less and less noticeable as the sixteenth century drew to a close, the individual and social needs once satisfied by saints and shrines were still there; the illnesses and un-certainties of this life and the next could hardly be eradicated by Articles and Injunctions. Ways were found to provide for at least some of these needs.

Although medieval villagers were well acquainted with local healers, after the destruction of the shrines these 'cunning men' and wise women seem to have become more important in everyday life. No one in Elizabethan Essex, for instance, was more than ten miles from a known cunning man (and there were others who wished to remain *un*known to all but their friends). They gained their reputations, as Keith Thomas points out in his admirable study, in much the same way 'as that which had in the Middle Ages enabled the shrines of saints to attract great concourses of people'.[36] The greater prominence given to lay healers may have had additional, very unfortunate, consequences: in 1584 Reginald Scot tried to defend the poor old women put on trial 'for working of miracles, otherwise called witchcraft'.[37] Not all healers were ancient crones who dabbled in black as well as white magic, of course. In the seventeenth century certain Puritans laid claims to the gift of healing, such as George Fox who in his *Book of Miracles* claimed to have cured about 150 people.[38]

Wizards, white witches and their charms and potions were not the only sources of *auxilium* in a world without saints and relics. It is probably no coincidence that although hydrotherapy was certainly not unknown in the Middle Ages, the popularity of English watering-places and the number of 'newly-discovered' spas grew tremendously from the later sixteenth century, when, in the words of a contemporary, 'Rumours are now spread almost of every spring, and vain tales fly about in manner of every water.'[39] In the first book about the curative effects of Bath, published in 1562, the author described how he experimented with 'certaine diseased persones'; the first to advertise the properties of curative springs other than Bath was John Jones, who praised Buxton in 1572. One of Cromwell's commissioners had taken away an image of St. Anne from Buxton in 1536 and locked up the baths and wells, but presumably Buxton was sufficiently secular by Jones's time to re-open the place.[40] The standard account of the healing virtues of natural baths was published in 1631,[41] and by the later seventeenth century crowds were flocking to English spas as much for fashionable gregariousness as for cures, a trend we saw at Becket's shrine where lepers soon gave way to medieval holiday-makers. Defoe put it this way, describing Bath in the early eighteenth century in words which also recall a typical medieval custom:

> In former times this was a resort hither for cripples; and we see the crutches hang up at the several baths, as the thank-offerings . . . But now we may say it is the resort of the sound, rather than the sick.[42]

The old social and curative needs once satisfied by shrines were partially satisfied by the baths and wells of early modern England.

Sometimes the link between baths and the old religion was quite strong, for example at Holywell or St. Winifred's Well in north Wales, where cures were recorded from the Middle Ages to the nineteenth century. The place was not closed down in the Reformation, presumably, because the relics of St. Winifred had been translated to Shrewsbury in the twelfth century. It was an open secret that after the Reformation Catholics visited the spring—actually a large pool—but the many cures of non-Catholics (even of a Quaker) and the apparent divorce from idolatry in the medieval period, prevented its closure in Henry's day. The accounts of seventeenth-century pilgrimages are almost indistinguishable from earlier, medieval descriptions, even down to the bending of a coin (a three-pence piece, in 1627) to God 'in

honour of St. Wenefrid'.[43] Later on in that century Celia Fiennes
visited Holywell and noted that bits of moss and stones were taken
away as relics. 'There I saw', she continued, 'abundance of the devout
papists on their knees all round the Well', and in the early eighteenth
century Defoe, after turning up his nose at the legend of St. Winifred,
went on, 'the Romanists indeed believe it, as 'tis evident, from their
thronging hither to receive the healing sanative virtue of the water'. He
suggested that the 'Romanists' confused the *medicinal* powers of the
water, with supposed *miraculous* powers.[44] The close association
between Holywell and Catholicism is also shown in the fact that one of
Cantilupe's bones, which had passed from family to family since the
time of Henry VIII, was kept by the Jesuits in the Old Star Inn at
Holywell from 1664 to 1835.[45] It is probable that many of the Catholic
pilgrims who came for the healing waters also visited the Old Star to
pay their respects to the Hereford wonder-worker, one of England's
last canonized saints of the Middle Ages.

After the shrines were destroyed, then, English society developed
means to compensate for some of the loss. Their curative function, for
example, was carried on in other ways including an increasing use of
natural baths, and by the seventeenth century these watering-places
had absorbed yet another role once played by medieval pilgrimage
centres, in providing for the gregarious instinct and the need for
'entertainment'. But these had always been minor, secondary benefits
of the shrines. Their most important role had been to provide spiritual
support, to allay the spiritual as well as the physical anxieties of this
life, and to soothe the souls of all men who contemplated the life to
come. It may be that Tudor England never managed to find satisfactory
alternatives to this more fundamental and socially significant function
of medieval saints' shrines. In any case, regardless of these later developments we cannot doubt that for a great part of the population the
destruction of their shrines, relics and statues in the sixteenth century
had been a painful experience. The wounds would only begin to heal in
the generations which grew up when Canterbury was no longer a
pilgrimage centre, and owls shrieked amidst the ruins of Walsingham
where

> Toades and serpents hold their dennes wher the palmers
> did thronge.

Conclusion

In the first pages of this study we described how Augustine led his missionary-monks into Kent and brought with him the full paraphernalia of relics and miracles and saint-veneration, and we have seen in the final chapter how these rites and beliefs and objects were swept away from English shores a thousand years later. The pragmatic approval of relic-miracles in the early missionary ages became less and less acceptable in a more settled European Christian Church. The conflicts, inherent in the very earliest saint-veneration of primitive Christianity, became more serious in the central and later Middle Ages, exacerbated by the tremendous diversity found within the Church itself. A shift in direction toward Marian and Christocentric piety in the later Middle Ages really had little deep effect upon majority (or lay) attitudes toward miracle-working shrines and magical relics. Ultimately these issues were decided only in the sixteenth-century Reformation: in some countries the practices were placed on a more regulated basis, in others—as in England—they were prohibited, though with some resistance from some among the clergy and laity.

As to the miracles themselves, we have found that in most cases the events can be accepted as 'real' although we would not interpret them as miracles or miraculous cures. The medieval attitude to cures and other supernatural occurrences must be considered, not our own; and we find that even limited, partial or temporary improvements in health were thought to be 'cures', and that the element of coincidence was usually not even considered. Not only this, but the squalid conditions of life and ignorance surrounding the causes and treatment of diseases and the make-up of the human body itself make these attitudes toward 'miracles' more understandable. In addition certain types of ailment— the chronic/remissive, self-limiting, and psychogenic—lend themselves especially well to such 'cures', a phenomenon as true of modern 'faith-healing'.

Individually, shrines differed in their earliest gatherings of miracle-touched pilgrims in varying degrees, basically, it would seem, because of differences between the particular saints enshrined and the circumstances of their deaths. In addition we found that cults had their own internal development, for certain changes were noted after the posthumous miracles had begun—the pilgrims tended to come from more distant places, the dominant sex changed to males, the frequency of miracles dropped and the type of miracle changed, over the active period of wonder-working (usually no more than a decade). Collectively, we discovered that most people involved in miracles in France as well as in England, were men, roughly divided into lower and other social classes, but the women were practically all lower-class individuals. Most of the miracles reported by all these pilgrims were physical cures, and one of the clearest findings in this regard was the fact that in England and France, and to the same degree in both countries, different sexes and social classes reported different categories of miracles. This indicates not only a difference in susceptibility to certain illnesses but also a difference in attitude toward illness and 'miracles', from one social class to the next and between the sexes.

The physiological, sociological and psychological functions of the shrines—as sources of 'healing', social coherence and spiritual strength and assurance—tended to vary in relative importance over the years at any given shrine, the final function being most lasting. The needs of society were so deep that after the destruction of the shrines in England alternative means were found to carry on at least some of those functions.

The miracles—though we would not think of them as such—provide valuable information about the 'real' people who became involved in wonder-working shrines—who they were, where they came from, what miraculous things happened to them. Through them we can observe medieval saints' shrines in action, and draw closer to understanding the important part these holy places played in contemporary life. Though the registrars may have gathered their data in order to provide a basis for future canonizations, or merely to advertise the wonders of the relics, their records, with all their biases and imperfections, are among the most valuable and unexploited documents of medieval popular Christianity.

Abbreviations

AASS	*Acta Sanctorum*
AB	*Analecta Bollandiana*
Ann. Mon.	*Annales Monastici*, ed. Luard, 5 vol. (1864-9) *RS* 36
Cantilupe	Life and Miracles, in *AASS* I Oct (1765)
C & Y	*Canterbury and York Society*
DuCanda	C. du Canda, *La Vie de S. Thomas*, 1615
Frideswide	Life and Miracles, in *AASS* VIII Oct (1853)
Gilbert	R. Foreville, *Le livre de saint Gilbert*, 1943
Godric	*Libellus de vita et miraculis*, ed. Stevenson, SS 20, 1847
HBS	*Henry Bradshaw Society*
Hedwig	Life and Miracles, *AASS* VIII Oct (1853)
Henry	R. Knox and S. Leslie, *Miracles of King Henry VI*, 1923; refs are to miracle numbers, not page
HMC	*Historical Manuscripts Commission*
Lawrence	C. Plummer, 'Vie et Miracles de S. Laurent', *AB* 33, 1914
Louis	St. Louis of Toulouse, *Processus Canonizationis, Analecta Franciscana*, VII, 1951
LP	*Letters and Papers Foreign and Domestic, Henry VIII*
LRS	*Lincoln Record Society*
Mat.	*Materials for the History of Thomas Becket, RS* 67
NRA	*National Register of Archives*
OHS	*Oxford Historical Society*
Osmund	A. Malden, *The Canonization of Saint Osmund*, 1901
Pap. Reg.	*Calendar of Entries in the Papal Registers relating to Great Britain and Ireland* (ed. Bliss *et al.*, 1893-1960)
PL	*Patrologiae Cursus Completus, Series Latina*, J. Migne
RS	*Rolls Series* (Chronicles and Memorials of Gt. Britain and Ireland)
Simon	*Miracles of Simon de Montfort*, ed. Halliwell, Camden Soc. 1840
SS	Surtees Society
Wilkins	D. Wilkins, *Concilia Magnae Britanniae et Hiberniae*, 1737
William	A. Jessopp and M. James, *Life and Miracles of St. William of Norwich*, 1896
Wulfstan	R. Darlington, *Vita Wulfstani*, Camden Soc. 3d ser. 40 (1928)

Notes

INTRODUCTION

1 R. Brentano, *Two Churches: England and Italy in the Thirteenth Century*, Princeton, 1968.

2 The word 'saint' includes popularly-venerated as well as papally-canonized individuals.

3 In this study the word 'cult' refers to the belief in the sanctity and miraculous powers of a particular dead individual, the group of people who believe, and their actions consequent upon that belief—particularly pilgrimage or devotion to his shrine or tomb, and the attribution of specific miracles to him.

4 Cantilupe, 613.

5 The clerics who sat by the shrines and noted the details of miracles, which were supplied by pilgrims or by letters, are called 'registrars', 'scribes', 'tomb-guardians', 'monks' (whether monks or not) and so on indiscriminately; their contemporary designations varied.

6 For references to some of these recent works, cf. R. Finucane, 'The Use and Abuse of Medieval Miracles', *History*, vol. lx (Feb. 1975), 1-10, which also includes some of the references from which we have reconstructed the macabre scenes in Becket's crypt.

CHAPTER 1

1 Augustine, *Letters*, ed. M. Dods, Edinburgh (1872), No. 136 (pp. 174-5).

2 Justin Martyr, *Dialogue with Trypho*, in *Writings*, ed., tr. T. Falls, Washington (1948), 260. Cf. *Luke* 11:15-20.

3 Ambrose, *Letters*, M. Beyenka, N.Y. (1954), No. 61; Paulinus, *Life of Ambrose*, in F. Hoare, *The Western Fathers*, London (1954), 159; Augustine, *Confessions* IX.6 and *Letters* No. 78 (p. 309); cf. *City of God* XXII:8.

4 Augustine, *City of God* XXIII:8-10; H. Delehaye, 'Les recueils antiques de miracles des saints', *AB* XLIII (1925), 74-85. For Augustine's part in the miracles, Peter Brown, *Augustine of Hippo*, London (1967) esp. 413-17.

5 D. R. Dendy, *The Use of Lights in Christian Worship*, London (1959), chap. 7, 'The Cult of the Saints', and J. Fowler, 'On a Window Representing the Life and Miracles of S. William of York', *Yorkshire Archaeol. and Topographical*

Journal, III (1875), 198-348, an excellent introduction (despite the limited subject suggested by the title) to early customs of Christian worship at saints' shrines.

6 Augustine, *Retractions,* M. Bogan, Washington (1968), 55, 61-2.

7 Cf. A. Momigliano, ed., *The Conflict between Paganism and Christianity in the Fourth Century,* Oxford (1963), 17-18.

8 Gibbon, 28th Chapter, section four.

9 Life of Germanus in Hoare, *The Western Fathers,* 307, cf. 289; Life of Leoba, ed. C. H. Talbot, *The Anglo-Saxon Missionaries in Germany,* London (1954), 213.

10 Life of Saint Martin in Hoare, *Western Fathers,* 29.

11 Bede, *Ecclesiastical History of the English Nation,* tr. J. Stevens, London (1910), 52-3.

12 H. Chadwick, *The Early Church,* (1967), 253.

13 Bede, *Eccl. Hist.,* 37, 54.

14 Life of Willibrord in Talbot, *Anglo-Saxon Missionaries,* 12.

15 When a previously unsuspected holy body was discovered (often as a result of a vision or dream), this was called 'invention' or *inventio* (Lat. *invenire,* to find). The next step might be a simple raising of the remains from the earth, *elevatio,* rather than a fully ceremonious *translatio.*

16 R. Roussel, *Les Pèlerinages,* Paris (1954), 67.

17 'Skulls and bones were heaped up in charnel-houses along the cloisters, . . . and lay there open to the eye by thousands, preaching to all the lessons of equality . . . Such was the place which the Parisians of the fifteenth century frequented . . . Day after day, crowds of people walked under the cloisters . . . In spite of the incessant burials and exhumations going on there, it was a public lounge and a rendezvous'. J. Huizinga, *The Waning of the Middle Ages,* N.Y. (1954), 148-9.

18 A. Mirgeler, *Mutations of Western Christianity,* tr. E. Quinn, London (1964), 48.

19 C. Dawson, *Religion and the Rise of Western Culture,* N.Y. (1950), 34.

CHAPTER 2

1 William, 175.

2 *Mat.* II. 186-7.

3 F. Stenton, *Anglo-Saxon England,* 3rd ed., Oxford (1971), 651; Orderic Vitalis, *Ecclesiastical History,* ed. M. Chibnall, vol. II, Oxford (1969), 173; Giraldus Cambrensis, *Opera,* ed. Dimock (1868), RS 21: VI.27.

4 Gregory of Tours, *Libri Miraculorum,* PL 71, col. 729.

5 The following is from Edmund Bishop, *Liturgica Historica,* Oxford (1918), Ch. II, 'The History of the Christian Altar', esp. 24-7.

6 C. R. Cheney, *Medieval Texts and Studies,* Oxford (1973), 350.

7 E. Bishop, *Lit. Hist.,* 30.

8 Bede, *Eccl. Hist.,* 220, and cf. 116; William, 123-7.

9 *PL* 77, 701.

10 *The Chronicle of Jocelin of Brakelond,* ed. H. Butler, London (1949), 114;

Self and Society in Medieval France: The Memoirs of Guibert of Nogent, ed. J. Benton, N.Y. (1970), 225.

11 B. Ward, St. Edmund, London (1903), 195-6.

12 Chronicon Monasterii de Abingdon, ed. J. Stevenson (1858), RS 2:II.155-8.

13 Adam of Eynsham, Magna Vita Sancti Hugonis, ed. tr. H. Farmer and D. Douie, 2 vols, London (1961-2), 169-70, 153.

14 R. Brentano, Two Churches, 229. This recalls the death of Father Zossima in Brothers Karamazov: 'Seeing that his end was near, they anticipated miracles and great glory to the monastery in the immediate future from his relics'.

15 Wm. Durand, Rationale divinorum officiorum, tr. J. Neale and B. Webb, Leeds (1843), 134; HMC VIII:I.348b-349a.

16 RS 13:182.

17 Froissart, Chronicles, ed., tr. G. Brereton (1968), 319; G. G. Coulton, Five Centuries of Religion, Cambridge (1936), vol. III.111, and Cheney, Medieval Texts, 362.

18 F. Henschen, The Human Skull: A Cultural History, London (1965), 112-22, 124-6.

19 D. Bethell, 'The Making of a Twelfth-century Relic Collection', Studies in Church History, vol. VIII (1972), 71.

20 R. Glauber, PL 142, col. 673.

21 G. R. Owst, Preaching in Medieval England, Cambridge (1926), 100.

22 Reg. Sutton, LRS 60:V.76, an inspeximus of 1295; E. Dooley, Church Law on Sacred Relics, Canon Law Studies No. 70, Washington D.C. (1931), 29; Wm. of Malmesbury, de gestis pontificum Anglorum, ed. H. Hamilton (1870), RS 52, 120.

23 One relic-catalogue compiled by a French savant approaches the bawdy, noting among other things the six breasts of St. Agatha and the two penises of St. Bartholomew, one of 'extraordinary size'. Collin de Plancy, Dictionnaire critique des reliques, vol. I (Paris, 1821), 8-9, 78.

24 Augustine, Confessions, VI.2.

25 Bede, Eccl. Hist., 53; R. W. Southern, Western Society and the Church in the Middle Ages, Pelican Hist. of the Church (1970), 174, from Capit. I.45.

26 A. L. Poole, Domesday Book to Magna Carta, 2nd ed., Oxford (1955), 274.

27 E. W. Kemp, Canonization and Authority in the Western Church, London (1948), 63-5; F. A. Gasquet and E. Bishop, eds., The Bosworth Psalter, London (1908), 27 f., 76-119; M. Brett, The English Church under Henry I, Oxford (1975), 83.

28 Cal. Patent Rolls 1321-24, 378; Chancery Warrants I.542; E. F. Jacob, The Fifteenth Century, Oxford (1961), 61-2.

29 William, 171, 214; Martene and Durand, Thes. Nov. Anec., III col. 1820; Godric, 339, 389-91, 417-18.

30 Simon 107-8, D. Bethell, 'The Miracles of S. Ithamar', AB 89 (1971), 436; Cantilupe 663; Gilbert 45.

31 Mat. II.206. This is actually a summary (except for the quoted words) of a much longer Latin passage. Most of the longer examples from the miracles, as in this case, have been paraphrased in the interests of brevity. Particular words or phrases of importance, however, have been directly translated and retained

in the longer examples. Most shorter passages and single phrases are direct translations.

32 *Mat.* I.160-62, II.229-34; William, 177.

33 A. Edwards, 'An Early Twelfth-Century Account of the Translation of St. Milburga of Much Wenlock', *Trans. Shropshire Archaeological Soc.* Vol. LVII (pt. II, 1962-3), 151; Walter Daniel, *Vita Ailredi* ed. F. M. Powicke, London (1950), 62, 77; Adam of Eynsham, *Vita Hugonis*, 206, and cf. 199 f. and 209.

34 B. Colgrave, 'Bede's Miracle Stories', in *Bede: His Life, Times and Writings*, ed. A. H. Thompson, Oxford (1935), 204, 208; Adam of Eynsham, *Vita Hugonis*, 122. Some early hagiographers invited their readers to go to the Old Testament, for wonders even more incredible than those they related, B. Gaiffier, *Études Critiques d'hagiographie et d'iconologie*, Brussels (1967), 60.

35 *Enchiridion Symbolorum: Definitionum et Declarationum de Rebus Fidei et Morum*, ed. H. Denzinger, Barcelona, 34th ed. (1965), 224: *ut honor redundet in Dominum.* Later medieval popes attempted to meet the demand for saints by allowing local veneration, but this half-way procedure—beatification—was not fully operative during the Middle Ages.

36 Reg. Swinfield, *C & Y* VI (1906), 490-1; Wilkins, III.636-9.

CHAPTER 3

1 Wilkins, I.48-50.

2 Life of Boniface in Talbot, *Anglo-Saxon Missionaries*, 129; *Mat.* I.472-4; R. Robbins, *Secular Lyrics of the Fourteenth and Fifteenth Centuries*, Oxford (1956) quoted by B. Stone, *Medieval English Verse* (1964), 106.

3 D. Rock, *The Church of Our Fathers*, ed. G. Hart and W. Frere, vol. III, 387-8; D. Knowles, *The Monastic Order in England*, 2d ed. Cambridge (1963), 481-2; Wm. Malmesbury, *Gest. Pont. Angl.*, 438.

4 Jocelin's *Chronicle*, 54.

5 H. Bradshaw and C. Wordsworth, eds., *Statutes of Lincoln Cathedral*, pt. II, Cambridge (1897), 56-7, xliv.

6 A. Gransden, *The Letter-Book of William of Hoo, Sacrist of Bury St. Edmunds*, Suffolk Rec. Soc. vol 5 (1963), 246; E. Bowen, *Britain and the Western Seaways*, London (1972), 110, 123; Reg. Drokensford, *Somerset Rec. Soc.* I (1887), 17, 133.

7 *Mat.* II.112-3; J. Capgrave, *The Chronicle of England*, ed. F. Hingeston (1858), *RS* 1, 284; *Vita Hugonis*, 162-3; Jointville, *The Life of Saint Louis*, M. Shaw, 1963, 195.

8 *Manuale et Processionale ad Usum Insignis Ecclesiae Eboracensis*, ed. W. Henderson, SS vol. 63 (1875), 103-4, 26*-28*; 121*; 208*-210*.

9 Joinville, *Life* of St. Louis, 254.

10 Cheney, *Medieval Texts*, 18-19.

11 Reg. Hethe (Rochester), ed. C. Johnson, *C & Y* vols 48-9 (1948), I.467-9; Gransden, *Letter-Book*, 81; Gaiffier, *Études*, 401 ff.

12 *HMC* VIII:1, 352a.

13 *Chronicon Abbatiae de Evesham ad annum 1418*, ed. W. Macray (1863), *RS* 29, 93.

14 C. Jenkins, 'Christian Pilgrimages, A.D. 500-800' in A. Newton, ed., *Travel and Travellers of the Middle Ages*, London (1926), 47; cf. Gerald of Wales, *Opera, RS* VI. 24: *exquisito furti genere.*

15 Guibert, *Memoirs*, 196.

16 Frideswide, 579; Wulfstan, 179-80.

17 B. Charles and H. Emanuel, 'A Calendar of the Earlier Hereford Cathedral Muniments', *NRA*, 3 vol. (1955), II.585, 588, 802, 815 *bis*; *Reg. Orleton, C & Y* vol. 5 (1908), ed. A. Bannister, 142-3; *Reg. Martival, C & Y* vol. 57 (1963), ed. C. Elrington, II.299-300; Cantilupe, 598; *NRA* (Hereford), II.821, 845, 867.

18 R. Cole, 'Proceedings Relative to the Canonization of John de Dalderby, Bishop of Lincoln', *Assoc. Archit. Soc. Reports and Papers*, vol. 33 (1915-16), 271; J. Chélini, *Histoire religieuse de l'occident médiéval*, Paris (1968), 471; J. Purvis, 'St. John of Bridlington', *Jour. Bridlington Society*, no. 2 (1924), 36-7, 41.

19 Gransden, *Letter-Book*, 157.

20 D. Erasmus, *Pilgrimages to Saint Mary of Walsingham and Saint Thomas of Canterbury*, ed., tr. J. G. Nichols, London (1875), 214.

21 William, 200.

22 H. Harrod, 'Extracts from Early Wills in the Norwich Registries', *Norfolk Archaeology*, vol. IV (1855), 338.

23 *Mat.* II.211, 253-4.

24 J. Jusserand, *English Wayfaring Life in the Middle Ages*, 1889 (ed. of 1961), 63; see *RS* 77: I. xlix-l.

25 *Mat.* I.160, II.186, 229-34; William, 167-8; *RS* 21.VII.130-33 (Hugh); Richard Wych, *AASS* I Apr., 310; Osmund, 37-9.

26 *Mat.* I.395, II.209-11; Henry 88; *Mat.* I.500-501; the woman's words are rendered by the medieval registrar as *abite trutanni.*

27 *MS Vatican Lat.* 4015, f. 86ᵛ, 107ʳ.

28 Gilbert, 70-1; Bodley *MS Fell 2*, f. 7ᵛ (Edmund Rich); Du Canda, 234.

29 Jusserand, 198; *Mat.* II.126.

30 *Mat.* II.118.

31 Henry of Huntingdon, *Historia Anglorum*, ed. T. Arnold, *RS* (1879), 74.xxvi; Edwards, *Milburga*, 149.

32 M. Glasswell, 'The Use of Miracles in the Markan Gospel', in C. Moule, ed., *Miracles: Cambridge Studies in their Philosophy and History*, London (1965), 151-62.

33 2 Kings 13:21.

34 Godric, 245; *Mat.* II.xlix-l; Gaiffier, *Études critiques*, 60; John of Salisbury, *Memoirs of the Papal Court*, tr. M. Chibnall, London (1956), 26; F. Kempf et al., *Handbook of Church History*, vol. III, London (1969), 313-4.

35 L. Thorndike, *A History of Magic and Experimental Science*, N.Y., vol. I (1923), 326-7; *Dialogues* of Pope Gregory, tr. O. Zimmerman, N.Y. (1959), 29-30; Caesarius of Heisterbach, *The Dialogue on Miracles*, tr. Scott and Bland, 2 vols. London (1929), II.172-3 (and cf. the Latin edition by J. Strange, 2 vol. Cologne, 1851).

36 *Vita Hugonis*, 219.

37 William of Malmesbury, *Gestis Pont.*, 436-9.

38 Walter Daniel, *Vita Ailredi*, 69-70.
39 *Selected Letters of Pope Innocent III*, ed. C. R. Cheney and W. H. Semple, London (1953), 28; Caesarius, *Dialogue*, II.171-2.
40 *Sum. Theol.* PP Quaes. 105, Art. 7-8; *Sum. Contr. Gentiles*, III. c. 101; cf. A. Van Hove, *La Doctrine du Miracle chez Saint Thomas*, Belgium, 1927.
41 F. Powicke and C. Cheney, *Councils and Synods*, Oxford (1964), 1044; G. Owst, *Literature and Pulpit in Medieval England*, 2d ed., Oxford (1961), 141; J. A. Mac Culloch, *Medieval Faith and Fable*, London (1932), 181-2; *LRS* 48, vol. III, 37; *LRS* 60, vol. V, 143, 176, 212; *LRS* 64 vol. VI, 103-4, 186.
42 Cantilupe, 590.
43 H.-F. Delaborde, 'Fragments de l'Enquete faite a saint-denis en 1282 en vue de la canonisation de saint-louis', *Memoires de la société de l'histoire de Paris et de l'Ile de France*, tome xiii (1896), 1-71; Ward, *St. Edmund*, 191-2.
44 Wilkins, III.637-8, s.a. 1494.
45 *Opus Maj.* II.397-9 ed. Bridges; R. Foreville, 'Une Lettre inédite de Jean de Salisbury', *Rev. d'Hist. de l'Eglise de France*, tome xxii (1936), 183.
46 B. Hareau, 'Les Recits d'Apparitions dans les sermons du moyen âge', *Memoires de l'Inst. National de France*, vol. xxviii (1876), 239-64; *Vita Hugonis*, 124.

CHAPTER 4

1 Bede, 227; and for other evidence that this danger was recognized in pre-Conquest England, cf. S. Rubin, 'The Medical Practitioner in Anglo-Saxon England', *J. Roy. Coll. Gen. Practit.* 20 (1970), 67; Wulfstan, 128, 153, *Mat.* I.173-4, II.216-7; *Vita Hugonis*, 178; Hugh in Gir. Cambren. *RS* 21:VII.142; Thorndike, *Magic* I.728—similar claims were made for coffee in seventeenth-century England.
2 E. E. Evans-Pritchard, *Theories of Primitive Religion*, Oxford (1965), 90.
3 J. Grattan and C. Singer, *Anglo-Saxon Magic and Medicine*, London (1952), 199; U. Maclean, *Magical Medicine: A Nigerian Case-Study*, 1971, 19. 'Egyptian days' were ill-omened days.
4 Godric, 441, 378, 407-8, 433.
5 Godric, 385, *potiones acerbissimas*; Frideswide, 587; Gilbert, 51-2 and 61; *Mat.* I.395-6.
6 *Mat.* I.416-7, II.242-3; *Gesta Stephani*, ed. R. Howlett, *RS* 82.III.38.
7 *Mat.* I.162-4, 187-8, 287; II.39-40; Gilbert, 50; *MS Vat Lat 4015* f. 109ᵛ.
8 L. Mac Kinney, *Medical Illus. in Medieval Manuscripts*, London (1965), 10-11, 15; Frideswide, 587-8; Wulfstan, 144-5; *Mat.* I.278-9; *HMC* IX.92a.
9 *Mat.* I.162, 169-70, 261-2, 332-4; II.259-60; Simon, 98, Wulfstan, 121; Henry 121, 132.
10 *Mat.* I.158-60, 188-9, 199-200, 210, 382-3; II.93-4, 153; Godric, 391-2; Wm. of York, Raine, *RS* 71:II.533, Bodl. *MS Dodsworth 125*, f. 132.
11 *Mat.* II.228; Giraldus, *RS* 21.VII.185 (Hugh of Lincoln); Grattan and Singer, 44.
12 Cantilupe, 610-21; Lawrence, 166.

13 Grattan and Singer, 189; *Mat.* II.252; M. Leproux, *Dévotions et Saints Guérisseurs*, Paris (1957), 40.

14 Grattan and Singer, 10; *Mat.* I.380-81; Thorndike, *Magic,* I.631-2, *Mat.* I.244-45; Godric, 406 ('sortes').

15 *Mat.* I.375-7, 240-1, 245; Simon, 103-5; Wulfstan, 154; Giraldus Camb., *RS* 21: VII.124-6 (Hugh of Lincoln); Godric, 445, William, 176-7.

16 Godric, 374 (St. James twice), 398 (Becket twice), 409, 441; Simon, 73, 109; Gilbert, 55, 65-7; Wulfstan, 134; *Mat.* I.220-1, 238-9; for *benedictio oculorum infirmorum* cf. *Manuale . . . Eborac.,* ed. Henderson, SS 63, a Salisbury rite p. 32*; and for holy oil in a twelfth-century miracle, Gilbert, 51.

17 Frideswide, 569-70, Hedwig, 255.

18 *Mat.* I.228-9, II.255; Cantilupe, 700; L. Hector, *The Handwriting of English Documents,* London (1958), 104-5; E. Hammond, 'Incomes of Medieval English Doctors', *Jour. Hist. Medicine* XV (1960), 162; Langland (Goodridge ed., 1959), 288; Chaucer (Coghill ed., 1952), 29; Froissart, 401.

19 Augustine, *City of God* VIII.22; Lawrence, 174, Simon, 96, Frideswide, 588-9; *Mat.* I.456-7, 472, 499, 503-4.

20 William of York, Raine, *RS* 71: II.537.

21 Gilbert, 51; *Catal. Cod. Hagiographicorum Latinorum,* BN Paris, tome III, Brux. (1893), 296-7 (Richard Wych); Lawrence, 177; Rubin, 'Medical Practitioner', 67.

22 C. Woodruff, 'The Miracles of Archbishop Winchelsey', *S. Pauls Ecclesiological Society,* vol. 10 (1938), 122; Bodley *MS Fell 2 f. 10ᵛ* (Edmund Rich); Wulfstan, 144-5; *Mat.* II.221-2.

23 *Mat.* I.164-5, 187-8; Cantilupe, 702.

24 Gilbert, 68.

25 *Mat.* I.184-7; Bodl. *MS Fell 2 f. 11ʳ* (Edm. Rich); W. Pantin, *The English Church in the Fourteenth Century,* Notre Dame (1963), 231; Du Canda, 263-4; Henry, 130; Lawrence, 170-71; R. Wych, Cat. Cod. III.296-7.

26 Cantilupe, 654, 663; William, 196; *Mat.* I.158-60; Simon, 72; Wulfstan, 130.

27 *Mat.* I.261-2, 440.

28 A.-J. Festugière, *Personal Religion among the Greeks,* Berkeley (1960), ch. VI, 'Popular Piety: Aelius Aristides and Asclepius', and R. Blum and E. Blum, *Health and Healing in Rural Greece,* Stanford (1965), 168-9.

29 Langland, 200.

30 Thorndike's paraphrase in L. Thorndike, *Michael Scot,* London (1965), 78.

31 Blum and Blum, 90.

32 *MS Vat Lat 4015,* f. 189 et sqq., Cantilupe 626 ff.; Reg. Baldock, *C & Y* vol. 7 (1911), 148; the papal bull in W. Capes, *Charters and Records of Hereford Cathedral,* Hereford (1908), 192, mentions the boy.

33 *MS Vat Lat 4015,* f. 46ᵛ.

34 *MS Vat Lat 4015,* 46ʳ-47ᵛ, 86ʳ.

35 More, *Dialogues,* I. ch. 14; *Henry VI* act II, scene 1.

36 *Mat.* II.57-8, 245-7; Gilbert, 42-3; Wulfstan, 131, 146; Cantilupe, 651, 665, 686, 692; Godric, 417; Louis, 296.

37 Wulfstan, 129; Mac Culloch, *Medieval Faith,* 39-40.

38 *Mat.* I.269-70, 340, 332-4, 431-2; II.67-8, 259-60; Lawrence, 165; cap. 22 of Fourth Lateran Council, Mansi, *Sac. Conc. Nov.* XXII, col. 1010; H. Sigerist,

On the History of Medicine, ed. F. Marti-Ibañez, N.Y. (1960), 137.

39 *Mat.* I.151-4, 165-6, 193-5, 383-4, 496-7, 410, 478; II.79, 167-8; Cantilupe, 653, 657, 661, 666, 689; William, 189, 247, 252; Frideswide, 574, 575; Godric, 391-2, 471-4, 477-8; William of York (Raine), 535, 540; Hedwig, 254; Lawrence, 180; Wulfstan, 124; Giraldus, *RS* 21.VII.121-4 (Hugh of Lincoln); Louis, 292.

40 Blum and Blum, 52-3, 115.

41 W. Tebb and E. Vollum, *Premature Burial and How it May be Prevented*, London (1896), 96; R. Blythe, *Akenfield*, 1969, 330.

42 Henry 145, 128; Wulfstan, 121; Simon, 109; Cantilupe, 611, 617 ff.

43 Cantilupe, 619; Frideswide, 573; Lawrence, 171, Louis 284, 305; Walter Daniel, *Vita Ailredi, a pulsu motus omnis abscesserat*, 43.

44 *MS Vat Lat 4015*, f. 13ᵛ; *Mat.* I.444; William, 68; Henry, 28; cf. *Mat.* I. 523-4, *facta est contentio inter circumstantes utrum excessisset a corpore*.

45 Simon, 83-4, 97; Osmund, 76.

46 *Mat.* II.115, 203, 223-4; Bodley *MS Fell 2*, f. 10ʳ; *MS Vat Lat 4015*, f. 69ʳ; Simon, 90, 93; Wm. of York (Raine) *RS* 71.II.534; Wulfstan, 136; Frideswide, 572, 580.

47 Godric, 376, 397-8; Frideswide, 585.

48 P. Lambertini (later Pope Benedict XIV), *De Servorum Dei Beatificatione et Beatorum Canonizatione*, Bologna (1734-8), IV:i.p. 93, no. 2.

49 Wulfstan, 159; Henry, *page* 58-9; William, 147, 158; Gilbert, 47.

50 Wulfstan, 135, 128; *Mat.* I.330, 339; II.150; *RS* 21.VII.124-6 (Hugh of Lincoln); Frideswide, 583-5; Godric, 455-8.

51 Lawrence, 177; Henry, 133.

52 William, 244-46; *Mat.* II.244-5.

53 *Mat.* II.183; Exon. Coll. *MS 158*, f. 47ʳ; William, 176; Godric, 446.

54 Frideswide, 588, a clear example of illness returning as soon as the pilgrim left the shrine, but disappearing when she came back to the holy bones; Wulfstan, 136; *Mat.* I.448-9.

55 Frideswide, 570; Godric, 398.

56 Frideswide, 574-5; Wulfstan, 140.

57 *LP* XIII:2.719.

58 *MS Vat Lat 4015*, f. 89ʳ.

59 U. Maclean, 'Sickness Behaviour Among the Yoruba', *Witchcraft and Healing*, ed. R. Willis *et al.*, Edinburgh (1969), 39.

60 D. Herlihy, *Pisa in the Early Renaissance*, New Haven (1958), 49.

61 I. Veith, in *Hysteria: The History of a Disease*, Chicago (1965), imagines that hysteria is past its heyday, a proposition rebutted by Carl Brownsberger in 'Hysteria—A Common Phenomenon?', *Am. Jour. Psychiatry*, vol. 123:110 (July, 1966), 110. Cf. J. C. Nemiah, 'Conversion Reaction' in A. Freedman and H. Kaplan, *Comprehensive Textbook of Psychiatry*, Baltimore (1967), 870-885. Incidence of conversion hysteria in F. Ziegler et al., 'Contemporary Conversion Reactions', *Am. Jour. Psychiatry*, vol. 116 (1960), 901-10, and F. McKegney, 'The Incidence and Characteristics of Patients with Conversion Reactions', *Am. Jour. Psychiatry*, vol. 124 (1967), 542-5; cf. also H. Kaplan, 'The Concept of Psychogenicity in Medicine' in Freedman and Kaplan, 1120-4.

62 M. Melinsky, *Healing Miracles*, London (1968), 51; R. Cranston, *The Miracle of Lourdes*, N.Y. (1955), 103; D. West, *Eleven Lourdes Miracles*, 1957, *passim.*

63 Maclean, *Magical Medicine*, 21.

64 J. Frank, *Persuasion and Healing*, Baltimore (1961), 62, 72; A. Kiev, 'The Study of Folk Psychiatry' in Kiev, *Magic, Faith and Healing*, Glencoe (1964), 26; *Mat.* II.216; Bede, 95; Mt. 13:58.

65 *The Ordinale and Customary of the Benedictine Nuns of Barking Abbey*, 2 vol. ed. J. Tolhurst, *HBS* 65-66 (1927-8), II.348; Frank, *Persuasion and Healing*, 54-8.

66 E. Fulda, *And I Shall be Healed*, London, 1959, *passim.*

67 T. Wright, *Essays on Archaeological Subjects*, I (1861), 227; W. Hutton in *The Lives and Legends of the English Saints*, London (1903), 296.

CHAPTER 5

1 F. Bullard, 'Malden in Retrospect and Prospect', *Atlantic Monthly* (Apr. 1930), 537-40, and *New York Times* for Nov.-Dec. 1929; M. Field, *Search for Security: An Ethno-Psychiatric Study of Rural Ghana*, Evanston (1960), 105-6.

2 *Mat.* II.60.

3 William, lxv, 84, 149-50; *Mat.* I.160-62; II.145-7, 229-34, 107; E. Dodds, *The Greeks and the Irrational*, Berkeley (1951), ed. of 1966, 109, 119—all of chapter four, 'Dream-Pattern and Culture-Pattern' is worth careful attention; Thorndike, *Magic*, II.290-4; B. Cron, ed., tr., *A Medieval Dream Book*, London, 1963, and Bodley *MS Bodl. 581*, ff. 7r-8v.

4 Thorndike, *Michael Scot*, 89; Henry, 122; Cantilupe, 624, 691; Wulfstan, 159; *Mat.* I.221.

5 *Mat.* I.446; Simon, 85-6; C. Talbot, ed., *The Life of Christina of Markyate, a Twelfth-Century Recluse*, Oxford (1959), 177; William, 118-21; *Decline and Fall*, chap. 58, intro.

6 Wulfstan, 135-6.

7 Gilbert, 55.

8 Gilbert, 66-7; Wulfstan, 134; Frideswide, 572; Wm. Malmesbury, *gest. regum*, *RS* 90a, 273; Exon. Coll. *MS 158*, f. 38v, the fourteen-year peregrination.

9 *Mat.* I.244-5; Godric, 406 (*more simpliciorum*); cf. Leproux, *Dévotions*, 76 ff.

10 *Mat.* I.451; Hedwig, 256; cf. J. Sumption, *Pilgrimage*, London (1975), 152.

11 Frideswide, 572; Hedwig, 255; William, 205; Wulfstan, 186; Lawrence, 175.

12 Cantilupe, 622-3, 650, 689; Simon, 82, 108; William, 242, 245, 275.

13 M. Harrison, 'A Survival of Incubation', *Folk-Lore*, vol. xix no. 3 (1908), 313.

14 Frideswide, 578; Edmund Rich in Bodley *MS Fell 2*, f. 7r-v, 12v, 19v; Godric, 403; Gilbert, 56-7; *Libellus de Admirandis Beati Cuthberti virtutibus*, Reginald of Durham, ed. J. Raine, vol. 1 SS (1835), 152.

15 *Mat.* II.42, 62; Wulfstan, 135; Lawrence, 176; Gilbert, 48; Hugh of Lincoln in Giraldus, *RS* 21:VII.126-7; Harrison, 'Incubation', 314.

16 Godric, 480-1, Du Canda, 263.

17 Harrison, 'Incubation', 314, and cf. the old standard by M. Hamilton, *Incubation*, London, 1906.

18 Wulfstan, 187; cf. Mt. 20:31—*increpabat eos ut tacerent*; Edmund Rich, *MS Fell 2*, f. 7ʳ.

19 Wulfstan, 188;*Mat*. II.86.

20 *Mat*. II.62-3, 76, 80, 86-7, 124-5, 140-1; cf. William, 155; Hedwig, 255; Wulfstan, 139; Frideswide, 572; for an exception see Osmund, 76-7, 'crackling sinews' at home the night after measurement for a candle.

21 *Mat*. II.77.

22 *Mat*. II.66; Frideswide, 571.

23 Cantilupe, 622.

24 *Mat*. II.82, 83; Louis, 309.

25 Simon, 107; Edmund Rich, *MS Fell 2*, f. 8ᵛ.

26 Gilbert, 47, 52-3; Frideswide, 579, 587; Wulfstan, 120; Simon, 106-7; Godric, 369, 389; William, 180; Cantilupe, 697; H. Farmer, 'The Canonization of St. Hugh of Lincoln', *Lincs. Architect. and Archaeol. Soc. Papers* (1956), 101.

27 A. Neame, *The Happening at Lourdes*, London (1968), 233.

28 *Mat*. II.64, 68; Edwards,*Milburga*, 146; Wulfstan, 126, 132.

29 William, 249 (editors' trans.); Wulfstan, 128, 137; Frideswide, 575.

30 Godric, 478-9.

31 Louis, 281; Frideswide, 574; G. Dawson, *Healing: Pagan and Christian*, London (1935), 262 n. 4; L. Rose, *Faith Healing*, 1971, 76; cf. Gregory of Tours, Dalton ed., *History of the Franks*, Oxford (1927), 372-5. I am indebted to Mr. S. Rubin (Children's Hospital, Liverpool) for particulars concerning certain aspects of physiotherapy.

32 Freud, *Selected Papers on Hysteria*, Chap. I (1893).

33 Frideswide, 572; Richard Wych, *AASS* April I, 310; Cantilupe, 693; *Mat*. I.306.

34 Giraldus, *RS* 21.VII.134-5; William, 226-7 (editors' trans.); Frideswide, 573.

35 Godric, 423.

36 Cantilupe, 703; Louis, 305; *Mat*. I.248; William, 200; Gilbert, 57, Henry 92, 109, 116;*MS Fell 2*, f. 14ᵛ-15ʳ.

37 *Mat*. I.169-70; cf. I.251-2; II.224, 257-8; Cantilupe, 688.

38 Cantilupe, 673, 690.

39 Louis, 291.

40 Louis, 303;*Mat*. I.393; Cantilupe, 682, 685; Du Canda, 241-2.

41 *Mat*. II.191-3; Wm. York (Raine) *RS* 71.II.539-40; *MS Fell 2*, f. 10ʳ; William, 135-6, 174-7; cf.*Mat*. I.211, 308-9, 354-7, 384; II.131, 205-6.

42 Cuthbert, ed. Raine, 231; Rich Wych, *AASS* Apr I.309; William, 268; Wulfstan, 156.

43 Cantilupe, 655, 669; L. Salzman, 'Some Sussex Miracles', *Sussex Archaeological Soc.*, vol. LXVI (1925), 73, without further ref.

44 Cantilupe, 702. Some writers have assumed that such coins were *tied* to the patient, and although the verb (*plicare*) might indicate this, and it did in fact happen in this way in a few cases, the usual interpretation is that the coin was *bent* while held above the victim.

45 Simon, 84; Osmund, 62; Henry 119;*Mat*. I.198.

46 *PL* 88 col. 509; *Mat*. II.265; Henry 128; Frideswide, 579. Though evidence

from *Thómas Saga Erkibyskups*, ed. Magnusson, *RS* 65, II.165, indicates that the measured-thread was not *always* incorporated in wax.

47 *Acta Sanctorum Ordinis S. Benedicti*, VI.392; Du Canda, 269-70, 241-2; William, 153-4; Wulfstan, 151; Cantilupe, 670; Henry 121.

48 Wulfstan, 125; Cantilupe, 635; Wilkins, II.490;*Mat.* II.106-7; Godric, 411.

49 Dendy, *Lights in Christian Worship*, 97.

50 P. Kemp, *Healing Ritual: Studies in Techniques and Tradition of the Southern Slavs*, London (1935), 121-3; M. D. Anderson, *A Saint at Stake: The Strange Death of William of Norwich, 1144*, London (1964), 185-6.

51 *MS Fell 2*, f. 18ᵛ; William, 200; *Mat.* I.359, 467-8; Godric, 419-20; Cantilupe, 667, 663, 677, 690; Simon, 73-4.

52 *Mat.* I.372; II.123, 189, 227, 281; Godric, 441-2; Wulfstan, 134-5; Simon, 89; Osmund, 68, Henry, 112, 120.

53 Henry, 90; *Mat.* I.181, 274-5, 423-4; II.105, 108-9; Edwards, *Milburga*, 146; Cantilupe, 681; Wilkins II.486;*MS Fell 2*, f. 11ᵛ, 14ʳ; Du Canda, 242-3.

54 Cantilupe, 670; Louis, 299, 309.

55 MS *Vat Lat 4015*, f. 9ᵛ.

56 Cantilupe, 622; Henry, 108.

57 Dawson, *Healing*, 49; Fowler, *St. William*, quoting Theodoret, 305.

58 U. Radford, 'The Wax Images found in Exeter Cathedral', *The Antiquaries Journal* XXIX (1949), 164-8.

59 *MS Vat Lat 4015*, the first list is on f. 74ʳ⁻ᵛ, the second on 312ʳ-313ʳ.

60 Purvis, *John of Bridlington*, 1924, 36, 41.

CHAPTER 6

1 William, 207;*Mat.* II.123, 125.

2 *MS Fell 2*, f. 9ʳ; *Mat.* II.116, 127; Frideswide, 572, 578, 582; William, 208-9; Cantilupe, 700, 702, 704, and*MS Vat Lat 4015*, f. 80ʳ.

3 *Coram Rege Roll*, Hen. III no. 13 and F. W. Maitland, *Pleas of the Crown in the County of Gloucester*, case 87—these references are supplied by the editor, Wulfstan, 174; Wm. of York (Raine) *RS* 71:II.536-7;*Mat.* I.177; II.95.

4 Farmer, 'Canonization of St. Hugh', 102.

5 Giraldus, *RS* 21:VII.124-6, and cf. Farmer 'Canonization of St. Hugh', 110-11.

6 William, 289-94.

7 *Mat.* I.347, 523; II.85, 171, 224;*MS Fell 2*, f. 14ʳ; Godric, 426.

8 *Mat.* II.140.

9 Simon, 72 and 77. There are also some interestingly different versions of the same miracles supplied by the editor of Godric's miracles.

10 *Mat.* I.138.

11 *RS* 71.II.531 ff., and Bodley *MS Dodsworth 125* sqq.; the miracle collection for St. Osmund covers a long period, as does that for St. Edmund, in *RS* 96:I.26-92, 107-208, and III.327-45 (ed. Arnold).

12 *Mat.* I.524.

13 Hutton, *English Saints*, 293-5; P. Brown, *The Development of the Legend of Thomas Becket*, Phila. (1930), 159-60.

14 Cf. C. Loomis, 'Hagiological Healing', *Bull. Hist. Medieval*, 8 (1940), 636-42, and P.-A. Sigal, 'Maladie, Pèlerinage et Guérison au xiie siècle. Les miracles de saint Gibrien à Reims', *Annales*, xxiv (1969), 1522-39, an important study.

15 Godric, 416.

16 Simon, 85; *Mat*. II.144.

17 Cantilupe, 658.

18 William, 253-4.

19 See S. Rubin, *Medieval English Medicine* London (1974), ch. 6 'The Problem of Leprosy'; E. Micklem, *Miracles and the New Psychology*, Oxford (1922), 44; R. Clay, *The Mediaeval Hospitals of England*, London (1909), 48-9 and Appendix; W. MacArthur, 'Mediaeval "Leprosy" in the British Isles', *Leprosy Review*, vol. xxiv (1953), 8-19; Z. Gussow, 'Behavioral research in chronic disease: a study of leprosy', *Journal of Chronic Diseases*, 17 (1964), 183.

20 Cantilupe, 686; E. Ladurie, 'Famine Amenorrhoea' in *Biology of Man in History*, ed. R. Forster and O. Ranum, London (1975), 163-78.

21 *Mat*. I.227−8, 469-70; II.222-3; *MS Fell 2*, f. 7^v, 14^{r-v}, 22^r; Godric, 424; William, 78-9; Simon, 76; Farmer, 'Canoniz. of St. Hugh', 100-101; Cantilupe, 666-7.

22 *MS Fell 2*, f. 10^r.

23 Rich. Wych, *AASS* Apr. I.309; Louis, 301; Cantilupe, 624; *MS Fell 2*, f. 19^r.

24 A. Sandison, 'Diseases of the Eye' in A. Sandison and D. Brothwell, eds., *Diseases in Antiquity*, Springfield (1967), 458; C. Berens, ed., *The Eye and its Diseases*, London (1949), 397, 842-3; M. Pyke, *Man and Food*, London (1970), 127; J. Drummond and A. Wilbraham, *The Englishman's Food*, rev. Hollingsworth, London (1958), 80.

25 William, 218; *Mat*. I.403.

26 O. Temkin, *The Falling Sickness*, Baltimore (1945), 94, and Veith, *Hysteria*, though caution is needed in Veith's treatment of medieval hysteria.

27 William, 204; J. Fuller, *The Day of St. Anthony's Fire*, N.Y. (1968), 84, 97, 93, 111, 165.

28 Wulfstan, 123-4; Wm. Malmesbury, *gest. pont.*, 439; *MS Fell 2*, f. 16^r; Hedwig, 257; *Mat*. I.518-20; II.208-9; Cantilupe, 668; Du Canda, 231-2; *Vita Hugonis*, 117-8; Erasmus, *Praise of Folly*, tr. Radice (1971), 202; T. Oesterreich, *Possession, Demoniacal and Other*, London (1930), 185; Osmund, 40; *MS Vat Lat 4015*, f. 106^v.

29 Gilbert, 72-3; *Mat*. I.306; G. Rosen, *Madness in Society*, London (1968), 140.

30 *Mat*. II.44-5; Godric, 417-8; Owst, *Literature and Pulpit*, 112; Gregory the Great, *Dialogues* (Zimmerman ed.), 59, 66, 43-4; MacCulloch, *Medieval Faith*, 35.

31 *Mat*. II.209; Wulfstan, 146; Farmer, 'Canonization of St. Hugh', 102; *MS Fell 2*, f. 19^v.

32 Lawrence, 172; Cantilupe, 631.

33 Pantin, *English Church in the Fourteenth Cent.*, 199; J. Moorman, *Church Life in England in the Thirteenth Century*, Cambridge (1945), 81-2; *MS Fell 2*, f. 14^v-15^r.

34 Osmund, 81, 83; Henry, 111, 113, 104, 10; Simon, 79-80; *Mat*. I.207, 253-7, 273-4; Gilbert, 51-2; *MS Fell 2*, f. 22^v.

35 Wulfstan, 118, 124-5; Cantilupe, 642; *Mat*. I.410, 424-8; IV.429.

36 Cantilupe,682.
37 Wm. York (Raine), *RS* 71:II.539; Wulfstan, 168-75; *Mat.* 155-8, 419-23; II.173-82.
38 Gaiffier, *Études*, 'Un thème hagiographique: la pendu miraculeusement sauvé', 194-232; R. H. C. Davis, *King Stephen*, Berkeley (1967), 92; *Thómas Saga* (*RS* 65), II.115; Langland, 266, 359; N. Hurnard, *The King's Pardon for Homicide before AD 1307*, Oxford (1969), 43-4, 176, 246-7; *MS Vat Lat 4015*, f. 12ʳ; Henry, 40.
39 *Mat.* II.156.

CHAPTER 7

1 S. Bhardwaj, *Hindu Places of Pilgrimage in India*, Berkeley (1973), Appendix.
2 For example, in 1929 Russell counted fourteen knights in the de Montfort miracle collection; we can only find nine. He may have included witnesses. J. C. Russell, 'Canonization of Opposition to the King in Angevin England', *Essays pres. to C.H. Haskins*, Boston (1929), 279-90.
3 William, 222-3; *Mat.* I.452.
4 Simon, 92-3; William, 157 & n.; *Mat.* I.403.
5 Cantilupe, 654, 662.
6 *Rot. Hun.* II.689, 691, 808; Simon, 82-3, 87; H. Salter, *Survey of Oxford*, ed. Pantin, *OHS* 1960, 69, II.51-4, 191.
7 Frideswide, 581; Cantilupe, 694.
8 Osmund, 36-9; cf. Cantilupe, 701-4.
9 Cantilupe, 697, 699; *Mat.* I.251-2.
10 *Mat.* II.104.
11 Huizinga, *Waning of the Middle Ages*, 145-6.
12 Whitelock ed., 200.
13 William, 192-3, 275, 286.
14 William, 84.
15 William, 279; R. Taylor, *Index Monasticus*, London (1821), 66; *The Customary of the Cathedral Priory Church of Norwich*, *HBS* vol. 82 (1948), vii, 73; *VCH* Norfolk, II.321, 225.
16 William, 294, 158, 150; 207, 279, 163, 227.
17 Among the innumerable historical and biographical works on Becket, the most important recent contribution is R. Foreville, ed., *Thomas Becket: Actes du colloque international de Sédières*, Paris, 1975. See also the essays in *Canterbury Cathedral Chronicle* no. 65 (1970); a readable popular study is *Thomas Becket* by R. Winston, N.Y., 1967, and Becket's biographer David Knowles has published several studies of the archbishop, e.g. *Thomas Becket*, London (1970). A projected study of the shrine by Dr. William Urry will be a welcome addition to the literature. Older works which are still very useful are the various editions of A. P. Stanley, *Historical Memorials of Canterbury*, and E. A. Abbott, *St. Thomas of Canterbury, his death and miracles*, London, 1898, 2 vols. The *Materials for the History* is, of course, the indispensable source.

18 Gervase of Canterbury, ed. Stubbs (1879-80), *RS* 73:I.18, 229; Wm. Fitzstephen in *Mat.* III.149-50; *Mat.* II.15-16.
19 *Mat.* II.37-48, 56; *Mat.* III.151; *Thómas Saga*, I.551 and II.71.
20 *Mat.* II.60, 77, 81, 91, 134.
21 *Mat.* I.2, 137-8; Gervase, I.18, 236-7.
22 *PL* 200, col. 725-6, 735-6, 872-4, 900-902; *Mat.* VII.428, 463, 469, 523; Kemp, *Canonization*, 82, 87-8.
23 *Mat.* VII.523-4, 564; A. Luchaire, *Social France at the Time of Philip Augustus*, tr. Krehbiel, N.Y. (1967), 323; Gervase, I.293.
24 Gervase, I.26.
25 B. Schlyter, *La Vie de Thomas Becket par Beneit: poème anglo-normand du xiie siècle*, Etudes Romanes de Lund, IV (1941), 154.
26 R. Foreville, *Le Jubilé de Saint Thomas Becket*, Paris (1958), *passim*; M. Caviness, 'A Lost Cycle of Canterbury Paintings of 1220', *The Antiquaries Journal*, vol. LIV (1974), 66-74; J. Russell and J. Heironimus, *The Shorter Latin Poems of Master Henry of Avranches*, Cambridge [Mass.] (1935), 64-78; Stephen Langton, 'Tractatus de translatione beati Thomae', *PL* 190, col. 407-24; *Mat.* IV.426-30; *Ann. Mon.* II.293, III.58.
27 R. Foreville, 'Le culte de saint Thomas Becket en Normandie', *Colloque*, 139; Du Canda, 227-72 (the relic was removed from the Abbey of Dommartin to Arras cathedral in 1790; it is still there, Foreville, 'Le culte de saint Thomas Becket en France', *Colloque*, 180).
28 W. Urry, 'Some Notes on the Two Resting Places of St. Thomas Becket of Canterbury', *Colloque*, 196, and plate II; B. Rackham, *The Ancient Glass of Canterbury Cathedral*, London (1949) is the authoritative study. For other iconographical remains cf. T. Borenius, *St. Thomas Becket in Art*, London (1932); new work in P. Newton, 'Some New Material for the Study of the Iconography of St. Thomas Becket', *Colloque*, 255-63.
29 R. Southern, *The Making of the Middle Ages*, London (1953), 255.
30 *Mat.* II.35, 37, 60-61, 202-7; E. Walberg, *La tradition hagiographique de Saint Thomas Becket avant la fin du xiie siècle*, Paris (1929), 57.
31 Walberg, 62-74.
32 Godric, 366-8, 371-2.
33 C. Peers, 'Finchale Priory', *Archaeologia Aeliana*, 4th ser., vol. IV (1927), 193-220; *The Priory of Finchale*, ed. Raine, SS vol. 6 (1837), 25, 26-7, 46, 59, 83-5, 117, 170-87.
34 Prior Philip's account of the translation of 1180 and the subsequent miracles found in *AASS* Oct VIII is the primary source, but unfortunately when the printed edition is compared with the original manuscript, Bodley *MS Digby 177*, it is clear that there are many transcription errors in the *AASS* version. Many mss., relating to the Saxon traditions especially, have been transcribed from various sources and collected under one cover, now Bodley *MS Lat. Misc. c 72*.
35 S. Wigram, ed., *The Cartulary of the monastery of St. Frideswide at Oxford*, *OHS* vol. 28, 31 (1895-6), I.412, 64, 102, 109, 204, etc. The translation of 1289 in *Ann. Mon.* IV.318; fourteenth-century indulgence, A. Wood, 'Survey of the antiquities of the city of Oxford', ed. A. Clark, *OHS*, vol. 17 (1890), II.136. For later commemoration, Reg. Henry Chichele, ed. E. F. Jacob, *C & Y*

vol. 46 (1945), III.256; letters from the University in *Epistolae Academicae,*
OHS vol. 35, 36 (1898), II.359-62; Wilkins, III.612-13, and *The Hereford*
Breviary, ed. W. Frere and L. Brown, 3 vol., *HBS* vol. 26, 40, 46 (1904-15),
II.375-7.

CHAPTER 8

1 M. Colker, 'Latin Verses lamenting the death of S. Wulfstan of Worcester', *AB*
   89 (1971), 321-2.
2 *Ann. Mon.* II.289.
3 Halliwell's edition of Simon's miracles is based upon BM *MS Cotton Vespas.*
   A.vi, a manuscript containing many errors, particularly as to dates.
4 Bliss, *Pap. Reg.,* I.431; C. Bemont, *Simon de Montfort,* Oxford (1930), 41; R.
   Treharne in *The Battle of Lewes,* Lewes (1964), 64-5, 85.
5 R. Hilton, *Med. Society* (1966), 59; E. Jacob, *Studies in Bar. Reform* (1925),
   297; M. Powicke, *The Thirteenth Cent.,* 2nd ed., Oxford (1962), 174.
6 Simon, xxxii; *Ann. Mon.,* II.365; *Chronica de Mailros,* ed. J. Stevenson,
   Bannatyne Club, 50 (1835), 202-4.
7 *Ann. Mon.* II.365; IV.170-1, 175-6; Simon, 92-3; D. C. Cox, *The Battle of*
   Evesham, Evesham (1964), 17-19.
8 Powicke, *Thirteenth Cent.,* 203; Simon, 91.
9 Bliss, *Pap. Reg.* I.435; *Ann. Mon.* II.367; A. Gransden, *Chronicle of Bury S.*
   Edmunds, London (1964), 33.
10 *Ann. Mon.* II.365; Simon, xxix; F. W. Maitland, 'A Song on the Death of
   Simon de Montfort', *Engl. Hist. Rev.,* xi (1896), 315-7; T. Wright, *Political*
   Songs of England, Camden Soc. 6 (1839), 125-8; Simon, 84: *credimus te*
   martirizatum pro justitia; G. W. Prothero, *Life of Simon de Montfort,* London
   (1877), 391: *ad renovandum britannie*—there are several other examples in
   Prothero. D. C. Cox has drawn the writer's attention to additional songs about
   the dead earl in Cambridge, Gonville and Caius Coll. *MS 349/542,* f. 10ᵛ, and
   the examples in I. Aspin, *Anglo-Norman Political Songs,* Oxford (1953),
   24-35.
11 Bodley *MS Laud 529,* f. 64ʳ (alt. 71ʳ).
12 Gransden, *Chron. Bury S. Edm.,* xxxvii.
13 *Ann. Mon.* II.365, IV.175-8, xxii; *MS Laud, 529* as above; *Pap. Reg.* I.434;
   Cantilupe, 671; *Officium ecclesiasticum abbatum secundum usum*
   Eveshamensis monasterii, ed. H. Wilson, *HBS,* 6 (1893), *passim.*
14 *DNB* and D. Maclean, 'The Cantilupe Family', *Woolhope Transactions,* vol.
   xxxvi (1958), 5-21, and cf. Bodley *MS Dugdale 15* and *MS Dodsworth 64* for a
   letter from one of his sisters, discussing their family background.
15 *MS Vat Lat 4015,* f. 56ʳ.
16 W. Wallace, *St. Edmund of Canterbury,* 1893, 29-39.
17 C. Lawrence, *St. Edmund of Abingdon,* Oxford (1960), 112, 309-10.
18 *Life* by Matthew Paris, in Lawrence, *St. Edmund,* 274.
19 Martene & Durand, *Nov. Thes.* III. col. 1847-8.
20 Ward, *St. Edmund,* 195-6 (Ward's trans.).
21 Lawrence, *St. Edmund,* 278-9 (Mt. Paris); Gransden, *Letter-Book,* 82; *HMC*

V:460 (A.D. 1327); Reg. Sutton, *LRS* 48:III.37; Lawrence, *St. Edmund*, 4-5.

22 See M. Toynbee's *S. Louis of Toulouse and the process of Canonisation in the Fourteenth Century*, Manchester (1929), which includes a number of comparisons with Cantilupe's canonization process. Biographical material and an excellent ed. of the miracles and other docs. are found in *Processus Canonizationis*, etc. (1951); cf. *Bibliotheca Sanctorum* (1966), vol. VIII.

23 M. H. Laurent, *Le Culte de S. Louis d'Anjou à Marseille au xive Siècle*, Rome (1954, *Temi e Testi* 2), documents number 26, 33, 40, 42, 43, 45, 50.

24 Certain church historians (Moorman, Coulton) have suggested that the clergy constituted no more than about 2% of the entire population of England in the thirteenth century. If so, the proportion of upper clergy would have been infinitesimal. In order to emphasize the relationship between 'normal populations' and our 'pilgrim populations' we shall use the figure 3% for the general distribution of lower clergy, and 1% for upper clergy, admitting that both figures are probably very generous. Likewise, we shall rate the normal distribution of the nobility at a high figure, 1%, and the knighthood at 3% (remembering that we have included all family members along with the nobles and knights themselves). The artisans, craftsmen, and nascent bourgeoisie will be rated at 7%. The remaining group (according to our classification system, the unskilled, the peasants, the poor, the unspecified) will then constitute 85% of medieval English society, according to our model. What one historian wrote for the west midlands was generally applicable to much of the rest of England as well: 'The aristocratic hierarchy was no pyramid. It could better be likened to a collection of skycrapers towering above the plain'. Hilton, *Med. Society*, 58. We have found that the actual social class distribution for 1933 English pilgrims was: noble, 3%, upper clergy, 4%, knights, 6%, lower clergy, 11%, merchant/artisan, 9%, lower classes, 67%. Comparing the 430 French pilgrims for the same classes, the figures are 2%, 1%, 3%, 4%, 13%, and 77%.

25 Langland, 298; see Ladurie, *Famine Amen.*, 167, 178 n. 54.

26 For example, by Maclean, *Magical Medicine*, 50.

27 Langland, 298.

28 *Mat.* I.403. Another reason would be the inclusion in the upper class—via membership in the upper clergy—of educated *magistri*, many of whom were themselves trained in medicine. For differential recourse by upper- and lower-class modern patients, see D. Apple, ed., *Sociological Studies of Health and Sickness*, N.Y. (1960), 82.

29 Blum and Blum, *Healing in Rural Greece*, 56, 63; I. Sanders, *Rainbow in the Rock: The People of Rural Greece*, Harvard (1962), 49.

30 *Mat.* I.459.

31 R. Loomis and L. Loomis, *Medieval Romances*, N.Y. (1957), 251.

CHAPTER 9

1 Gilbert, 44-5; William, 162.

2 *Mat.* I.196; William, 135-6; Cantilupe, 638.

3 William, 263-4; Cantilupe, 673; Farmer, 'Canoniz. St. Hugh', 100-101.

4   Hedwig, 256; Cantilupe, 619; *Mat.* II.106; William, 147, 159; Cantilupe, 690: *de consilio vicinorum et peregrinorum.*
5   Simon, 74; Giraldus, *RS* 21:VII.128-9; Cantilupe, 610 ff., 615; *MS Fell 2*, 15ʳ.
6   *Mat.* I.187-8, 310; II.165-77 ff. (there is another Kentish Newington, near the medieval archiepiscopal castle of Saltwood); Wulfstan, 135.
7   Cantilupe, 665; Lawrence, 171.
8   Godric, 436-7; *Mat.* II.197-8.
9   Cantilupe, 614-6.
10 *Mat.* I.471.
11 And the roads, for all their ruts and bumps, were well-used, in some regions at least: one twelfth-century traveller encountered two hundred people on horse and foot in a fifteen-mile stretch of Sussex road, *Mat.* I.320.
12 *Mat.* II.161-2, 147; *MS Fell 2*, f. 8ᵛ.
13 Godric, 427-9; *Mat.* I.262-4.
14 Cantilupe, 662 and Exon Coll. *MS 158*, f. 5ᵛ.
15 Giraldus, *RS* 21:VII.124-6; Henry of Huntingdon, ed. Arnold, *RS* 74, xxvi, xxviii; Salzman, 'Sussex Miracles' 62, and Bodley *MS Dodsworth 125*, f. 132, as Raine, *Hist. York, RS.* 71:II.531.
16 Giraldus, *RS* 21:VII.143-7; Jocelin's *Chronicle*, 110.
17 *Mat.* II.161-2; Simon, 80-1, 87-8; Wm. York, *RS* 71:II.531, 533-5.
18 *Mat.* II.191-3.
19 *Mat.* III.152.
20 *Mat.* I.354.
21 *Mat.* I.250.
22 *Mat.* II.40; Owst, *Literature and Pulpit*, 126-34.
23 As our source explains, 'to the greater glory of the blessed Wulfstan, on the same day by divine providence justices itinerant were in the self-same church with episcopal permission, dealing with matters of the realm', Wulfstan, 167.
24 *Mat.* II.252, xxi.
25 *Mat.* I.340.
26 *Mat.* I.458-60; VII.431, 462-3, 524; Foreville, 'Une lettre inédite' etc., (1936), 183.
27 *Mat.* I.xxxiii.
28 Frank, *Persuasion and Healing*, 55; B. Aitken, a review in *Folklore*, vol. 41 (1930), 115-16.
29 *Mat.* I.287, 397-402, 517-20; II.145.
30 One could cite dozens of examples: between A.D. 1195 and 1205 a relic was sent from Clairvaux to a French abbot, with a letter sealed with Becket's seal, kept at Clairvaux, BN MSS Lat. Nouv. Acq., *Lat. 1543*, in *BN MSS latin et Francais acquisitions 1875-91*, II.618.
31 *Mat.* II.39-41.
32 Jacob, *Studies in Baronial Reform*, 290.

CHAPTER 10

1   Cantilupe, 696, and *MS Vat Lat 4015*, f. 308ᵛ. The 1674 work was by a Jesuit, Robert Strange.

2 Cantilupe, 618 f. or *MS Vat Lat 4015*, f. 157ᵛ *et sqq.*

3 As one chronicler put it, 'his corpse was boiled' and where the water was thrown out, a miraculous spring appeared, *Ann. Mon.* IV.483; *MS Vat Lat 4015*, f. 98ᵛ, 101ʳ, 109ᵛ-110ʳ, 118ᵛ.

4 Reg. Swinfield, *C & Y* 6, 67-8, 234-5, 281-2, 369-70, 358; Reg. Sutton, *LRS* 60, 32; *MS Vct Lat 4015*, f. 260ᵛ *et sqq.* The king's letter to Swinfield in Reg. Swinfield, 440-1, with answer on 420-1; the royal letters to pope and cardinals in Rymer, *Foedera*, II.972-3.

5 Reg. Swinfield, 430. For the file in Rome cf. pope's letter in *MS Vat Lat 4015*, f. 1ᵛ-2ʳ, and Reg. Gandavo (Sarum), *C & Y* 40 (1934), I.247-8.

6 *MS Vat Lat 4015*, f. 2ʳ-ᵛ, Reg. Gandavo, I.248-9. A similar case arose in 1300 when, in the examination into his reputed sanctity, an Italian 'saint' was discovered to be a heretic, F. Heer, *Medieval World*, N.Y. (1963), 219-20.

7 This unpublished process—a curious document among the annals of canonizations which have succeeded—is *MS Vat Lat 4016*, of 148 folios.

8 *MS Vat Lat 4015*, f. 54ᵛ.

9 The rest of the proctors' witnesses discussed miracles, and though most of the commissioners' witnesses discussed Cantilupe's life, much of it was hearsay. The whole question of the number of witnesses has been misunderstood in the past; the same must be said for the number of miracles.

10 *MS Vat Lat 4015*, f. 123ʳ.

11 *MS Vat Lat 4015*, f. 241ʳ; the figure of 204 miracles is also given in the MS.

12 *Foedera*, III.39-41 (12 Dec. 1307).

13 *Foedera*, III.77, 347-8.

14 *MS Ottob. Lat. 2516*, f. 44ʳ-46ᵛ, a Vatican MS.

15 L. Labande, 'La ceremonial Romain de Jacques Cajetan', *Biblio. de l'Ecole des Chartes*, LIV (1893), 55-59. For the bull, cf. Reg. Martival, 277, or Reg. Cobham, ed. E. Pearce, *Worcestershire Hist. Soc.* 38 (1930), 94; Bliss, *Cal. Pap. Reg.* II.199, Capes, *Charters and Records*, 190-4, *Bull. Rom.* I.292.

16 *NRA*, Heref. D & C. II.814-15.

17 Capes, *Charters*, 186-90, *NRA* Hereford, D & C. II.816-7, *CPR* (1317-21), 526, *Foedera*, III.863-4; *NRA* Heref. II.811 for the £45.

18 The intervention of a grand-nephew of Cantilupe, Nicholas de Gresley, was important too. Some historians have (incorrectly) given 1348 as the translation date.

19 Hereford Breviary, ed. Frere (*HBS* 1911), II.380-6.

20 Heref. Breviary, above, and for *verbatim* repeat of miracles taken from papal bull, the 2 Oct. lections in Bodley *MS Laud 299*, f. 467ʳ-68ʳ. On iconography, F. Havergal, *Ancient Glass in Credenhill Church*, Walsall, 1884, and G. Marshall, 'Some Remarks on the Ancient Stained Glass in Eaton Bishop Church', *Trans. Woolhope* (1921-3), 101-14.

21 *MS Vat Lat 4015*, f. 80ᵛ, 83ʳ, 97ᵛ-98ʳ.

22 *MS Vat Lat 4015*, f. 122ᵛ.

23 *MS Vat Lat 4015*, f. 18ʳ-ᵛ; Reg. Sutton, *LRS* 60, 143, etc., see chapter III above for these mandates.

24 *MS Vat Lat 4015*, f. 28ᵛ. For the list of votives actually found, cf. Ch. V, above.

25 *MS Vat Lat 4015*, f. 73ᵛ-76ʳ, 312ʳ.

26 Reg. Hethe (Rochester), I.200, 217, 467-9.
27 Wilkins, II.486-90.
28 W. Yates, 'The Fabric Rolls of Hereford Cathedral 1290/91 and 1386/7', *The Natl. Library of Wales Jour.*, xviii (1973), 79-86. Such figures, when found in isolation, as in this case, must be used with caution. They could mean that oblations at the shrine had declined by 1387, or that in 1387 the oblations were for the most part diverted from the fabric to some other fund. And cf. the *caveat* in K. Edwards, *The English Secular Cathedrals in the Middle Ages*, Manchester (1949), 242: 'The system of accounting at the Hereford exchequer was among the most complicated in use at any English secular cathedral in the middle ages'. For the pope's notice of falling revenues, *Cal. Pap. Reg.*, II.531.
29 Reg. Booth, *C & Y*, vol. 28 (1921), 172, 302, xiv.
30 G. Marshall, 'Shrine of St. Thomas de Cantilupe', *Trans. Woolhope* (1935), 34-50, believes that the superstructure was added before the 1287 translation, and a miracle in Cantilupe, 625, bears this out.
31 Cantilupe, 641.
32 *MS Vat Lat 4015*, f. 221^r *et sqq.*, f. 85^v, 88^r, 110^r; cf. Cantilupe, 632, 697.
33 Five years does seem a long time to delay a mere funeral courtesy. Swinfield himself was one of the executors.
34 *MS Vat Lat 4015*, f. 265^r *et sqq.*
35 Cantilupe, 622.
36 *MS Vat Lat 4015*, f. 212^r.
37 Exon. Coll. *MS 158*, f. 60^r.
38 Forty-three out of the first hundred pilgrims were men, but sixty-nine out of the last hundred were of this sex.
39 Sigal, 'Maladie, pèlerinage', etc., *Annales*, xxiv (1969), 1522-39.

CHAPTER 11

1 Huizinga, *Waning of the Middle Ages*, 27.
2 J. Fowler, *Extracts from the account rolls of the abbey of Durham*, SS 100 (1899), 420 ff.; R. Snape, *English Monastic Finances in the Later Middle Ages*, Cambridge (1926), 74; E. Venables, 'The Shrine and Head of St. Hugh of Lincoln', *Archaeol. Jour.* vol. 50 (1893), 54. For Becket, see C. Woodruff in *Arch. Cantiana* xxix (1911), 47-84, and *Arch. Cant.* xliv (1932), 13-32; *Lit. Cantaur*, RS 85:II,xliv ff., *HMC* IX:i.124, 126, and *Valor Eccles.* I:8.
3 *Lit. Cantuar*, RS 85:III.26-9, 191-2; *Christ Church Letters*, ed. J. Sheppard, Camden Soc. ns. vol. xix (1877), 29.
4 *HMC* V.460; IX.i.90; Grandisson wrote the biography.
5 *HMC* IX.i.112; *Christ Ch. Lett*, 37-8; *Fifty Earliest English Wills*, ed. F. Furnivall, *EETS* os 78 (1882), 65 ff.; *Testamenta Eboracensis*, ed. J. Raine, SS xxx (1855), 283.
6 R. Hart, 'The Shrines and Pilgrimages of the County of Norfolk', *Norfolk Archaeology*, vi (1865), 277; T. Wright, 'On the Municipal Archives of the City of Canterbury', *Archaeologia* xxxi (1846), 207-9, and *HMC* IX:i.148-9; *LP* III.ii.p. 1538, 1541.

7 P. Grosjean, ed., *Henrici VI Angliae Regis Miracula Postuma*, Brussels, 1935, and R. Knox and S. Leslie, *The Miracles of King Henry VI*, Cambridge, are the basic sources.

8 This may be due to shifting attitudes toward the traditional curative saints, which we saw indicated in Cantilupe's miracles where the number of purely physical cures was lower than earlier cults; in Henry's, it is even lower than in Cantilupe's.

9 Cf. R. Pfaff, *New Liturgical Feasts in Later Medieval England*, Oxford (1970).

10 Cole, 'Canonization of John de Dalderby', *Assoc. Archit. Soc.*, 243-76.

11 *Handbook of Church History*, ed. H. Jedin and J. Dolan, London (1970), IV. 571-2; L. Eisenhofer and J. Lechner, *The Liturgy of the Roman Rite*, London (1961), 143.

12 Reg. Orleton, *C & Y* 5, 347 (A.D. 1326).

13 *Fifty Early Engl. Wills*, 117-8; Jusserand, 196; D. Owen, 'Bacon and Eggs: Bishop Buckingham and Superstition in Lincolnshire', *Studies in Church History* VIII (1972), 141.

14 Quoted by J. Dickinson, *The Shrine of our Lady of Walsingham*, Cambridge (1956), 128.

15 *HMC* 35 (Kenyon MSS).

16 F. Rapp, 'Les pèlerinages dans la vie religieuse de l'occident medieval aux xive et xve siecles' in M. Philonenko and M. Simon, edd., *Les Pèlerinages*, Paris (1973), 140-3; *De codicibus hagiographicus Iohannis Gielemans*, Bruxellis (1895), 194-6, 526-8, and cf. 190-4, 435-45, 483-4.

17 Radulphi de Coggeshall, *Chronicon Anglicanum*, RS 66 (1875), 202.

18 *Sermons and Remains of Hugh Latimer*, ed. G. E. Corrie, Parker Soc. (1845), 363-4, 233.

19 Kemp, *Canonization*, 113; Reg. Trefnant, *C & Y* 20 (1916), ed. W. Capes, 392-3, 314-5 (A.D. 1391).

20 *Fasciculi zizaniorum*, RS 5, 364-5.

21 A. Pollard, *Fifteenth-century Prose and Verse* (1903), 137, 139-41.

22 Dickinson, *Walsingham*, 27; J. Thomson, *The Later Lollards*, Oxford (1965), 126.

23 Thomson, *Later Lollards*, 246; F. Wormald, 'The Rood of Bromholm', *Jr. Warburg Inst.* I (1937-8), 41-2; cf. W. Simpson, 'On the Pilgrimage to Bromholm in Norfolk', *Jour. Brit. Archaeol. Assn.* xxx (1874), 52-9.

24 Langland, 106.

25 Quoted by E. Gibson, *The Thirty-nine Articles*, London (1904), 561.

26 *Middle English Sermons*, ed. W. Ross, EETS 209 (1940), 42; *Speculum Sacerdotale* ed. E. Weatherly, EETS 200 (1936), 13-16.

27 *A Relation . . . of the Island of England*, tr. C. Sneyd, Camden Soc. vol. 37 (1847), 30; Stanley, *Mem. Canterbury*, 10th ed. (1909), 255-8.

28 Stanley, *Mem. Canterbury*, 237, 232, 243.

29 *LP* III.I.p. 499; Dickinson, *Walsingham*, 44-45; *LP* III.II.p. 1446; *LP* XIII:II.p. 1280.

30 H. Gillett, *Shrines of Our Lady*, London (1957), 347.

31 *LP* III.I.p. 497; *LP* XIII.II.p. 1280, 5b.

32 F. Haslewood, 'Our Lady of Ipswich', *Proc. Suffolk Instit. Archaeol.* vol. x (1898), 53; Gillett, *Shrines*, 82.

33 *LP* III.I. no. 1285; 'Journal of Prior William More', ed. E. Fegan, *Worces. Hist. Soc.* vol. 30 (1914), 314.

CHAPTER 12

1 G. Burnet, *History of the Reformation*, 2 vols., London (1850), II.lxxxii.
2 C. Wriothesley, *A Chronicle of England*, ed. W. Hamilton, Camden Soc. n.s. vol. xi (1875), I.31; T. Wright, *Letters Relating to the Suppression of the Monasteries*, Camden Soc. (1843), 58, 85. The monastic visitors had instructions to suppress relics used 'for increase of lucre', J. Youings, *The Dissolution of the Monasteries*, London (1971), 151.
3 W. Frere and W. Kennedy, *Visitation Articles and Injunctions of the Period of the Reformation*, 3 vols., 1910, II.41, 57-60; Wriothesley, I.84, 88.
4 *LP* XIII.I.1177, 1501; XIII.II, 256, 346; *The Pilgrim, by Wm. Thomas, Clerk of the Council to Edward VI*, ed. J. Froude, London (1861), 147.
5 *LP* XIII.II.1280; Wriothesley, 83; Dickinson, *Walsingham*, 61; Wright, *Letters*, 186, 190-1, 224-5; *Valor Eccles.* III.344; Latimer, *Sermons*, ed. G. Corrie, Parker Soc. (1844), I.55.
6 Bodley *MS Tanner 105*, f. 65ʳ and *Tanner 343*, f. 18 (cf. *LP* XIII.II.126); Wright, *Letters*, 185-6.
7 *LP* XIII.II.224.
8 *LP* XIII.I.604, 686, 1066, 1150, 1199, 1345; XIII.II.111, 345, 361, 830, 964, 1243.
9 Bodley, *MS Tanner 105*, f. 58ʳ⁻ᵛ.
10 Wriothesley, I.76, 90; *LP* XIII.I.347, 580; XIII.II.409, 709-10, 856.
11 G. Elton, *Policy and Police: The Enforcement of the Reformation in the Age of Thomas Cromwell*, Cambridge (1972), 215.
12 *The Pilgrim*, 36-7.
13 *LP* XIII.I.231; Wriothesley, 74.
14 *LP* XIII.I.339, 754, 348; Wriothesley, I.76; G. Gorham, *Reformation Gleanings*, London (1857), 17-19.
15 *LP* XIII.II.880.
16 M. McKisack, *Medieval History in the Tudor Age*, Oxford (1971), 136.
17 W. Lambarde, *A Perambulation of Kent* (1576), 183, 185 (Bodl. 4° Rawl. 263).
18 H. Smith, *Pre-Reformation England*, London (1938), 178-80; *LP* XIV.I.p. 155; *The Pilgrim*, 38. See A. Deane, *The Life of Thomas Cranmer*, London (1927), 136, where these 'mechanical toys' are said to have 'deluded few' but given pleasure to many.
19 Sumption, *Pilgrimage*, 56: the Rood 'rolled its eyes, shed tears, and foamed at the mouth'.
20 Caesarius of Heisterbach, *Dialogue* II.70-2; *Fasc. zizanior.*, 364-5; Thomson, *Later Lollards*, 246; J. Davis, 'Lollards, Reformers and St. Thomas of Canterbury', *Univ. Birmingham Hist. Journal*, vol. ix (1963), 4-9.
21 F. Furnivall, ed., *Political, Religious, and Love Poems*, EETS, o.s. 15 (1866), 62; Wright, *Letters*, 6.

22 Burnet, II.713; Wilkins III, 823-4; Stanley, *Mem. Canter.* (1909), 239-40; *HMC* IX.i.129.

23 *LP* XIII.I.754.

24 Cf. A. Mason, *What Became of the Bones of St. Thomas?*, Cambridge (1920), *passim*, despite its rather lurid title a scholarly attempt to unravel the mystery. Mason thinks that the bones were not burned, but Dr. W. Urry, who is to publish a study of the shrine, suggests that they were.

25 The 'process' is in Wilkins III.835-6.

26 Elton, *Policy and Police*, 257.

27 *LP* XIII.II.542, 880, 684, 741.

28 *LP* XIV.I.76, 444, 1052-4.

29 Frere and Kennedy, *Visit, Art.*, II.67; Wilkins III.857-8.

30 Frere and Kennedy, *Visit. Art.*, II.105, 109, 126; Wilkins IV.22.

31 Burnett, II.clxxxv; Latimer, *Sermons*, I.231; Gibson, *Thirty-nine Articles*, 80.

32 Davis, 'Lollards and Reformers', 14; *HMC* IX.i.155.

33 'Church-Wardens Accts.', 1349-1560', *Somerset Rec. Soc.* vol. 4 (1890), 160-72.

34 *HMC* IX.i.156; McKisack, *Medieval Hist.*, 96; Frere and Kennedy, *Visit. Art.* III.381; Gibson, *Thirty-nine Art.*, 357.

35 J. Purvis, *Tudor Parish Documents of the Diocese of York*, Cambridge (1948), 163.

36 K. Thomas, *Religion and the Decline of Magic*, London (1971), 299. This invaluable work contains much which illuminates medieval beliefs as well as those of sixteenth- and seventeenth-century England.

37 Reginald Scot, *The Discouverie of Witchcraft*, London (1584), ix (Bodley, Douce S 216). There were 'witches' in medieval England, but the problem did not assume significant proportions until the later sixteenth century. K. Thomas also links the rise of witchcraft with the decline of traditional charitable institutions, and the loss of ritual support once provided by the Catholic Church during the Middle Ages.

38 H. Cadbury, ed., *George Fox's Book of Miracles'*, Cambridge (1948).

39 W. Harrison, *The Description of England* [1587] , ed. G. Edelen, N.Y. (1968), chap. 23, esp. p. 287.

40 W. Turner, *A Booke of the Natures and Properties as well of the Bathes in England as of other Bathes in Germany and Italy*, London, 1562 (Bodley CC 58 Art); C. F. Mullett, *Public Baths and Health in England*, 16th to 18th centuries, Suppl. to *Bull. Hist. Medicine* no. 5 (1946), 4; Wright, *Letters*, 143-4.

41 C. Webster, *The Grand Instauration* (1975), 298.

42 *Tour*, ed. P. Rogers (1971), 360.

43 *AB* IV (1887) 305-52, esp. 345-6, 329-30; *AASS* Nov. I, 744 ff.

44 *Journeys*, ed. C. Morris, London (1947), 181. She also saw Papists kneeling in the water of St. Mungo's Well with 'so much Zeale', 82. Defoe, *Tour*, 388-9, cf. 468.

45 J. Morris, 'English Relics, I: St. Thomas of Hereford', *The Month*, xliv (Jan-Apr, 1882), 125-6.

Select Bibliography

I *Miracle collections and other contemporary materials*

Adam of Eynsham. *Magna Vita Sancti Hugonis*, ed., tr. H. Farmer and D. Douie, 2 vols., London, 1961-2.

Caesarius of Heisterbach. *The Dialogue on Miracles*, tr. H. Scott and C. Bland, 2 vols., London, 1929. For the Latin ed. cf. J. Strange, ed., 2 vols., Cologne, 1851.

Cantilupe. The Life and Miracles of St. Thomas Cantilupe, Bishop of Hereford, are found in *AASS* I Oct., 610 ff. (1765), a transcript of the process of canonization. Because of certain editorial adjustments, however, the manuscript itself should be consulted, *MS Vat Lat 4015*.

Darlington, R. R., ed. *Vita Wulfstani*, Camden Soc. 3rd ser. vol. 40 (1928).

Delaborde, H.-Francois, 'Fragments de l'Enquête faite à saint-denis en 1282 en vue de la canonisation de saint-louis'. *Memoires de la société de l'histoire de Paris et de l'Ile de France*, tome xiii (1896), 1-71.

Du Canda, C. *La Vie de S. Thomas*, S. Omer, 1615.

Edmund Rich. The miracles are found in Bodley *MS Fell 2* and, in a slightly different but less satisfactory form, in E. Martene and U. Durand, *Thesaurus Novus Anecdotorum*, vol. III, 1775 ff.

Edwards, A. J. M., 'An Early Twelfth-Century Account of the Translation of St. Milburga of Much Wenlock', *Trans. of the Shropshire Archaeological Soc.*, vol. LVII:2 (1962-3), 134-51.

Erasmus. *Pilgrimages to Saint Mary of Walsingham and Saint Thomas of Canterbury*, tr., ed. J. G. Nichols, London, 1875.

Farmer, D. H., 'The Canonization of St. Hugh of Lincoln', *Lincs. Archit. and Archaeol. Soc. Papers* (1956), 86-117.

Foreville, R., 'Une lettre inédite de Jean de Salisbury évêque de Chartres', *Rev. d'Hist. de l'Eglise de France*, tome xxii (1936), 183.

Foreville, R., *Un Procès de Canonisation à l'aube du xiiie siècle (1201-1202). Le Livre de saint Gilbert de Sempringham*, Paris, 1943.

Frideswide. Her miracles are found, transcribed from Bodley *MS Digby 177*, in *AASS* VIII Oct. 568 ff. (1853); there are some transcription errors.

Gervase of Canterbury. *Historical Works*, ed. W. Stubbs, 2 vols. (1879-80), *RS 73*.

Gielemans. *De codicibus hagiographicis Iohannis Gielemans*, Brussels, 1895.

Giraldus Cambrensis. *Opera,* ed. J. Dimock, 8 vols. (1861-91), *RS* 21, esp. vol. VII, *Vita S. Hugonis.*

Grosjean, P., ed. *Henrici VI Angliae Regis Miracula Postuma,* Brussels, 1935.

Halliwell, J. O., ed. *The Chronicle of William de Rishanger; The Miracles of Simon de Monfort,* Camden Soc., vol. 15, 1840. Though the miracles were carefully transcribed by Halliwell, the manuscript itself is a poor copy, with several errors, of an earlier version. (BM *MS Cotton Vespas. A.vi,* f. 162^r-183^r, modern foliation.)

Hedwig. Life and Miracles in *AASS* VIII Oct. (1853).

Jessopp, A., and James, M. R., eds., *The Life and Miracles of St. William of Norwich by Thomas of Monmouth,* Cambridge, 1896.

Jocelin of Brakelond. *The Chronicle concerning the acts of Samson Abbot of the Monastery of St. Edmund,* London, 1949, ed. H. Butler.

Knox, R., and Leslie, S. *The Miracles of King Henry VI,* Cambridge, 1923.

Labande, L. H., 'La ceremonial Romain de Jacques Cajetan', *Biblio. de l'Ecole des Chartes,* LIV (1893), 45-74.

Laurent, M.-H. *Le Culte de S. Louis d'Anjou à Marseille au xive Siècle,* Rome, 1954.

Louis. *Processus Canonizationis et Legendae variae Sancti Ludovici O.F.M. epis. Tolosani. Analecta Franciscana,* tom. VII, Florence, 1951.

Malden, A. R., ed., *The Canonization of Saint Osmund,* Wilts Rec. Soc., 1901.

Plummer, C., ed., 'Vie et Miracles de S. Laurent', *AB* 33 (1914), 121-86.

Raine, J., ed., *Historians of the Church of York,* 3 vols. (1879-94), *RS* 71, vol. 2 for St. William of York.

Reginald of Durham. *Libellus de Admirandis Beati Cuthberti virtutibus,* ed. J. Raine, *SS* I (1835).

Reginald of Durham. *Libellus de vita et miraculis S. Godrici, Heremitae de Finchale,* ed. J. Stevenson, *SS* 20 (1847).

Richard Wych. Miracles in *Catal. Codicum Hagiographicorum Latinorum BN Paris,* tome III, Brussels, 1893, 294-8.

Robertson, J., ed. (with J. Brigstocke in vol. 7). *Materials for the History of Thomas Becket,* 7 vols. (1875-85), *RS* 67.

Wright, T., ed. *Letters Relating to the Suppression of the Monasteries,* Camden Soc., 1843.

2 Some Useful Secondary Sources

Abbott, E., *St. Thomas of Canterbury, his death and miracles,* 2 vols., Lond., 1898.

Brown, P., *The Development of the Legend of Thomas Becket,* Phil., 1930.

Bishop, E., *Liturgica Historica,* Oxford, 1918.

Bhardwaj, S., *Hindu Places of Pilgrimage in India,* Berkeley, 1973.

Bethell, D., 'The Making of a Twelfth-century Relic Collection', in *Studies in Church History,* VIII (1972), 61-72.

Colgrave, B., 'Bede's Miracle Stories', in *Bede: His Life, Times and Writings,* ed. A. H. Thompson, Oxford, 1935, 210-29.

Dawson, G., *Healing: Pagan and Christian,* London, 1935.

Dickinson, J. C., *The Shrine of our Lady of Walsingham,* Cambridge, 1956.

Dooley, E., *Church Law on Sacred Relics* (Canon Law Studies, 70), Washington, 1931.

Field, M. J., *Search for Security: An Ethno-Psychiatric Study of Rural Ghana*, Evanston, 1960.

Foreville, R., ed., *Thomas Becket: Actes du colloque international de Sédières*, Paris, 1975.

Frank, J., *Persuasion and Healing*, Baltimore, 1961.

Gaiffier, B., *Études Critiques d'hagiographie et d'iconologie*, Brussels, 1967.

Grabar, A., *Martyrium. Recherches sur le culte des reliques et l'art chrétien antique*, 3 vols., 1943-46.

Hutton, W., *The Lives and Legends of the English Saints*, London, 1903.

Kemp, E. W., *Canonization and Authority in the Western Church*, London, 1948.

Lawrence, C. H., *St. Edmund of Abingdon*, Oxford, 1960.

Leproux, M., *Dévotions et Saints Guérisseurs*, Presses Univ., 1957.

Maclean, U., *Magical Medicine: A Nigerian Case-study*, Penguin, 1971.

Maclean, U., 'Sickness Behaviour among the Yoruba' in *Witchcraft and Healing*, ed. R. Willis *et al.*, Edinburgh, 1969.

Moule, C., ed., *Miracles: Cambridge Studies in their Philosophy and History*, London, 1965.

MacCulloch, J., *Medieval Faith and Fable*, London, 1932.

Philonenko, M., and Simon, M., eds., *Les Pèlerinages*, Paris, 1973.

Rock, D., *The Church of Our Fathers*, 3 vols. in 4, ed. G. Hart and W. Frere, London, 1903-4.

Rose, L., *Faith Healing*, London, 1968 (Penguin, 1971 ed. B. Morgan).

Roussel, R., *Les Pèlerinages à travers les Siecles*, Paris, 1954.

Rubin, S., *Medieval English Medicine*, London, 1974.

Sandison, A., and Brothwell, D., eds., *Diseases in Antiquity*, Springfield, 1967.

Sigal, P.-A. 'Maladie, Pèlerinage et Guérison au xiie siecle; Les miracles de saint Gibrien à Reims', *Annales*, xxiv (1969), 1522-39.

Sumption, J., *Pilgrimage*, London, 1975.

Thomas, K., *Religion and the Decline of Magic*, London, 1971.

Thorndike, L., *A History of Magic and Experimental Science*, 8 vols., N.Y., 1923-58.

Toynbee, M. R., *St. Louis of Toulouse and the Process of Canonisation in the Fourteenth Century*, Manchester, 1929. (Cf. *AB* 49 (1931), 211-13 for a review by Grosjean.)

Index